Guide to
Lump Sum
Investment

THE DOGS' HOME BATTERSEA
Registered Charity: 206394

As the oldest and most famous rescue organisation in the world, we launched our very first major appeal in our 130 year history in 1990 to help pay for a £2 million multi-storey kennel block. The kennel block is now in operation but we still have to rebuild a further 300 kennels which are now over 30 years old.

The Home was instituted in 1960 to:
- provide food and shelter for the lost, deserted and starving dogs in the Metropolitan and City Police areas.
- restore lost dogs to their rightful owners.
- find suitable homes for unclaimed dogs at nominal charges.
- provide a merciful and painless death for those that are old, injured or diseased.

The Home continues to receive worldwide acclaim by leading the way in caring for stray dogs and cats at Battersea and Old Windsor which also acts as a convalescent home and canine maternity home. We are constantly striving to find new homes for the many thousands of dogs and cats which pass through our doors every year.

Please help us to care for these unfortunate animals by making a donation, covenant or bequest.
Further details available from: **The Secretary, The Dogs' Home Battersea, 4 Battersea Park Road, London SW8 4AA. Telephone: 071-622 3626.**

The Daily Telegraph
Guide to
Lump Sum
Investment

SIXTH EDITION

Liz Walkington

KOGAN PAGE

First published in 1985
by Telegraph Publications
Author: Diana Wright

Sixth edition 1994
Author: Liz Walkington

Kogan Page Limited
120 Pentonville Road
London N1 9JN

© Telegraph Publications 1994

British Library Cataloguing in Publication Data

A CIP record for this book is available from the British Library.

ISBN 0-7494-1406-5

Typeset by DP Photosetting, Aylesbury, Bucks
Printed and bound in Great Britain by
Clays Ltd, St Ives plc

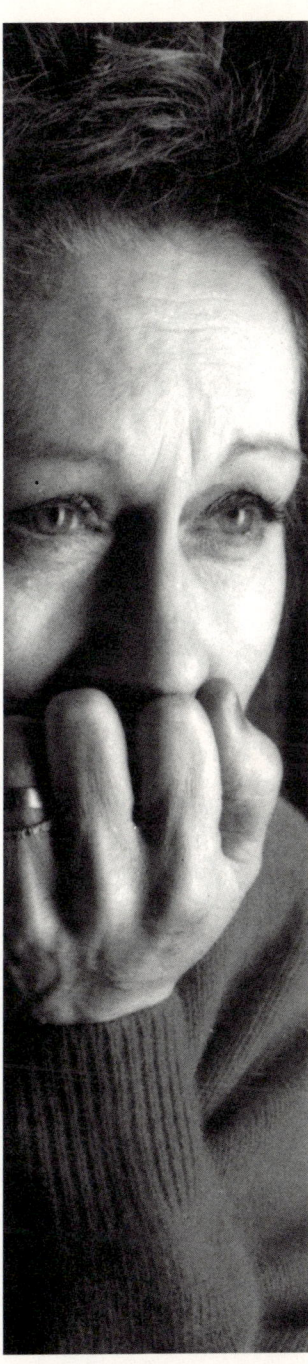

"Tom had Health Insurance, House Insurance, Car Insurance.

If only he'd thought of making a Will."

Most people with family responsibilities take great trouble to protect their loved ones.

But sadly, too many neglect to take one essential precaution.

They don't make a Will. And the result can be a disaster for those they leave behind.

For a widow it can mean that financial worries are added to her grief. Without a Will to protect her, the security she thought she had may turn out to be an illusion. She may even lose her home because other family members have a claim on it.

For the whole family it can mean distressing legal proceedings over "who gets what".

Now the British Red Cross has produced a booklet telling you how to protect your family by making a Will.

For a free copy of **The most precious gift of all**, the British Red Cross Guide to Wills and Legacies, simply post the coupon below to: British Red Cross, FREEPOST, 9 Grosvenor Crescent, London SW1X 7BR. Or phone 071 201 5044 now.

SEND FOR THIS FREE BOOKLET TODAY.

Please send me a free copy of
The British Red Cross Guide to Wills
and Legacies (BLOCK CAPITALS PLEASE)

Mr/Mrs/Ms/Miss: _____

Address: _____

_____

_____

Postcode: _____ Tel: _____

Registered Charity No. 220949

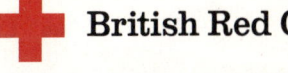

British Red Cross

Send to: British Red Cross, FREEPOST, 9 Grosvenor
Crescent, London SW1X 7BR.   4032

Cold, hungry, out of touch..

that was <u>yesterday</u>!

Like many other older people. Mary is living below the poverty line. Sudden incapacity turned her life into a nightmare. Now a grant from Aid for the Aged in Distress has given her the practical help she so urgently needed.

Enhancing the quality of life

Aid for the Aged in Distress is concerned first and foremost with helping people, like Mary, to cope in their own homes, by making personal grants towards the cost of necessary equipment or other exceptional expenditure. We also provide essential funds for schemes such as minibus transport, taking frail elderly people to and from Day Centres and lunch clubs, giving help with shopping, heating, home visits etc.

But the help we can give is limited to the amount our generous supporters can donate! With the number of elderly people growing all the time, we desperately need your help, through donations, covenants or – best of all – a legacy in your Will. Please help us not to let them down.

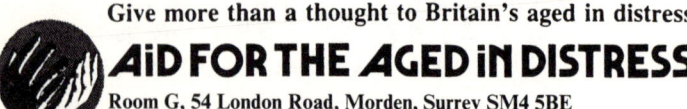

Contents

NEW TELEPHONE SAVINGS SERVICE CREATES A LOT OF INTEREST

It had to happen. We've had telephone banking, telephone insurance, and now we have a telephone saving service. From the comfort of your own armchair you can now plan your savings at your own convenience at any time of the day or night. Asset is great news for serious investors and busy people. So, will Asset be good news for you?

Well, if you have a substantial sum to invest, if you want intererst rates that are guaranteed to be competitive and if you're looking for building society security, then it is well worth looking at Asset.

Asset has been aimed directly at you.

It recognises that when provided with good information you are quite happy to make your own financial decisions.

The best currently available?

Asset is the very first telephone savings service in the UK. It was launched by the Bristol & West Building Society on New Year's Day – and judging by the response so far, the Bristol & West has a real winner on its hands, with new customers exceeding expectations.

The Asset proposition is simple, logical and timely. Interest rates are high and they're guaranteed. Since Asset cannot predict what might become available from other societies, they guarantee that your Asset account will <u>always remain</u> competitive whatever else happens in the market.

You know what you're doing

There is a third element in the Asset proposition which is at least as important as the other two. Asset guarantees its standard of service; and guarantees that every Asset investor is kept fully informed.

Bristol & West Operations Director Ian Kennedy explains:

"Research has told us that nothing irritates people more than discovering that the rate they're earning could have been bettered, if only the building society had informed the customer of new and more competitive products."

"Asset therefore <u>guarantees</u> to keep every customer fully informed. At any time of the day or night, 365 days a year, the customer is entitled to call Asset for an immediate telephone review of his or her investments. Every quarter he or she is issued with a comprehensive Performance Report detailing changes in the balance, and interest earned, as well as any new Asset products. At any time, Asset Account Managers are available to receive calls."

Not on the 'High' St.

In setting up a 'better' savings service, Asset has had to make some savings of its own. There are no High St locations with their associated high costs. There is also a high point of entry – only people with at least £10,000 to invest need apply.

Ian Kennedy says:

"We've planned our business so that we're able to concentrate on the things that really matter to customers – high interest rates, and high standards of service. If we tried to do it for everybody, we wouldn't be able to do it for anybody."

"Our policy is not to attract as many customers as possible. We are developing a relatively small base of serious investors to whom we can demonstrate our standards through real performance. We know that by servicing our customers well we will keep them."

The Asset Portfolio currently carries a range of six products:
Instant Access, 90 Day Notice, High Interest Cheque, Monthly Income, Term and TESSA Accounts.

You can, of course, make enquiries by telephone – call free on 0800 30 33 30

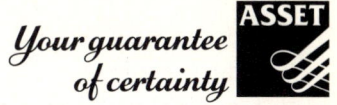

Your guarantee
of certainty

OF THIS YOU
CAN BE CERTAIN

Asset is a 24 hour,

365 day telephone savings service from the Bristol & West.

It offers clear guarantees on interest rates, on long term competitiveness,

and on keeping you fully informed.

The minimum investment level on all Asset savings products is £10,000.

Asset is determined to become recognised as the finest

financial service available.

☎
Telephone free on 0800 30 33 30.
24 hours, 7 days a week.

ASSET, PO BOX 1045, 41 CORN STREET, BRISTOL BS99 1UF.
Asset is a division of the Bristol & West Building Society.

HIGH INTEREST CHEQUE ACCOUNT. TERM ACCOUNT. TESSA.
INSTANT ACCESS. 90 DAY NOTICE.

UK Residents only.

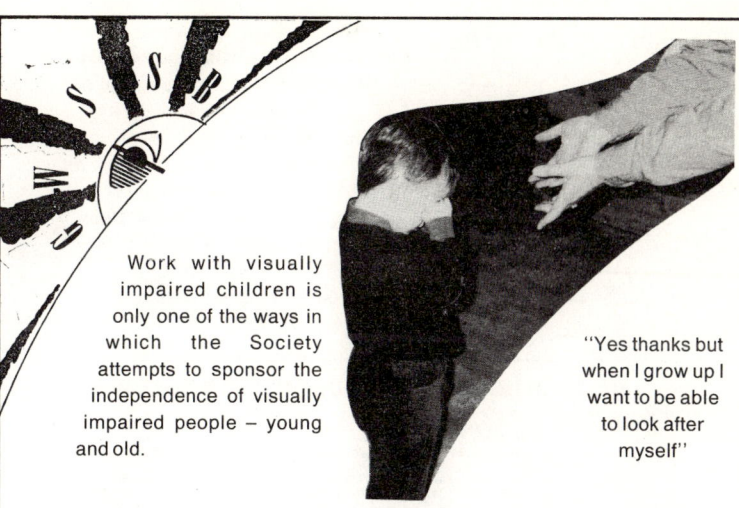

Work with visually impaired children is only one of the ways in which the Society attempts to sponsor the independence of visually impaired people – young and old.

"Yes thanks but when I grow up I want to be able to look after myself"

GLASGOW AND WEST OF SCOTLAND SOCIETY FOR THE BLIND
2 Queens Crescent, St. George's Cross, Glasgow G4 9BW
Telephone – 041 332 4632

Supporting visually impaired people in the West of Scotland since 1859.

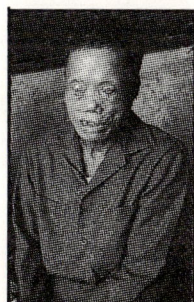

We can't turn our backs on leprosy – the cost is too high.

There are over 8 million people in the queue for leprosy treatment.
If we don't act swiftly, many will develop needless deformity.
Yet the medical cure costs as little as £10.

If you would like to help, write or send your gift to:
The Leprosy Mission, Box No S1
FREEPOST, Edinburgh EH3 0EP
Telephone: 031-226 6338

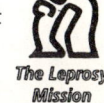

The Leprosy Mission

Lord Whisky Sanctuary Fund
DEDICATED TO SAVE LIFE

Lord Whisky

Lord Whisky Sanctuary Fund is a small charity based in Kent and Sussex but has members all over the UK. The sanctuaries are dedicated to save life and no healthy animal is ever put down, permanent sanctuary is given if a home cannot be found. Over the past year hundreds of creatures have been rescued: there are so many animal waifs and strays in modern day society, unfortunately some people seem to think that animals can be thrown away like an unwanted or broken toy.

All creatures are welcome at Lord Whisky Sanctuaries where, if necessary, they are nursed back to health and then found new loving owners who will hopefully repay the faith these animals still show towards mankind after the most appalling ill-treatment at our hands. Please support this work by sending a donation, becoming a member, and/or remembering us in your will. Everything helps. Our fund-raising is done by volunteers, so you may be assured that all money raised will go directly towards the work of the sanctuaries.

Park House, Stelling Minnis,
Nr. Canterbury, Kent CT4 6AN
Tel: Folkestone (0303) 862622
(Charity 283483)

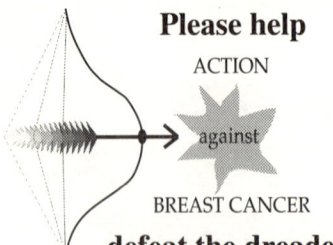

1

Introduction

Money makes the world go around, or so the song says, and it is a valid point of view. But from another angle, the world makes money go around, and many of us, in different ways, are playing catch-as-catch-can trying to get a share of it. This book is, in very broad terms, about making the most of that share.

Given the chance, most people like to save money, whether it is for a short-term purpose, such as a holiday, a long-term purpose, such as retirement, or simply for unspecified 'emergencies'. Saving is effectively deferred consumption: you save today to spend tomorrow. This is true even if your savings pass on to a future generation and 'tomorrow' is 50 years hence; sooner or later, the savings will be spent.

While savings could be simply money stuffed under the mattress, investment implies some added value – either actual or potential. Generally, this would take the form of a monetary reward; *Chambers English Dictionary*, for example, defines investment as 'the placing of money to secure income or profit'.

But for some people, the actual rewards may be secondary in importance to the pleasure of going after them. Just as there is enjoyment to be had from horse-racing, so there is in, say, playing the stock market, and there are similar opportunities to study 'form' and look for attractive odds. Of course, it is always good to win, but there can be pleasure in taking part even if some ventures fail.

So before you can decide how to invest, you need first to be clear why you want to. It may be to fulfil a particular need at a specific time, for example, to meet expected school fees; it may be a less definite saving for retirement or for the future in general; it may be that you have spare money you feel should be put to good use; or it may be simply for the fun of it.

Having settled the why, you should then have some idea of what you expect to achieve from the investment, which is a first step to deciding the how. Other factors to take into account are:

- the amount of money you have available;
- your attitude to risk;
- your tax position;
- the time you are prepared or able to devote to managing your investments.

As regards the size of investment, there are few limits in either direction. Much of the information in this book could be as well used by someone with just a few hundred pounds to invest as someone right at the other end of the scale, although the majority of readers will perhaps fall into the middle band, with somewhere between a few thousand and a six-figure sum.

Risk and protection

As to risk, again the book aims to cover a wide range. To start with, Chapters 2 and 3 look at various types of investment which provide capital security. Those who prefer rather more spice to life may want to skip these and move straight on to unit trusts or shares. Nevertheless, most people will find some use for this type of investment.

As well as short-term cash-flow management – putting aside money for bills and so on – vehicles such as bank and building society deposits can be useful over the longer term for 'emergency' cash. Most of us like to feel we have some money that is not only safe, but also readily accessible; fixed capital investments can provide this security while also offering some return.

The drawback is that security can become a habit. The amount of safe money that it is sensible to have will differ from person to person: single people with no dependants may need less than families, while those whose only recourse for loans is the bank manager may want to tuck aside rather more than those who have obliging relatives. Deciding when you have enough and can start

Table 1.1 *Inflation*

What £1000 would be worth in the future, in today's terms

Years ahead	Annual rate of inflation		
	3%	5%	8%
1	970	950	920
2	941	903	846
3	913	857	779
4	885	815	716
5	859	774	659
6	833	735	606
7	808	698	558
8	784	663	513
9	760	630	472
10	737	599	434
15	633	463	286
20	544	358	189
25	467	277	124

to move up the risk scale can be like letting go of the side of the swimming pool.

The other important point to remember is that 'safe' investments that guarantee capital security are almost always open to a different kind of danger – inflation. An investment that is not growing in money terms will be shrinking in real terms, as measured by its purchasing power.

To get an idea by how much, you need only look at Table 1.1, which shows how much £1000 would come to be worth, valued in today's terms, given different rates of inflation. Even at the modest rate of 3 per cent, more than a quarter of the value would be eroded over 10 years. At 8 per cent, more than half would be lost.

So far, the 1990s have seen reduced inflation and it is tempting to think that it has been controlled, if not wholly overcome. But the long-term record, as shown in Table 1.2, should act as a warning. After the extreme levels seen in the 1970s and at the beginning of the 1980s, inflation reached a low point in 1986 that was similar to the 1992 level. Yet four years later it had climbed back up to 9.5 per cent, and there is no guarantee the same thing will not happen again. In fact, in the run-up to the

Table 1.2 *Average annual inflation rates*

Year	%
1980	15.1
1981	12.0
1982	5.4
1983	5.3
1984	4.6
1985	5.7
1986	3.6
1987	4.1
1988	4.9
1989	7.8
1990	9.5
1991	5.9
1992	3.7
1993	1.6

next General Election it is likely that government spending will be increased and inflation will creep up.

It is possible to have an inflation-proofed investment, in the shape of index-linked National Savings Certificates (outlined in Chapter 2) or gilts (outlined in Chapter 4). These will guarantee to give you back your capital uprated by inflation, so in real terms you get back what you started with.

The downside is that this security comes at a price. The current seventh issue of index-linked National Savings Certificates pays tax-free interest equivalent to 3 per cent a year compound, for five years, on top of the index-linking. This may currently look better than some building society accounts that lack the inflation proofing, but if inflation rises, so will interest rates, so in neutralising the inflation risk you are paying an opportunity cost.

Once you venture beyond the realms of fixed capital investments, you lay yourself open to investment risk. Broadly speaking, this operates on a tit for tat basis – the greater the potential for capital growth, the greater the potential for capital loss. In theory, the upside and downside should be roughly in balance, either in actual amount or when adjusted for likelihood. For example, if an investment is more likely to lose than gain, the

A success story for children

Over the years Tadworth Court has developed services specifically for children with multiple disabilites, becoming a lifeline for their families and a reassuring source of knowledge, support and experience. Imagine the outcry in the early 1980s, therefore, when it was threatened with closure. The public's response was tremendous and parents and staff were joined by celebrities, MP's and the national media in a heartfelt and successful campaign to save Tadworth Court.

Tadworth Court Trust now provides nursing care, treatment, rehabilitation and special education for up to 60 children from all over the UK and, occasionally, from around the world. In any given year more than 200 different children and their families will benefit from its work.

Rehabilitation for brain-injured children

60% of children coming to Tadworth for rehabilitation are the victims of road traffic accidents. Others have been affected by illness or other accidents such as falling out of a window. One minute they are perfectly happy, healthy and active, the next they are at Tadworth Court sometimes unable to speak, walk or eat for themselves.

The Rehabilitation Unit has pioneered an intensive approach to each child's needs. Teams of physiotherapists, teachers, psychologists, nurse therapists, occupational, speech, recreational and play therapists work on and plan the child's rehabilitation together. Progress can be slow, taking anything between 3 and 18 months and funding for the placement can be a pressing issue.

The trauma of such dramatic change affects the whole family deeply and it is widely acknowledged that, since being established in 1985, this unit has developed a unique expertise in dealing with the problems that these families face. In 1990 rehabilitation moved into purpose-built premises.

Residential Special Education

St Margaret's School at Tadworth Court is an independent, residential special school for children aged 8-19 years with 'profound and multiple learning difficulties' (this means they usually have physical, mental and sensory disabilities). Many of the children will also have complex medical needs which call for special feeding requirements and medical supervision.

St. Margaret's varied curriculum takes into account every minute of the child's waking day and each pupil follows a curriculum which is tailor-made to their individual needs following a lengthy assessment. Pupils stay at school for 48 weeks of the year and return home to their families every other weekend.

Brand new school buildings and accommodation were officially opened in 1989 by HRH the Duchess of Kent.

Respite and Residential Care

Our Cedar and Meadow units provide residential care for children with the most profound disabilities. Children with the degenerative condition cystic fibrosis come to us for intensive treatment whilst those with other profound disabilities stay at Tadworth Court when the family needs a break, for instance, or when parents, brothers and sisters go away on holiday. Our highly skilled nursing staff and therapists also give 'terminal care' when a child is in the last stages of a chronic illness and the whole family needs extra special support. Doctors are on-site 24 hours a day to give medical back-up whenever it is needed.

Although each child's place at Tadworth Court is fully funded, the Trust relies on charitable donations to meet the need to expand and develop services and for new classroom and therapy equipment, vehicles, excursions, improvements to accommodation, and much-needed research.

Tadworth Court has a staff of 350 plus more than 100 volunteers. Last year just 10% of its total income came from voluntary donations. If the Trust is to realise plans to expand and increase its services for children and their families then more funds will be sorely needed.

Belma is a little girl of four years old who was rescued from war-torn Sarajevo on the very first children's mercy flight to the UK. She is now on a rehabilitation programme at Tadworth Court's Head Injury Unit.

Little Belma, whose mum, Ziba and sister, Samira, eight, are with her, was referred to Tadworth Court by an expert team of Neurological Consultants at Great Ormond Street Children's Hospital where she first received treatment.

She was diagnosed there with a rare and severe form of brain damage possibly caused by an infection brought on by the war conditions.

Dr Robert Surtes, who was on the team said, "Belma's is such an unusual and special case that we only wanted the very best for her – there was no other choice but Tadworth Court."

HOW TO GET 'MANY HAPPY RETURNS' FOR YOUR MONEY

Children who have profound disabilities or complex medical needs come to Tadworth Court for a very special kind of care, treatment and education.

A sanctuary in 22 acres of open gardens, Tadworth Court was saved from closure in 1984 but has no government grant. Yet it is a lifeline for many disabled or chronically sick children and their families who come from all over the UK and even from around the world.

It would not survive today without financial support from the public.

1994 is Tadworth Court's 10th anniversary year - your donation or covenant could really make it worth celebrating. *And what better return for your money?*

TADWORTH COURT TRUST

Please contact the Fundraising Department, Tadworth Court, Tadworth, Surrey KT20 5RU

Telephone: (0737) 357171

Charity Registration No. 288018

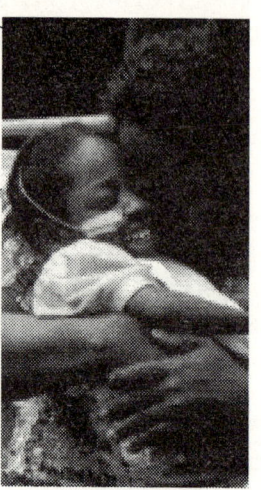

In favour of Sense

A small change can make a big difference to someone <u>who is deafblind</u>

It's impossible for us to imagine what life must be like for a person who is deafblind. Deprived of the sight and sound we take for granted, he must make sense of the world without visual clues or friendly words from those around him.

That's why the work of **Sense,** the national deafblind charity, is so important. Whether it's support for parents bringing up a child with special needs or residential care for those who cannot cope alone, **Sense** aims to help people who are deafblind, whatever their situation.

Would someone you know wish to leave a legacy to **Sense**? It only takes a small change to a client's Will to make a world of difference to a person who is deafblind.

Helen Andralojc, Fundraising Department (A94)
Sense, 11-13 Clifton Terrace, Finsbury Park, London N4 3SR
Registered Charity No. 289868

The National Deafblind and Rubella Association

possible gain needs to be larger than the possible loss to persuade people into it.

In practice, there are other factors to take into account, not least of which is the investment period. Take, for example, the UK stock market, as measured by the FT-Actuaries All-Share index. Over the long term, the trend is broadly upwards; the 1987 crash, for instance, appears on a long-term graph as only a temporary blip. But for an investor who put money into the market in, say, July 1987 and took it out again at the end of October that year, the loss would have been considerable.

The lesson from this is that the odds improve if you are prepared to commit your money for some time and to be patient. If the market turns down, you may be tempted to cut and run, but if you hold on, the loss is only on paper and may eventually turn round to profit. Conversely, if you have only a short time horizon, the risk becomes much greater and you may be better advised to stick to fixed capital investments. The stock market is not the best home for money that may be needed at short notice.

Help AFASIC break through the communication barrier

Amy has a condition which prevents her from speaking and understanding what others are saying. She often feels lonely and frustrated, unable to make friends or cope at school. AFASIC helps children like Amy overcome their difficulties and make the most of their lives.

Please help by making a donation – and show Amy you understand

347 Central Markets,
Smithfield,
London EC1A 9NH
Tel: 071 236 3632/6487
Reg Charity No 256289

AFASIC was formed 25 years ago to help children and young people who have speech and language impairments. Every aspect of our lives requires an ability to communicate with other people; to use spoken language. It is easy to take speech for granted – as something that is picked up naturally in childhood. But there is a group of children for whom this is not the case. They have neurological conditions which prevent them from developing speech and language.

There are at least half a million children in the UK – 1 in 20 – who have difficulty in speaking or understanding what is said to them to some degree. Their inability to communicate with other people leaves them isolated in a confusing and frightening world. They need special help to have a chance of participating at school, at work and in society.

AFASIC is the only organisation offering a broad range of services specifically for these youngsters and their families. We urgently need funds to provide information, support and training for children and young people throughout the UK. Our work is dependent on voluntary donations. Please help these youngsters gain the power of speech and make the most of their lives by making a donation to AFASIC. For further information about our work, please call Helen Sant on 071 236 3632/6487 or write to 347 Central Markets, Smithfield, London EC1A 9NH.

Your support could make all the difference.

Another means of controlling risk is to spread your investments around. One of the drawbacks of privatisation issues is that
many people who buy them own no other shares. So if the
company does badly, they stand to lose a disproportionate
amount. At the worst, if you put all your money into a single
company that then goes bust, you will lose everything. If, on the
other hand, you hold a collection of several different shares, a loss
on any one will only be a small part of your investment and may
be counteracted by gains elsewhere.

This is the principle behind collective or 'pooled' investments
such as unit trusts and investment trusts. Small investors, who
lack the resources to achieve a wide spread of direct shareholdings, can instead buy a stake in a large portfolio. A trust will
usually have at least 40 different holdings, so the chances of them
all failing together are pretty small.

Again, of course, there is a price for safety. If you hold ten
shares and one doubles in value, you may wish you had backed it
to the hilt and not bothered with the other nine. But if one out of
the ten halves in value, you will be grateful for the insurance of the
other holdings.

Even with banks and building societies, you should not take
safety for granted, bearing in mind the collapse some years ago of
the Savings and Investment Bank in the Isle of Man. In the UK,
and nowadays in several other locations, there is a deposit
protection scheme, which guarantees you will get back some, if
not all, of your money. But if you are putting money offshore, you
should check whether such a scheme applies; if not, only put in as
much as you would be prepared to lose, or steer clear altogether.

Tax

Tax is the next factor to consider. A few investments, such as
National Savings Certificates and personal equity plans, are tax
free; some are subject to income tax, while others are liable to
capital gains tax. Depending on your particular tax circumstances, this can influence the net returns you will make and
therefore your choice. The main tax rates and allowances are
summarised in Table 1.3.

Interest payments and dividends from shares are treated as

ChurchArmy
Reg Charity No. 226226

GIVE AS YOU EARN

PAYROLL
GIVING TO THE
CHURCH ARMY

Sharing Faith through Words and Action

CHURCH ARMY
YOUTH CENTRE

For further information contact:
CAPT. GORDON KITNEY, DEPT GKP,,
INDEPENDENTS ROAD, BLACKHEATH,
LONDON SE3 9LG.   TEL: 081 318 1226

Table 1.3   *Income and capital gains tax*

Rates of income tax 1994/95		
Taxable income £	*Rate* %	*Cumulative on top of band* £
0–3000	20	600
3000–23,700	25	5775
Over 23,700	40	—

Main tax allowances

Personal allowance	£3,445
Personal allowance (age 65–74)	£4,200
Personal allowance (age 75+)	£4,370
Married couple's allowance	£1,720*
Married couple's allowance (age 65–74)	£2,665*
Married couple's allowance (age 75+)	£2,705*
Single parent allowance	£1,720*
Widow's bereavement allowance	£1,720*
Blind person's allowance	£1,200
Age allowance income limit	£14,200

(Allowance is reduced by £1 for every £2 of additional income above the income limit.)

* Tax relief is restricted to 20 per cent in 1994/95 and will be reduced to 15 per cent in 1995/96

Capital gains tax

Annual allowance for individuals	£5,800

(Excess, after indexation allowance, is charged at the individual's highest rate of income tax.)

Annual allowance for trusts	£2,900
Chattel exemption	£6,000
Retirement relief (age 55+)	£250,000 plus 50% of gains between £250,000 and £1,000,000

Major exemptions
- Principal private residence
- National Savings Certificates
- Gilts
- Assets gifted to charity
- Life assurance policies, for the original owner
- Betting winnings, including the pools and premium bonds

income and taxed at your highest rate. Interest from bank and building society accounts is normally paid net of basic rate tax, although you can register for gross payments if you are a non-taxpayer, while higher rate taxpayers will have to pay the difference. Share dividends are also paid net and accompanied by a tax credit, with which non-taxpayers can reclaim what has been paid.

In the 1993 Budget, the basic rate tax charged on dividends was reduced from 25 per cent to 20 per cent. For basic rate taxpayers, there is no material difference, since the value of the tax credit has also been reduced and therefore matches the liability just as it did before. Non-taxpayers, though, will only be able to reclaim 20 per cent, while investors subject to higher rate tax will now have to pay out an extra 20 per cent, to bring the total up to the 40 per cent rate, instead of the 15 per cent that applied before.

One consequence of this is that personal equity plans, on which all dividends are tax free, are now slightly less attractive than before to basic rate taxpayers, as the tax saving is only 20 per cent, which may be offset by the plan charges. Conversely, they are a little more attractive to higher rate taxpayers, because of the higher tax bill they face on shares not held through a plan.

Capital growth on investments is generally subject to capital gains tax at the time the profit is realised. This is charged at the same rate as income tax, but in practice it is paid by very few investors. This is because there are two types of allowance which, combined with a little management, can allow you to avoid a liability.

First, there is an indexation allowance, designed to avoid tax being charged on gains which are due only to inflation. The base date for the calculation is 31 March 1982; assets held since before then are assessed as if they had been bought at the market value on that date and gains made previously are no longer taxable.

For assets acquired after March 1982, the original purchase price is scaled up in line with the change in the Retail Price Index. Only gains made above that are liable to tax. If you make a loss on selling an asset, it can be used to offset any gains you have made elsewhere. But a provision in the 1993 Autumn Budget means that you can no longer use the indexation allowance to create or increase a loss to offset gains.

There is also an annual exemption allowance, currently £5800 a year, which applies to all individuals. Taking this together with the indexation allowance means you would have to make very profitable disposals in one year to become liable. If it does seem likely to happen, one way round the tax is to sell assets up to the point where you fully use the exempt allowance and buy the same assets again the next day. Your overall portfolio is then the same as before, but you will have established a new purchase price for the assets you sold and bought, on which the indexation allowance will be based in future.

This technique, known as 'bed and breakfasting', enables you to neutralise up to £5800 of gains over and above inflation, for the price of the dealing costs – and, as special deals are widely offered towards the end of the tax year, these are very small compared to the potential tax liability.

Tax should not be the only criterion when choosing an investment, nor even necessarily the prime one. But as a broad rule, the higher rate taxpayer will do better from a growth

MONEY IN YOUR POCKET...

Giving to charity makes everyone feel good. But wouldn't it feel even better to be able to give more without it costing you one extra penny?

As a registered charity working for animals, Compassion in World Farming Trust can offer you the chance to make your gift go further by taking advantage of the tax benefits of charitable giving. If you choose to make a donation using a covenant, payroll giving or gift aid, we can claim back the tax and use your generosity to even greater effect.

CIWF Trust is an educational charity, working with young people in schools and colleges, to encourage a spirit of care and compassion in our attitude toward the treatment of animals condemned to life in the intensive farming system.

If you would like to know more about our work and if you are interested in finding out how you can make your gift work harder for the animals, please write to us for your free *GUIDE TO TAX EFFICIENT GIVING* pack at the address below.

... AND MONEY IN OURS!

CIWF TRUST
Dept DT/I
Charles House
5a Charles Street
Petersfield
Hants GU32 3EH

Registration No. 295126

FREE
GUIDE TO
TAX-EFFICIENT
GIVING

TENOVUS

t h e   c a n c e r   c h a r i t y

Created in 1944 by ten businessmen, Tenovus has grown from modest beginnings into an Organisation that now raises over £2 million each year which is now devoted to cancer research, diagnosis, treatment and relief.

Tenovus scientists in Cardiff, Aberystwyth and Southampton and clinicians in Bournemouth are acknowledged to be amongst the world's leading experts.

They collaborate with research centres in many other countries and work closely with the staff of hospitals to ensure that patients benefit promptly from advances in basic research.

Additionally, the charity remains committed to providing support and counselling services for cancer patients and their families through the Tenovus Cancer Information Centre and the Freephone Cancer Helpline (0800 526527)

Your help is vital.
Join us in the fight against cancer.

TENOVUS, *The Cancer Charity*
11 Whitchurch Road, Cardiff CF4 3JN.
Phone: (0222) 621433 Fax: (0222) 615966
Tenovus Cancer Helpline: (0800) 526527
Registered Charity No. 223648

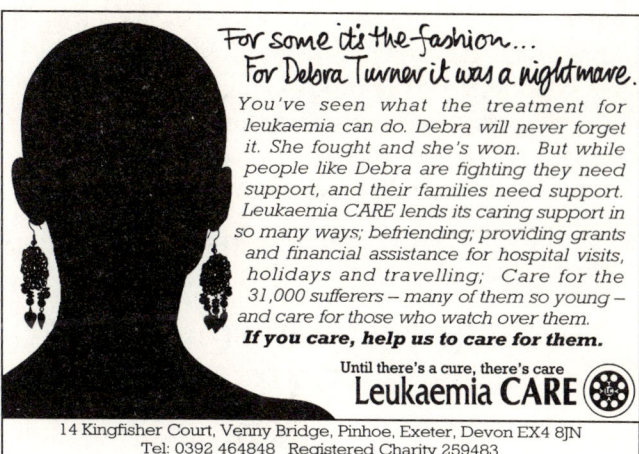
The Leukaemia CARE Society was formed in 1967 as the Leukaemia Society and aims to promote the welfare of persons suffering from Leukaemia and allied blood disorders.

Leukaemia CARE is funded solely by voluntary donations, covenants and legacies and receives no government help. It offers limited financial assistance, caravan holidays, moral support and friendship to sufferers and their families via volunteer Area Secretaries throughout the country.

A newsletter is published four times a year. A brochure and leaflets explaining the work of the Society are available, together with reports on various types/treatments of the disease.

PLEASE help Leukaemia CARE to continue to CARE. A donation or covenant now, and a legacy later, sent to the above address will be gratefully received and acknowledged, and make it possible.

investment, where he can use the capital gains exempt allowance, than from one that produces income on which he will immediately lose 40 per cent.

There are two other factors which may influence choice. First, since 1990, married couples have been taxed independently, whereas before that all investment income was imputed to the husband. They are still entitled to a married couple's allowance, but for the tax year starting in April 1994, this will attract tax relief at only 20 per cent, dropping to 15 per cent from the 1995/ 96 tax year.

Meanwhile, each of the couple has his or her own personal allowance, capital gains tax exempt allowance and tax rate. As a result, there may be benefits in transferring investments between you and your spouse – particularly as such transfers are exempt from inheritance tax. For example, income-producing investments could be put in the name of whichever partner has the lower tax rate, while those producing capital growth can be split so as to make the most of the annual CGT allowance. Bear in mind, though, that if you give assets away to your partner, you are not entitled to ask for them back if the marriage breaks down.

The other issue is age allowance. Individuals are entitled to a higher personal tax allowance when they pass the age of 65, with another increase when they reach 75, while a higher married couple's allowance is given where either partner reaches 65 or 75 during the tax year. The trap is that there is an annual income limit (based on the husband's income, for the married couple's allowance). If income goes above this level, the allowance is reduced by £1 for every £2 of excess income – a heavy penalty. Hence those who are at or near the limit may do better from growth-oriented investments which they can cash in if they need extra income.

Finally, there is inheritance tax. This does not affect an investor directly, since it only comes into play on death, and gifts between husband and wife are exempt. Nevertheless, with the increase in home ownership, many people may find their total assets go beyond the nil rate band, and it may be worth taking note of the exemptions, particularly if your investment plans extend to your heirs. Details are given in Table 1.4.

Table 1.4   *Inheritance tax rates*

Amount of transfer	Tax rate
Up to £150,000	Nil
Over £150,000	40%

Relief on transfers made within 7 years of death:

Years between gift and death	*% of full tax charge*
0–3	100
3–4	80
4–5	60
5–6	40
6–7	20

Main exemptions
Transfers between husband and wife
Transfers of up to £3000 a year
Gifts to anyone of up to £250 a year
Gifts out of income forming 'normal expenditure'
Gifts on marriage – up to £5000 for parents, £2500 for grandparents, £1000 for anyone else

Layout of the book

Investments can be categorised in a number of different ways: by product type, by what they achieve in terms of income or growth, or by risk factors. For the most part, this book goes by product type, although Chapters 2 and 3, as mentioned above, lump together investments that offer capital security. Chapter 2 covers high street institutions, such as banks, building societies and National Savings products which are largely available through post offices; Chapter 3 goes further afield into local authority bonds, insurance company guaranteed bonds and offshore money funds.

Chapter 4 covers gilts, which come halfway between fixed capital and risk investments. If you hold on to a gilt to its maturity date, you will get a fixed return, but meanwhile gilts can be traded, for profit or loss.

Chapters 5 to 9 deal with equity-based investments: shares

NATIONAL **ASTHMA** CAMPAIGN
getting your breath back

One in Seven children in the UK has Asthma – Help us improve their quality of life

Over three million people in the UK have asthma, one million of these are children.

Asthma is the most common chronic condition of childhood and hospital admission rates for childhood asthma have doubled since the mid-70s.

One child dies from asthma every ten days in the UK alone.

More than 5 million school days are lost each year because of asthma.

Taking time off school can seriously affect a child's education, often leading to under achievement, which in turn can jeopardise career prospects and the opportunity of fulfilling employment.

In short, asthma can seriously affect the quality of life of many children.

The National Asthma Campaign is the only charity which dedicates itself to all aspects of asthma by: funding more research than any non-commercial organisation; providing education about asthma; supporting and advising people with asthma and their carers through the provision of our information booklets and our National Asthma Helpline, which operates 12 hours a day, five days a week and is staffed by specialist asthma nurses.

This year we will spend more than £2 million on research and we rely entirely on voluntary contributions to continue this vital work.

Our ultimate aim is to eradicate asthma and we urgently need your help to do it.

By sending us a donation now or by leaving us a legacy you will ensure that we increase our chances of reaching that goal and of providing a better future for everyone with asthma.

If you can help and would like more information about out vital work, please write to:

The National Asthma Campaign, Providence House, Providence Place, London N1 0NT.   Tel: 071-226 2260

Registered Charity Number 802364

themselves, unit trusts, offshore funds, investment trusts and personal equity plans, which can be based on individual shares or trusts. While the chapter on equities is largely based on the UK market, a point to bear in mind is that the advantages of spreading your investments can apply equally well on a global scale as on a domestic one.

These days, the major world markets have a tendency to move roughly in line with each other, but there can still be short-term differences, as well as currency factors that will affect the returns. Smaller markets are a law unto themselves, usually displaying significant volatility.

'Smaller', however, is a relative term; the so-called emerging markets currently account for around 5 per cent of total world market capitalisation and the proportion is steadily increasing. While direct investment into these markets – and to some extent, any overseas markets – can be difficult, expensive and risky for the private investor, pooled funds such as unit and investment trusts offer a sensible and accessible route in. A glance at Table 1.5,

Table 1.5   *World stock markets*

Exchange	Capitalisation (£ billion)	Number of companies
Amsterdam	113.1	251
Australia	88.2	1038
Delhi	108.5	2114
Germany	217.9	425
Hong Kong	113.6	386
Johannesburg	98.2	642
Mexican	91.6	199
Montreal	130.7	556
New York	2508.3	1969
Paris	216.9	515
Switzerland	129.2	180
Tokyo	1583.5	1651
Toronto	159.8	1049
UK	624.4	1878

Note: Figures apply to domestic equities and companies at 31 December 1992.

Source: Stock Exchange Quarterly

which shows the capitalisation of the main markets, provides a clear picture of what you are ignoring if you focus on the UK alone.

Moving on, Chapters 10 and 11 cover investments with life assurance companies, which might more immediately be associated with regular savings. This is particularly true of pension plans, covered in Chapter 11; however, retirement planning can be so important, and so few people can expect the maximum benefits allowed, that topping-up provision should feature high on the list of priorities for investing windfall cash.

Chapter 12 rounds up so-called alternative investments, including tangibles such as precious metals and diamonds.

The final criterion for choosing investments that was mentioned at the outset of this chapter is the time you have to devote to your portfolio. While some investments take a while to come good, few selections will be right for all time, particularly as your own circumstances and needs will change over time. Constant chopping and changing will generally lose more in costs than it gains; nevertheless, reviews are an important part of the process.

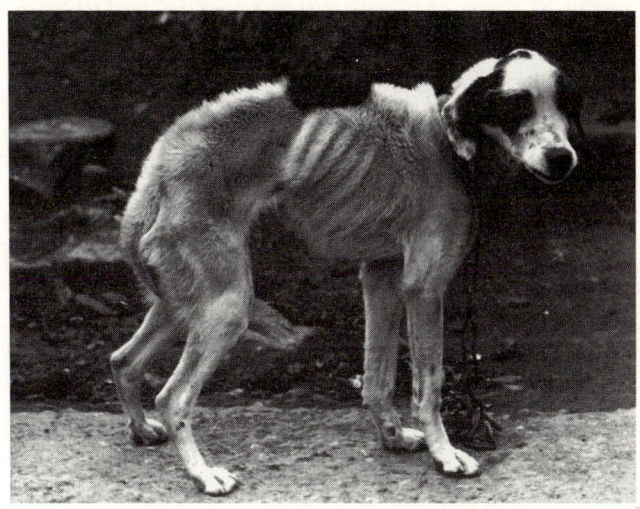

WE ALSO TAKE IN MONEY.

Financially, animal rescue is a risky business. The Mayhew Home's experience has served to underline this.

Too often we have been thrown into a crisis of existence by the sheer numbers of abandoned and abused animals.

We desperately need a guarantee of survival. So do the animals. Please help us move toward that goal, by naming us in your will.

Your bequest will be used as a long-term deposit where only the accrued interest will be withdrawn to help pay for the daily running expenses of the home.

And the daily saving of lives.

If you would like more information about our work with animals, and our child education programme, please contact Diane Conrad at the address below.

THE MAYHEW HOME

ONE HUNDRED YEARS OF ANIMAL RESCUE

Trenmar Gardens, Harrow Road, London NW10 6BJ

Registered Number: 208331

RIDING FOR THE DISABLED ASSOCIATION

National Agricultural Centre, Kenilworth, Warwickshire CV8 2LY
Tel: 0203 696510   Fax: 0203 696532
President: HRH The Princess Royal, LG, GCVO
Registered Charity No. 244108

We currently provide the opportunity for riding to over 25,000 children and adults of all disabilities at our 725 Member Groups throughout the United Kingdom. Funds are always needed to meet the growing demands of this very active charity in providing facilities, horses and saddlery. Supported by over 14,900 volunteers without whom the charity could not work, we have grown to our present size in 25 years. Many more disabled people would like the opportunity to ride with us. Help us to help them do so.

Riding for the Disabled Association
AVENUE R, NATIONAL AGRICULTURAL CENTRE,
KENILWORTH, WARWICKSHIRE CV8 2LY
Tel: 0203 696510   RCN: 244108

We currently provide the opportunity for riding to over 26,000 children and adults of all disabilities at our 710 member groups throughout the United Kingdom. Funds are always needed to meet the growing demands of this very active charity in providing facilities, horses and saddlery. Supported by over 14,600 volunteers without whom the charity could not work, we have grown to our present size in 24 years. Many more disabled people would like the opportunity to ride with us. Help us to help them do so.

It is not only your own circumstances that will change; the market is also in constant flux. In the past half-dozen years, there have been two major upheavals: Big Bang, which reorganised the operations of the Stock Exchange, and the Financial Services Act, which set up a new system of regulation for the industry.

Neither of these has proved conclusive, in that adjustments are still going on. In March 1993, the Stock Exchange abandoned the development of Taurus, a proposed electronic dealing system, and now intends to introduce a different and rather less ambitious system called Crest.

The Financial Services Act has undergone a series of alterations since it was introduced and is, at the time of writing, on the verge of a major change. The Act set up a system of self-regulation under the auspices of the Securities and Investments Board (SIB), which in turn delegates authority to self-regulatory organisations. Hitherto, there have been four of these: the Financial Intermediaries, Managers and Brokers Regulatory Association (Fimbra), which looked after independent financial advisers; the Life Assurance and Unit Trust Regulatory Organisation (Lautro), which covered insurance companies and unit

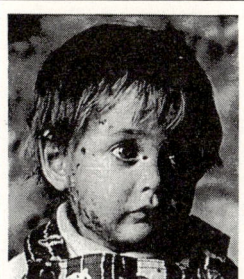

trust groups; the Investment Management Regulatory Organisation (Imro), which covered fund management groups (including some unit trust groups); and the Securities and Futures Association (SFA), which covered stockbrokers and the like. In addition, the SIB itself regulated a small number of companies.

The current intention is that a new body, the Personal Investment Authority (PIA), will become operational in July 1994. This will be responsible for all retail investment services, encompassing the operations of current Fimbra and Lautro members, plus Imro firms which primarily deal with private, rather than institutional, investors. The SIB has said that it plans to recognise the PIA as a self-regulatory organisation and subsequently to derecognise Fimbra and Lautro. At the same time, it would like ideally to relinquish its own position as a direct regulator, with this option being available only as a last resort.

While all these initials may be bemusing, they are not without relevance to private investors in general, and the time factor in particular. The less time you are able to devote to looking after your investments, the more you may need to rely on the services

MONEY <u>CAN</u> BUY HAPPINESS

..... if it's used for a good cause. And if animals are important to you, what better cause than the PDSA and its work of caring for sick and injured animals?

For 76 years, the PDSA has provided free veterinary care to the suffering animals of impoverished owners throughout the nation. Over 5,000 animal patients are treated in our hospitals and clinics every day.

This vital service is paid for entirely by public donation. Lump sum gifts are particularly important in providing the expensive but essential equipment which is needed - surgical equipment, x-ray machines and so on.

Why not talk to us about how <u>your</u> lump sum gift could be used - and also about how your generosity could be memorialised? And let us show you how to make your gift really tax-effective by giving through the Gift Aid scheme.

Having a lump sum to dispose of is a rare, perhaps unique, event in your life. What a wonderful opportunity it gives you to buy a little health and happiness .... for the animals!

Please telephone or write to the Director of Appeals at:
People's Dispensary for Sick Animals
Whitechapel Way, Priorslee, Telford, Shropshire, TF2 9PQ
Telephone: (0952) 290999   Registered Charity No. 208217

of an adviser, and the Financial Services Act aims to ensure that the advice you will receive is honest and competent. It also provides for redress in the case of malpractice.

Details of how the Act and its various creations operate are given in Chapter 13. This also discusses the various types of advice available and how to choose between different services. For example, one of the main planks of the Act is that advisers are 'polarised' into two categories: completely independent, which means offering advice across the full range of the markets in which they operate, or tied to a single company and able to offer only the products it supplies.

At the outset, one of the cardinal rules for independents was that they should offer 'best advice' – the best possible product, in terms of type and supplier, to fit their customer's needs. This has now been adjusted to read 'good advice', in recognition of the fact that no one can be expected to pick in advance the product which will turn in the best performance in some years' time.

While you may be happy to trust your adviser's judgement, you are likely to get more out of the relationship if you understand the

For Daniella, life is no longer a leap in the dark

Like any active youngster Daniella loves a rough and tumble now and again. It is one of the many reasons why she enjoys herself so much in the Ball Pool at her Nursery at Dorton House School, run by The Royal London Society for the Blind. Dorton House is one of the world's leading educational centres for blind and partially sighted children, and is just one of The RLSB's services providing education, training and employment for blind people of all ages.

The Society is 100% dependent on private donations, often in the form of bequests and legacies. The Royal London Society for the Blind produces a free booklet to take the confusion out of making A Will. For a copy, and a free RLSB lapel badge, please write to;

**ROYAL LONDON SOCIETY
FOR THE BLIND
FREEPOST, 105 Salusbury Road,
London NW6 1YA
Tel: 071-624 8844.
Fax: 071-328 4353**
Patron: Her Majesty The Queen
President: HRH The Duchess of Gloucester
Registered Charity No. 307892

basics of the selection process. This book is designed to help in that, and at the end of each chapter there are suggested sources of further information.

One final word of warning. The book only deals with lump-sum investments, hence it does not cover regular savings by way of monthly or annual premiums on life assurance policies or pension plans, or outgoings such as a mortgage. In practice, these may all impinge on your overall financial picture and any part should not be viewed in isolation from the rest.

Having said that, lump-sum investments may arise out of windfall gains such as inheritance, and therefore be additional to existing regular, and planned, savings. If you are happy that your basic needs are already catered for, you may be prepared to take a different tack with the lump sum, perhaps involving more risk.

Because the choices are so wide, it is impossible to categorise potential gains. But to whet your appetite, Table 1.6 gives a few key statistics. While there is no guarantee that taking risks will always provide rewards, it does suggest that, over the long term, a little care and imagination can prove fruitful.

Table 1.6   *Past performance comparisons*

Value of £100 invested over periods to 28 February 1994			
	3 years	*5 years*	*10 years*
Building society (90-day account)	121.9	151.4	231.6
Unit trust (offer to bid basis)	163.7	171.7	371.2
Investment trust	184.1	205.8	500.7
Retail Price Index	108.5	127.3	162.7
FT–SE Actuaries All Share Index	161.2	190.9	468.9
MSCI World Index (£)	163.3	159.0	421.9

Source: Association of Investment Trust Companies

WHO WILL ANSWER THE CALL?

The Samaritans volunteers

*A*re ordinary people who give their time freely to answer the call every 12 seconds from a person in crisis.

*B*ut it costs us £4 million every year to ensure that we're there when the call comes.

*P*lease remember us in your will so that we can always be there for people in crisis. Without The Samaritans, who will answer the call?

*W*rite to James Pollock, The Samaritans, Room 29, 10 The Grove, Slough, SL1 1QP for further details.

The Samaritans

A Registered Charity

2

Fixed Capital Investments (1)

As a starting-point, this chapter will look at the more familiar varieties of investment available through high street outlets. In particular, it will deal with fixed capital products: those which guarantee that the capital you get out will be the same as the capital you put in.

This can be reassuring, but the drawback is that old hidden enemy, inflation, which will progressively erode the value. The rate of inflation is one factor which influences the general level of interest rates; they are rarely substantially above inflation for very long, which means that the real rate of return on the investments discussed here is usually pretty small. Indeed, it can even be negative: in October 1990, for example, the gross return on an instant access deposit of £5000 hit a high of 14 per cent, but inflation was then running at 10.9 per cent – above the net return to a basic rate taxpayer. So these investments are suitable chiefly for short periods, 'emergency' money or the extremely cautious.

Fixed versus variable interest

Most of the investments covered in this chapter pay variable interest, which will move up and down in line with general market rates. But there are a few, including some National Savings products and fixed term deposits, which pay fixed interest over a predetermined period of time.

Fixed interest rates, like fixed mortgage rates, are something of a gamble: if general rates subsequently go up, you lose; if they go down, you win. As a gambler, you are probably betting on fairly long odds, since the rate offered will ultimately depend on the view of the money market, which has no crystal ball but is generally in a better position to make predictions than the average investor. On the whole, it is better to be guided by your needs and decide whether or not the certainty of a fixed income would outweigh any possible loss.

Variable rates tend to reflect the general economic environment, but different institutions react at varying speeds to underlying changes. It may seem that mortgage rates move up faster than down, while investment rates are sticky in the other direction; in practice the institutions are simply balancing their borrowing and lending against the demand and supply in the market. Broadly, when they are looking to attract investors they will be quicker to raise their interest rates; when they are seeking to increase their lending they will try to hold rates down.

Neither pattern is likely to be consistent for all time, so this should not be a prime factor in deciding where to invest. Of course, it is possible to gain by monitoring all the rates available and switching your investments around accordingly, but this is more valuable if you are locking into a fixed rate; with variable rates, the benefit is likely to be small and short-lived compared with the time and energy you would spend on the research.

The tax position

Until April 1991, bank and building society accounts paid interest net of composite rate tax. This was calculated by the Inland Revenue on the basis of the proportion of savers who were non-taxpayers and therefore worked out at slightly less than basic rate income tax, but the major drawback was that it could not be reclaimed by those not liable for tax.

Nowadays, non-taxpayers can register to have interest paid gross by completing the Inland Revenue Form R85, available at banks and building societies. Otherwise, interest will normally be paid net of basic rate tax, which can be reclaimed by those who are not liable to some or all of it. Basic rate taxpayers themselves will have no further liability, while higher rate taxpayers will have to pay the difference.

National Savings Certificates and tax exempt special savings accounts (TESSAs) are free of both income and capital gains tax (CGT), while the return on gilts is liable only to income tax and will be paid gross if they are held through the National Savings Stock Register (see Chapter 4). A handful of other products pay interest gross, although it will still be liable for tax. These include National Savings accounts, offshore bank and building society accounts (see Chapter 3) and fixed-term bank and building society deposits amounting to £50,000 or more.

Accounts that pay gross have the advantage that you can enjoy the money for a while before the tax falls due, but there is also a potential drawback. In the first year, and the second if you so elect, the tax charged is based on the actual interest received, but thereafter it moves to a 'preceding year' basis. So, for example, in the tax year 1994/5 your tax charge for the account will be based on the interest you actually received in 1993/4. When interest rates are rising, this means you will effectively pay too little tax, but conversely when they are falling you will be overcharged. In this case there is no right of appeal, because the procedure counts as an actual tax charge, rather than a provisional assessment. The only way around it, if interest rates are dropping and you are therefore losing out, is to close the account, as the tax will be calculated on the interest actually paid in the final year. However, the Inland Revenue is then entitled to reassess the previous year's charge and adjust that to the true amount if it is in its own favour to do so (note that it will not offer a rebate if you paid too much!).

In the long run, the overpayments and underpayments should tend to even out. However, when you decide to close the account, you should try to do so in a year when rates have been falling so that any final swing will be in your favour. If you subsequently open another account, this will not affect the tax assessment of the first.

Banks

Current accounts

Time was when a current account was simply a convenient alternative to keeping your money under the mattress. You earned no interest on it, but neither did it cost you anything to run, as long as you kept the account in credit. The high street

banks, at least, offered services that were more or less identical to each other, so most people picked the one that was nearest to their home or workplace, or possibly the one their parents used, and then stuck with it for life. This had the advantage, in theory at least, that if you established a track record with your bank you were likely to be looked on more favourably if you needed a loan.

Nowadays, competitive pressures have swept all that aside. There are a host of different accounts offering a variety of facilities and there is more point in shopping around to find one that suits your needs. For instance, there are some that offer, within limits, an interest-free overdraft, particularly on student accounts – students being potentially lucrative customers in the future. Others are linked to a savings account, with an automatic sweep between the two, or provide telephone banking through which you can juggle your money between accounts.

Also, since building societies began to provide cash card and cheque-book facilities, banks have introduced interest payments on current accounts. On the basic accounts, however, the rates are very low, so they should be considered as purely for cash flow purposes, not as investments.

Higher interest accounts
Just as current accounts have burgeoned, so have deposit-style accounts. These offer better rates of interest but do not normally provide cheque-book or money transmission facilities, though they may have a link to a current account and some offer a cash card.

For instant access accounts there is usually no minimum deposit. Notice accounts, where withdrawals require between one and three months' notice, may require a minimum of £1000 or £2500. Generally, these will allow immediate access with loss of interest equivalent to the notice period, but the penalty may be waived if there is a balance remaining in the account of £5000 or £10,000.

Interest rates rise with the amount deposited and the length of notice; examples of rates offered at the time of writing are shown in Table 2.1.

Money market and high interest cheque accounts
These were once the preserve of merchant banks and licensed deposit-takers, and there are still some that are essentially deposit

Table 2.1 *Bank account rates*

Amount deposited (£)	Instant access (%)	30 days' notice (%)	90 days' notice (%)
500–999	2.25	2.44	—
1000–2499	2.34	2.44	—
2500–4999	2.34	2.63	3.00
5000–9999	2.44	2.81	3.19
10,000–24,999	2.72	3.19	3.56
25,000–49,999	3.00	3.56	3.75
50,000+	3.19	3.56	3.94

Note: Rates net of basic rate tax, applicable as at March 1994. Bank base rate: 5.25%.

Source: Money Facts

accounts for large sums of money, with no money transmission facilities. However, most of the major banks now offer some form of high interest cheque account. The services provided are usually more limited than the standard current account; there may be a minimum withdrawal or cheque amount of anything up to £250, or only a limited number of withdrawals free of charge, so for daily purposes you would probably need an ordinary account as well.

But, as in other spheres, competition is leading to improved options and there are a growing number of accounts which have no minimum withdrawal and offer a full range of facilities such as overdrafts, cash card, cheque card, standing orders and direct debits, with free banking as long as you remain in credit. On top of this, the interest rates can be substantially more than the token offerings on basic current accounts.

The one drawback is that they do require a relatively high initial deposit, generally of £1000 or £2500. There are one or two which offer respectable rates of interest on sums from £1 upwards, but these do not provide the full range of services.

Term deposits

Fixed-term deposits pay a fixed rate of interest for a specified period of time, which may be anything from one month to five years. Some of the smaller banks offer these for as little as £500 but the minimum is usually £2500 or £5000. As a rule, no withdrawals are allowed during the term and the interest rate is fixed at the outset, but rates can vary on a daily basis, so check before you invest.

Very large sums of money, upwards of £50,000, can be placed in money market time deposits through banks. While these may be for a period of some months, it is also possible to place money on overnight deposit with automatic renewal on a daily basis, so that you can leave the money for as long as you like while having instant access to it. Interest rates are set daily or sometimes more frequently and, provided the deposit is at least £50,000, interest can be paid gross.

Building societies

Like the banks, building societies have vastly expanded their range of products in recent years. In terms of the banks versus building societies 'savings war' the societies have largely been the aggressors, moving in on the banks' traditional territory of cheque accounts. But at the same time, they have faced considerable competitive pressure from each other, with the result that a number of smaller local societies have merged with the larger ones that maintain a national network of branches. One society, Abbey National, changed its status to become a bank but, despite occasional rumours, at the time of writing no other has followed this lead.

Banking accounts

Banking accounts come in two types: those which are more or less deposit-style accounts but provide cash card facilities; and those which offer a cheque-book and other banking facilities such as standing orders, direct debits and even overdrafts, though this last is rather less common. The services are generally free as long as the account is in credit, but there may be a minimum opening balance – normally not more than £200.

Interest is paid on these accounts and, while it can be rather more generous than bank current accounts, the same caveat applies, that rates are too low for these accounts to be considered as investments proper. For larger deposits, however, the rates offered are comparable to banks' high interest cheque accounts, or similar facilities may be offered through a separate account. The minimum deposit in this case is generally upwards of £2500. Some societies offer postal accounts, which may still provide

NATIONAL COUNTIES

BUILDING SOCIETY

Consistently a "best buy"

for *growth*

or *income*

on lump sum investments

147-153 High Street, Epsom, Surrey KT19 4EN

0372 742211

instant access but carry higher interest rates than the basic cheque account.

Instant access and notice accounts

Despite the vast array of different accounts that come under this heading, there are just three main points to consider in making a choice: the minimum investment, the period of notice required for withdrawals and the interest offered. Table 2.2 shows examples of the better offerings around at the time of writing. As can be seen, the general rule is that interest rates increase with the amount deposited and the length of notice period, though there can occasionally be anomalies where one society's instant access account offers more than another's notice account.

Notice accounts usually allow withdrawals within the notice period subject to an equivalent loss of interest, but the penalty may be waived if, say, £5000 or £10,000 remains in the account. There are also some which offer a bonus if no withdrawals are made during the year. This can be attractive if you do not expect to need access to your money but are not quite prepared to tie it up in a longer term bond.

Deposit accounts are not shown in the table as they are scarcely heard of these days. Although some instant access accounts require a minimum of £500, a number are available for smaller

Table 2.2   *Building society variable interest account rates*

Amount deposited (£)	Instant access (%)	30 days' notice (%)	90 days' notice (%)
500–999	4.50	—	—
1000–2499	5.10	4.76	5.25
2500–4999	5.10	4.80	5.25
5000–9999	5.10	4.80	5.25
10,000–24,999	5.18	5.14	5.25
25,000–49,999	5.33	5.33	5.51
50,000+	5.33	5.44	5.51

Note: Rates net of basic rate tax, applicable as at March 1994.

Source: Money Facts

sums, right down to £1, so they have largely superseded the older deposit and paid-up share accounts.

When comparing interest rates you should always go by the Compound Annual Rate (CAR) figure. This takes into account how often interest is credited, whether monthly, half-yearly or annually. If interest is credited more than once a year, the interest paid will itself start to earn interest, so the total return over a year will be that little bit higher.

One other point to watch for is when an account is closed to new business in favour of a new version. Often the old account will carry a lower rate of interest than the new one, although the terms and conditions may be identical. Not all societies inform their investors in this case – the argument being that the postage would prove prohibitive – so you need to keep an eye on developments and be prepared to switch if necessary. Local society branches will have up-to-date information on closed and new accounts.

Fixed-term accounts

Fixed-term accounts fall into two types: those which offer a fixed rate of interest during the term and those on which the interest is variable but guaranteed to be a fixed percentage above the ordinary share account rate. The minimum investment is generally £1000 and terms may run from six months to four years. Withdrawals during the term may be disallowed altogether, or may be subject to a penalty (commonly of 90 days' interest). Examples of fixed rates are shown in Table 2.3.

Like banks, the larger building societies offer money market time deposits for sums from £50,000 upwards. Rates change frequently but, once you invest, are fixed for the full term.

Tax exempt special savings accounts

Tax exempt special savings accounts (TESSAs) first appeared in January 1991, having been announced in the previous year's Budget. In a way, they are like a little sister to personal equity plans (PEPs, detailed in Chapter 9); PEPs offer tax-free returns from equity-linked investments, while TESSAs offer tax-free returns from bank and building society deposit accounts.

Table 2.3   *Building society fixed-term account rates*

Term	Minimum investment (£)	Net rate (%)
6 months	500	4.50
6 months	5000	4.58
1 year	500	4.50
1 year	10,000	4.88
2 years	2000	3.83
2 years	5000	4.88
3 years	2000	4.09
3 years	10,000	4.80

Note: Rates net of basic rate tax, applicable as at March 1994.

Source: Money Facts

TESSAs are available to any UK resident over the age of 18 and run for a period of five years. The maximum investment that can be made is £3000 in the first year and up to £1800 in each subsequent year, subject to an overall maximum of £9000. You may have only one TESSA, which must be held individually (ie not in joint names), but if you become dissatisfied with your current provider, you may transfer the account to another, although not all institutions are prepared to accept transfers.

Provided the capital is left intact for the full five years, all the interest earned is tax free. You may make withdrawals equivalent to the interest earned net of basic rate tax, but any larger amount will invalidate the TESSA which will then revert to being an ordinary taxable deposit. However, if you die within the five years, the TESSA will be treated as maturing at that point. All interest earned to date will be free of tax, but from then on it will become taxable as usual.

Whether or not it is worth while to have a TESSA depends very much on your personal circumstances. At the time of writing, interest rates have been falling steadily, so even free of tax the returns are not too exciting. But if you are going to hold money in a deposit account anyway, you may as well hold it in a TESSA, particularly if you are subject to higher rate tax. Even if you suddenly need access to the money, and therefore lose the tax advantage, you will be no worse off than if you had put it in an ordinary account in the first place.

You may, however, find that the rate of interest does not turn out to be so good. This is because a number of TESSA providers offer a special bonus at the end of the five-year term, at the expense of a lower rate meanwhile. Transferring the account to a new provider may also trigger a penalty, sometimes in addition to a stipulated period of notice, so to get the full benefit, as well as the tax exemption, you have to be prepared to stay the course.

Because of these bonuses, and the various terms attached, it is difficult to compare different TESSAs to determine the best buy. Also, interest rates are variable, so there is no guarantee that today's best offer will still be among the leaders in a year's time. Since you are effectively locked in once you start a plan, providers may be rather more interested in attracting new business than looking after their existing customers; it has been known, for example, for a provider to close an account to new business and then drop the rate paid on it, while offering a more attractive rate on a new product. Although you can transfer in that instance, the penalty charged may mean you lose out anyway.

The choice may be influenced by how much you want to invest. TESSAs may be opened with as little as £1 or £10 a month for those that offer a regular savings option. Some of the best rates, though, apply only if you make the maximum £9000 investment over the term and a number require you to set up a separate 'feeder' account which itself carries a minimum balance, and from which withdrawals are made to fund the TESSA.

National Savings

National Savings products can be divided into three categories: those that pay a return completely free of tax, those that are taxable but pay interest gross, and a couple of one-offs, the First Option Bond and Premium Bonds, which do neither of these things.

Tax-free investments

National Savings Certificates
National Savings Certificates can currently be bought for a minimum of £100, with units of £25 thereafter. Recent issues have followed the same pattern: they run for five years with a fixed

Table 2.4 *National Savings Certificates 41st issue*

Years after purchase	Value at end of year (£)	% yield for year	Compound yield % pa
1	103.65	3.65	3.65
2	107.85	4.05	3.85
3	113.67	5.40	4.35
4	120.95	6.40	4.85
5	130.08	7.55	5.40

Note: Value for a £100 certificate; tax-free return.

rate of return in each year. The return increases over the five years, so although you can cash units in at any time, you lose out by doing so. Table 2.4 shows the interest build-up on the current 41st issue.

As Table 2.5 shows, issues are available for varying lengths of time and give different rates of return, depending on the market rates at the time and how anxious the government is to get a slice of the savings market. In 1993, it took a more aggressive stance by doubling the maximum holding in current issue certificates to £10,000 and also doubling the reinvestment limit to £20,000.

Reinvestment is an option at the end of the fixed period, when certificates mature. Instead of taking out your money, you can either continue to hold the certificates, or reinvest in the latest

Table 2.5 *National Savings Certificates, past issues*

Issue number	Dates of issue	Value of £100 certificate after 5 years (£)	Compound annual return over 5 years (%)
33rd	1.5.87–21.7.88	140.26	7.0
34th	22.7.88–16.6.90	143.56	7.5
35th	18.6.90–14.3.91	157.42	9.5
36th	2.4.91–2.5.92	150.37	8.5
37th	13.5.92–5.8.92	146.94	8.0
38th	6.8.92–4.10.92	143.57	7.5
39th	5.10.92–12.11.92	138.63	6.75
40th	13.11.92–16.12.93	132.25	5.75

issue, for which there is a £20,000 maximum holding on top of the £10,000 for new investment.

Once an issue has reached the end of its fixed period, the interest rate moves to the general extension rate, which is variable and currently 3.51 per cent for the 7th to 34th issues. The 1st to 6th issues come under different rules and are subject to a lower rate of interest. So you will do better to cash in any of these and reinvest in the current issue, rather than retaining them. More recent issues that are still within their fixed period are worth holding on to up to maturity, because the guaranteed return is higher than anything you could currently get from a comparable investment.

Index-linked certificates
Like the ordinary savings certificates, the current 7th issue of index-linked certificates has a minimum investment of £100 and a maximum of £10,000, with a further £20,000 allowed for reinvestment from mature certificates. The difference is that here the return is linked to movements in the Retail Price Index over the five-year period. In addition, extra interest is added at a guaranteed rate, which increases for each of the five years. Currently the compound return above inflation is equal to 3 per cent a year and is free of tax. All the interest earned is added to the capital value – so that after year 1 you are earning interest on the interest – and repaid in total when you cash in.

As mentioned at the start of this chapter, inflation can be a serious threat to fixed capital investments and the real returns above inflation offered by interest rates can be very small. So in principle, index-linking should be very attractive. In practice, though, it is like any fixed rate: in return for protection against doing worse, you give up the chance to do better. For example, if inflation remains at the current rate of around 2.5 per cent, the total return on index-linked certificates, including the extra interest, would be 5.5 per cent, just slightly above that offered on savings certificates. If inflation leaps up again, the in-built protection will be extremely worth while.

Yearly Plan
The Yearly Plan is outside the scope of this book as it is a monthly

Carr Sheppards and Retirement Income Planning

Carr Sheppards is the result of the amalgamation of two of the oldest names in the London Stock Exchange, W I Carr (founded 1825) and Sheppards (founded 1827).

Our directors and executives have been giving advice to clients on investment and financial planning matters since the 1960's, much of it relating to retirement income planning.

We are independent of any insurance companies and fund management groups and so can give entirely unbiased advice across the full range of investment products in the market. Carr Sheppards' solutions are tailored to the client, rather than fitting the client to a product, in marked contrast to Procrustes, the legendary criminal from the ancient Greek fable, who ambushed unwary travellers and strapped them to a bed. If they were too short he stretched them, and if they were too long he chopped off their limbs. Some advisers are wont to sell you packaged products in much the same way. The salesman may think to himself, "It nearly fits and I do need the commission."

Having shopped around and found an independent adviser, do remember that independent does not necessarily mean unbiased. There are some important questions which you must ask:

1. How are they remunerated? Is it mainly by salary or mainly commission? A salaried remuneration basis puts less pressure on the adviser to 'sell'.

2. How many years experience do they have? You should be seeking an absolute minimum of 5 years.

3. Do in-house products give them a larger 'credit' than other similar contracts? Are they making extensive use of insurance-based products? Both can create a bias towards products which may carry higher commission.

4. Will you be provided with a written report and recommendations that you can study at your leisure? This should summarise your present position, your needs, a recommended investment strategy and indicate the future tax and income position.

5. What happens if the adviser's firm gets into financial difficulties, or worse?

Do not be embarrassed to ask these questions. Selecting an adviser to assist you in creating your plan for retirement is an extremely difficult decision. Select an adviser who can satisfy these questions and you should not come to too much harm. If you feel you are being pressurised, do nothing. In fact, the best investment you can ever make is the time you spend finding someone good whom you can trust.

Carr Sheppards Limited is a member of the London Stock Exchange and the Securities and Futures Authority.
Registered Office: 122 Leadenhall Street London EC3V 4QH.
Registered in England No. 2122340

savings plan, rather than a lump-sum investment product. For the purposes of comparison, it offers a guaranteed return, currently equivalent to 5.4 per cent compound, if you save for a year and then hold the certificate for a further four years.

Taxable investments

Income bonds

Income bonds are available from a minimum of £2000 up to a maximum of £250,000 and offer a monthly income, paid on the 5th of each month. The interest rate is variable, but six weeks' notice is given of any change, which will be advertised in newspapers. The current rate is 6.5 per cent gross for sums up to £25,000 and 6.75 per cent gross for larger amounts, which compares favourably with offers from banks and building societies. Income is paid (gross, but liable to tax) direct to a bank, building society or National Savings investment account.

Capital bonds

Capital bonds run for five years and offer a guaranteed rate of return if they are held for the full term. For the current Series H bonds this is 7.25 per cent gross. You can cash in a bond early, but this would mean you lose out, as the interest rate increases each year, and the amount you get on cashing in is the value at the last anniversary plus a special interest rate since then. No interest is paid on bonds encashed before the first anniversary.

The minimum holding is £100, with a maximum of £250,000. This maximum applies to total holdings of all capital bonds, with the exception of Series A. At the end of the five years bonds are repaid in full, together with all the interest accumulated; no further interest is earned after the fifth anniversary.

National Savings Bank ordinary account

With a basic interest rate of 2 per cent gross, the ordinary account is slightly more lucrative than a bank current account, although the facilities are more limited. Withdrawals are generally restricted to £100 on demand, with written notice required for larger sums, although if you have used the account for at least six months at one particular post office you can apply for a regular customer account, which entitles you to take out up to £250 on demand.

If you keep an account open for a full calendar year, you are then eligible for a higher interest rate for each month that the balance is £500 or more. Even so, this higher rate is only 3.25 per cent gross. The one feature that does add some attraction for higher rate taxpayers is that the first £70 of interest, or £140 for a joint holding, is free of tax. Otherwise, this is more a home for ready cash than an investment.

National Savings Bank investment account
For smaller sums in particular, this can be an attractive alternative to bank and building society deposits, as the minimum is just £20. There are three tiers of interest rates which are currently 5.25 per cent for sums under £500, 5.75 per cent from £500 to £25,000 and 6 per cent for sums over £25,000. These are the gross rates; interest is credited gross, so you can enjoy the money for a short while before settling the tax bill. Withdrawals are at one month's notice and from May 1993 the maximum holding was increased to £100,000.

Pensioners Bond
The Pensioners Bond was announced in the 1993 Autumn Budget and introduced in January 1994. It is available only for people aged 65 or over, although younger people may buy them for a relative, as long as the recipient of the interest is over 65. The minimum investment is £500 and the maximum is £20,000, or £40,000 for a joint holding, for which both savers must meet the age requirement.

The interest rate is fixed for the first five years that you hold a bond and is currently 7 per cent gross. The interest is taxable but paid gross and will be credited on the 19th of each month direct to a bank or building society account or a National Savings investment account.

At the end of five years, National Savings will write to tell you the guaranteed interest rate for the next five years. The money can then be reinvested or withdrawn without penalty. If you want to cash in at any other time, you must give 60 days' notice and no interest will be paid during those 60 days. Partial withdrawals can be made from a minimum of £500 as long as at least £500 remains in your holding.

At the time of writing, the Pensioners Bond has proved popular and the return is attractive compared with building society accounts. The drawback is that interest rates are currently low and may rise significantly over the next five years, leaving the bond looking uncompetitive. Although you can cash in early, the penalty is quite severe – the loss of interest would amount to about £115 on a £10,000 holding. For some people, the benefits of having a regular fixed income will outweigh the possible loss if interest rates rise. Otherwise, you might do better with the Income Bond, which is currently paying slightly lower interest, but could pay more if rates rise and can be cashed in at three months' notice without any interest penalty.

First Option Bond

The First Option Bond was initially launched in July 1992 and caused something of a furore. The building societies saw it as a serious threat to their own ability to attract savings and Cheltenham & Gloucester took the bold step of raising its mortgage rate – on the grounds that it would have to raise its savings rate to compete with the bond and needed to maintain its margins. The last thing the government wanted, at a time when it was trying to bring down inflation, was to see mortgage costs rise, so it backed off and reduced the interest on the bond.

But governments do not remain intimidated for long and the bond was relaunched in the 1993 Budget. The minimum investment is £1000 and interest is fixed for 12 months at a time. At each anniversary, investors are notified of the new rate for the next year and have the option of continuing the bond or cashing it in. Between anniversaries, the return will be the full value at the last anniversary plus interest at half the fixed rate for the period since then, except that no interest is paid for encashments during the first year. Bonds can also be partially cashed in as long as the value remains above £1000.

Unusually for a National Savings product, interest is credited net of basic rate tax. Higher rate taxpayers will be liable for the difference, while non-taxpayers can apply for a refund. Interest is not paid out automatically, but you can apply for a part repayment equivalent to the amount earned. This should be timed for the anniversary date if possible.

At the time of writing the interest rate is 4.5 per cent net of basic rate tax, which compares well with building society accounts. There is also a bonus of 0.3 per cent where the value remains at least £20,000 during the year.

Premium Bonds

Premium Bonds are not exactly an investment, as there is no promise of a return – but then again, that could be said to apply to equities and at least with Premium Bonds your capital is always safe. The odds on winning a prize also improve with the size of your holding: at the maximum of £20,000, you should on average win sixteen prizes a year, while to win once a year on average you need to hold £1250-worth. Of course, averages do not always work out; although ERNIE is quite impartial, some people seem to be luckier than others.

The minimum investment is £100, with multiples of £10 thereafter. The prize fund is currently calculated at 5.2 per cent of all eligible bonds – they have to be held for one complete calendar month before they are entered for the draw. Every month there is a top prize of £1 million, going down to 25 prizes of £5000. The balance of the prize fund is divided between prizes of £50, £100, £500 and £1000, the numbers depending on how many bonds are eligible for the draw. All prizes are free of tax.

For a complete guide to all the National Savings products mentioned, see Table 2.6.

Where to find out more

Banks and building societies

Information on the types of account offered and current interest rates can be found in local branches. The Building Societies Association (071-437 0655) can also answer general questions, but will not advise on current rates offered by individual societies. *Money Facts*, a monthly subscription magazine aimed chiefly at professional advisers, gives comprehensive listings of bank and building society accounts, TESSAs, offshore accounts and

Table 2.6 *National Savings guide*

Product	Minimum and maximum holdings	Who may buy or invest	Income fixed or variable
National Savings Certificates 41st issue	Minimum £100, maximum £10,000 in addition to previous issues; may reinvest a further £20,000 from mature savings and Yearly Plan Certificates	Individuals (also jointly), trustees	Increasing at fixed rate for initial term; variable extension rate thereafter
National Savings Certificates 7th index-linked issue	Minimum £100, maximum £10,000 in addition to previous issues; may reinvest a further £20,000 from mature savings and Yearly Plan Certificates	Individuals (also jointly), trustees	Repayment value linked to changes in the RPI plus fixed annual supplement; variable after 5 years
National Savings income bond	Minimum £2000, maximum £250,000	Individuals (also jointly), trustees	Variable; paid monthly
National Savings capital bond	Minimum £100, maximum £250,000 for holdings in all Series, excluding Series A	Individuals (also jointly), trustees	Fixed if held for full five years; no interest paid after five years
Pensioners Bond	Minimum £500, maximum £20,000	Individuals over 65 (also jointly), trustees	Fixed for 5 years at a time; paid monthly
National Savings First Option Bond	Minimum £1000, maximum £250,000	Individuals (also jointly), trustees	Fixed for 12 months at a time
National Savings Bank ordinary account	Minimum £10, maximum £10,000	Individuals (also jointly), children, trustees	Variable; credited annually
National Savings investment account	Minimum £20, maximum £100,000	Individuals (also jointly), children, trustees	Variable; credited annually
Premium Bonds	Minimum £100, maximum £20,000	Individuals over 16; bonds can be bought for children by parents, guardians or (great) grandparents	No interest
National Savings Yearly Plan	Minimum £20, maximum £400 per month	Individuals, trustees	Guaranteed five-year return at time of buying

Tax position	Notice of withdrawal	How to buy/sell
Free of income tax and CGT	At least eight working days	Buy: through post offices Sell: repayment form from post offices
Free of income tax and CGT	At least eight working days	Buy: through post offices Sell: repayment form from post offices
Interest is taxable, but paid gross	3 months; in the first year, interest paid at half rate from date of purchase to date of repayment	Buy: application form at post offices, send with cheque to Blackpool Sell: repayment form from post offices
Interest is taxable, but paid gross	At least two weeks; no interest paid if cashed in in first year	Buy: through post offices Sell: repayment form from post offices
Interest is taxable, but paid gross	60 days; no interest paid during notice period	Buy: application form at post offices, send with cheque to Blackpool Sell: repayment form on bond
Interest is taxable; paid net of basic rate tax which non-taxpayers can reclaim	No notice; no penalty if repaid on anniversary date, otherwise interest paid at half the fixed rate since the last anniversary; no interest if cashed in in first year	Buy: application form from post offices to be sent with cheque to National Savings, Glasgow Sell: repayment form on investment certificate
First £70 (£140 joint) of annual interest is free of income tax	Up to £100 on demand; larger amounts require a few days' written notice	Opening and withdrawals at post offices
Interest is taxable, but paid gross	One month	Opening: through post offices Withdrawals: form from post offices to be sent to Glasgow
Prizes free of income tax and CGT	At least eight working days	Buy: through post offices Sell: repayment form from post offices
Free of income tax and CGT	At least 14 working days; lower rate of return if cashed in early	Buy: application form at post offices Sell: repayment form from post offices

National Savings products. It is available from Moneyfacts Publications, Laundry Loke, North Walsham, Norfolk NR28 0BD, telephone 0692 500765.

Money market accounts
Information can be found in newspapers.

National Savings
Booklets on the various products are available at post offices. General information can be obtained by phoning the Sales Information Unit on 0645 645000 during normal office hours.

The latest interest rates are also quoted by recorded message on the following numbers:

London: 071-605 9483/9484
Blackpool: 0253 723714
Glasgow: 041-632 2766.

3

Fixed Capital Investments (2)

The last chapter covered the major institutions that offer fixed capital investments, most of which can be bought through high street outlets. Going a little further afield, there are a number of other products which also offer capital security, but may offer a more attractive rate of income than the standard bank and building society accounts, particularly for smaller investments.

Local authority bonds

Local authority bonds are issued for a fixed term of between one and ten years, over which the capital value remains constant. The minimum investment starts at £500 and the interest rate is fixed throughout the term. The bonds used to be a popular way for local authorities to raise funds, but in the 1980s the administration involved and the availability of cheaper loans from other sources led to a decline in the number of issues. However, there has recently been something of a revival and the bonds that are available are open to any investor – it need not be your own local authority that you buy from.

One drawback is that there is no facility to make withdrawals during the term of the bond, so your money is effectively locked in until the maturity date, although it may be possible to transfer it to a third party on written request. When the fixed term expires, there may be an opportunity to continue the investment for a further period at whatever the going rate of interest is at that time, otherwise you can simply have your original capital returned.

As for the safety aspect, the bonds are backed by the local authority itself, not by central government. Hence they are marginally more risky than a government-issued security such as a gilt and usually offer slightly higher rates of return to reflect this. However, while there is no obligation for the government to help out or provide any compensation in the event of a default, there is a certain presumption that it would act if there was a danger of widespread losses, if only for the sake of political expediency.

Interest is paid out twice a year and will normally be paid net of basic rate tax. If you are a non-taxpayer, you can register to receive interest payments gross by completing Inland Revenue Form R85, in the same way as for bank and building society deposits. Once the bond has been issued, the interest rate will remain fixed for the full term. Hence the longer term bonds are most suitable for investors for whom security of income is a priority – others may find they lose out if interest rates rise in the future. The rates will vary between different authorities and across the different lifespans, and are reset on a regular basis – sometimes daily – so you should check the up-to-date position before investing. Examples of current rates at the time of writing are shown in Table 3.1.

Guaranteed income and growth bonds

Guaranteed income bonds are issued by life assurance companies and are available for terms of between one and ten years, although the widest choice is for periods of four or five years. The minimum investment is generally around £5000 and the interest rate is fixed for the whole term, so these bonds are attractive to investors seeking a regular income, perhaps in retirement, to supplement a pension.

Not all life offices operate in this market and some that do issue

Table 3.1 *Local authority bonds*

Years	1	2–5	6/7	8/9	10
Typical gross rates (%)	4.75	6.0	6.0	6.5	6.0

Source: Money Facts, March 1994

bonds only occasionally. In any case, specific offers will only be available for a limited period, as interest rates will be reviewed at regular intervals. The rates are generally based on the return available on gilts and should give a better deal than a building society deposit, but then again, you may be committing your capital for a longer period.

Interest payments are usually made once a year, though some bonds pay out half-yearly and there may also be a monthly income option on larger investments. Some examples of the rates available at the time of going to press are shown in Table 3.2. These are net rates and apply for an investment of £2000; in some cases higher rates may be available for larger sums.

In this case, the returns increase with the length of term of the bond. You might expect that the longer you are prepared to tie up your capital, the higher the return should be, but this is not always so. The companies have to match the rates that they offer to those they can obtain on their investments, so it depends on the pattern of market interest rates. Remember, too, that the rate is guaranteed throughout the term, so at the longer end you may be sacrificing a small measure of return in exchange for the security of a fixed income.

Once you buy a bond, you are effectively locked into it for the full term. Companies vary in their willingness to provide a surrender value on early encashment, but generally any amount offered will be small. Should the bond holder die, the original capital will be returned, but again, companies have different policies on whether they will add in any income accrued since the last payment. Where payments are annual, this could be a significant amount if the bond holder dies just before a payment is due. For married couples, one way around this problem is to take out a bond on a 'joint life, second death' basis, which means payments would continue to be paid to the surviving spouse for the rest of the term. Should both partners die, the capital sum would be repaid to the estate on the second death. As with annuities, however, this kind of 'extra' may mean the income level is slightly lower.

A variation on the theme is a rising income bond, which incorporates guaranteed increases in interest each year. A current example, for a minimum investment of £10,000, offers a starting

Buying The Future
Why Emerging Markets?

Do you ever look at where things are made? If you do, you may have noticed the growing number of products that have their origin outside the major western economies. This is just one aspect of the changing nature of the world economy. Companies in many developing nations now compete successfully with the best in the world, combining skilled, but low cost labour, with up-to-date technology. In turn these trends are opening up opportunities for investors in emerging markets to participate in the development process and spread of prosperity.

Where are the Emerging Markets?

'Emerging markets' is taken to describe markets and nations categorised by the World Bank as low or middle income, or those with a stockmarket capitalisation of less than 2 per cent of the MSCI-World Index. Over 80 per cent of the world's population lives in such countries, and they include much of South East Asia, the Indian sub-continent, all of Africa, Latin America, Eastern Europe and what was the Soviet Union, as well as parts of Southern Europe.

There are now over 100 emerging countries, but only around 24 can currently be accessed by foreign portfolio investors and, of these, some still have investment restrictions.

Why Do Developing Countries Grow Faster?

Fast population growth, the transferability of modern technology and the liberalisation of economies all play a role in generating faster growth. But gains in life expectancy and literacy standards are perhaps two of the most important factors. Advances in medicine and improving standards of health care are leading to significant gains in life expectancy. In turn, increasing life expectancy makes gaining skills and experience more worthwhile. Dramatic improvements in adult literacy have been witnessed in many countries. Less than 10% of the Indonesian population could read in 1930, but by 1980 this proportion had risen to 60%. Improved literacy encourages the use of modern methods. Educated farmers are more likely to apply new techniques – helping to explain why rapid population growth has not out-stripped food supply. Moreover, rising education standards allow for the introduction of the latest technology, and combining technology with low labour costs provides a base for export-led growth.

Market Performance

As in developed markets the performance of emerging markets can vary enormously. In the five years since the inception of the IFC Investable indices at the end of 1988, to 31 March 1994 some markets have produced quite staggering returns in sterling terms: Argentina is up by 1266.0%; Mexico by 869.6%; Chile by 840.6%; Malaysia by 244.1% and Thailand by 387.2%. Over the same period the MSCI World Index rose a modest 67.7%. This performance is reflected in the appreciation of emerging market funds. For example ordinary shares in Templeton Emerging Markets Investment Trust plc show a rise of 268% from inception in June 1989 to 29 April 1994.

Nor is it too late to share in the development of these markets. The opening of new markets, further liberalisation and privatisation measures, and temporary setbacks to individual markets and stocks, all present opportunities to the disciplined value investor.

Diversification Opportunities

Emerging markets can perform strongly but the performance of individual emerging markets is much more variable from year to year than that of the three largest developed markets.

Building a portfolio from shares drawn from a range of emerging markets brings two benefits. As the individual markets tend to move out of step, a fund investing across a range of markets will tend to have a much smoother path than a portfolio concentrating on only one or two emerging markets. And as emerging markets are also out of step with the developed markets their inclusion in an overall portfolio will add to its stability.

Emerging markets are here to stay. For many investors it is wise to build some exposure to these fast growing countries.

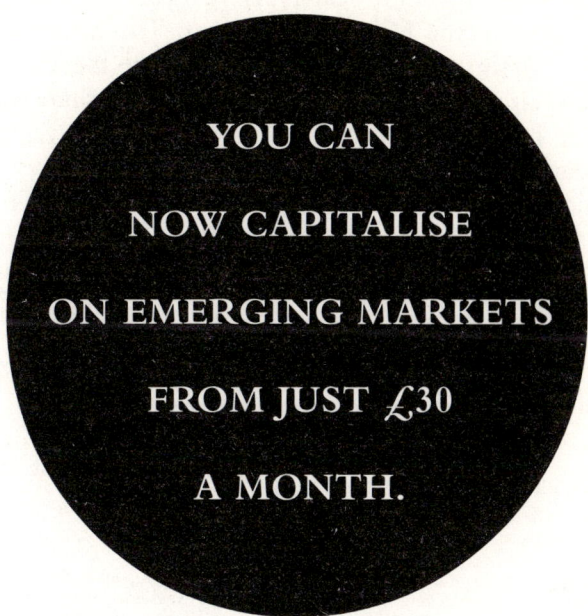

TEMPLETON INVESTMENT PLANS

Reaching the world's most exciting markets needn't cost you the earth ● Our Investment Plan will take a little a long way, in two Trusts investing across a wide range of developing economies. ● Now you can invest in both the new Templeton Latin America Investment Trust and the Templeton Emerging Markets Investment Trust. ● We believe this will give the best of both worlds – high potential rewards with increased diversification.

For more details, call 031-469 4000 or write to Templeton Investment Management Limited, Saltire Court, Castle Terrace, Edinburgh EH1 2EH.

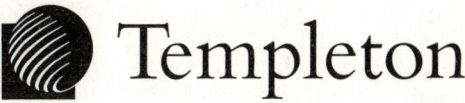

income of 5 per cent in year 1, rising by 0.5 per cent each year to 7 per cent in the fifth and final year. This will provide some defence against inflation, which can erode the value of a level income, although the increases are only small; there is also a price to pay in that the initial income will be lower than on a comparable fixed income bond.

Another version is the guaranteed growth bond. This operates on a similar principle to the income bond, but the interest earned is accumulated within the bond rather than paid out, so at the end of the term you receive back your capital plus a guaranteed profit.

Table 3.2 *Examples of guaranteed income bond rates*

Term	Income net of basic rate tax (%)
1 year	3.23
2 years	3.56
3 years	3.75
4 years	4.2
5 years	4.2

For comparison, these bonds were available when sample interest rates on competing products were as follows:

Product	Term or notice required	Rate net of basic rate tax (%)	Fixed/variable interest
NS Certificates 41st issue	5 years	5.40[a]	Fixed
NS First Option Bond (£1–20,000)	1 year	4.50	Fixed
Building society instant access (min £5000)	None	4.88	Variable
Building society 90-day account (min £10,000)	90 days	5.25	Variable
TESSA	5 years	7.25[a]	Variable

[a] Tax-free to all investors

Tax treatment of guaranteed bonds

The tax position of guaranteed bonds can be complex, partly because they are not all of the same structure. Longer term bonds are sometimes based on a combination of annuities: a temporary annuity, which provides the income payments, and a deferred annuity, which provides the return of capital at maturity. However, a change in the tax treatment of annuities at the beginning of 1992 made this route less attractive and the majority of bonds now issued are based on a single premium endowment policy with guaranteed bonuses.

For a basic rate taxpayer, the composition of the bond is of no concern. Income is paid net of basic rate tax, so you have no further liability. Non-taxpayers, however, cannot reclaim the tax paid from an endowment, so as a rule these bonds are not suitable to those investors.

Higher rate taxpayers are in a different position again. With an endowment, up to 5 per cent of the original sum invested may be withdrawn each year free of tax – it is counted as a return of capital – and any unused part of this allowance can be carried forward to subsequent years. Where a bond pays income annually, the mechanics are such that you will usually be 'in credit' with this allowance for most or all of the term. At maturity, however, tax may be charged on the 'profit', taking into account the money paid out and the amount originally invested. Further details of the taxation of single premium policies are given in Chapter 10.

Older investors who qualify for age allowance may also be affected by the tax rules. For these and higher rate taxpayers, an insurance broker or other professional adviser should be able to offer guidance on the best buy.

Cash unit trusts

Unit trusts are usually associated with equity investments, which are far from capital secure, but cash trusts are a fairly new breed. They invest chiefly in money market instruments and, by virtue of the size of the fund, they can secure top rates of interest. The minimum investment varies between £250 and £5000.

Cash trusts offer complete capital security and in most cases there is no initial charge. There is an annual management charge, which has to be met from the income the trust generates, but it is generally no more than 0.5 per cent. The return varies according to the interest rates available in the market; at the time of writing, gross yields are between 4.2 per cent and 5.95 per cent.

Income can be paid out or reinvested in the fund. Interest is credited net of basic rate tax, which can be reclaimed by non-taxpayers, while higher rate taxpayers will be liable for the extra amount due. A few trusts provide a cheque-book facility; otherwise, if you want to get your money out, the manager is obliged to issue a cheque within 24 hours of receiving the redemption form.

Further information on cash unit trusts can be found in Chapters 6 and 7.

Offshore deposit accounts

All the major banks and building societies now have offshore branches or subsidiary companies, situated in either the Isle of Man or the Channel Islands. Like their onshore parents, they offer a variety of accounts, depending on how much you want to invest and how quickly you want to be able to access your money. The choices include instant access, 90-day notice accounts, fixed interest term deposits with periods from a number of months to a number of years, money market accounts and high interest cheque accounts. All of these operate in very much the same way as their onshore equivalents.

Table 3.3 *Examples of offshore deposit rates*

Type of account	Gross annual interest rate (%)
Instant access, min £500	5.75
Instant access, min £5000	5.75
Instant access, min £50,000	7.00
60-day notice, min £10,000	6.30
90-day notice, min £10,000	6.80
Money market account, min £5000	3.75

Source: Money Facts, March 1994

As a rule, interest rates are tiered with the size of the deposit and the notice period (see Table 3.3 opposite). At the bottom end of the scale, minimum deposits start at £500, while money market accounts start at around £2500 and can go up to more than £100,000.

Offshore deposit accounts enjoyed particular popularity when onshore accounts were subject to composite rate tax, which was deducted at source and could not be reclaimed by a non-taxpayer. Nowadays that advantage no longer exists and for UK residents the tax liability will be the same either way. However, offshore accounts do have the slight advantage that interest is paid gross, so the tax bill is deferred for a while.

The other important consideration is how safe your investment is. 'Offshore' used to be synonymous with shady, or at least dubious, dealing, but the image has been considerably cleaned up in recent years. The Isle of Man, which had a salutary experience with the collapse of the Savings and Investment Bank in 1982, now has a compensation scheme for bank and building society deposits. In addition, building society subsidiaries are covered by their parents for the full amount of their liabilities. The Channel Islands keep a tight rein on financial businesses by having a strict vetting procedure for any institutions applying to set up in the islands.

Offshore money funds

Sterling offshore money funds are similar to the money market funds mentioned in the last chapter, investing in much the same kind of holdings, such as bank deposits and certificates of deposit. In addition, however, there are offshore money funds denominated in a variety of different currencies. These range from major currencies, such as the US dollar, the German D-Mark, the Swiss franc and the Japanese yen, to the less obvious, such as the Belgian franc, the Danish krone and the Swedish krona.

After the UK left the Exchange Rate Mechanism in September 1992, there was increased interest in foreign currency funds, which may offer higher rates of interest than their sterling counterparts. However, there is a greater risk involved because of currency fluctuations. This may be reduced if you invest in a managed currency fund, where the manager will switch between various currencies according to their perceived prospects. Even so, while there is the opportunity for gain on the exchange rates, there is equally the chance of capital loss.

Some money funds have no set minimum investment, while others may require £1000 upwards. One point to watch for is that these funds carry an annual management fee. The usual figure is around 1 per cent and anything higher than this should be treated with caution, as it will cut into the returns available.

Taxation of offshore funds

The tax position of offshore funds is a little complex, as they are classified into two types: those with 'accumulator' status, also known as 'roll-up' funds, and those with 'distributor' status.

Prior to 1984, all funds were of the roll-up type, which meant that all interest earned was accumulated within the fund and added to the capital value. As a result, when investors came to sell, they were liable only to capital gains tax on the profits. Since there was the annual exempt allowance to make use of, and the top rate of capital gains tax at that time was only 30 per cent, this provided excellent tax efficiency, for higher rate taxpayers in particular.

Since 1984, however, the Inland Revenue has introduced new tax rules based on the dual classification. Roll-up funds still accumulate all the interest in the old way, but when you come to sell your holding, all the profits – whether they arise from capital gains or interest – are taxed as income.

For investors who are not in need of a regular income, there are still some advantages in roll-up funds, because the tax liability is deferred until you cash in your investment. This means that, meanwhile, you continue to earn interest on the full amount. Also, you will benefit if you wait to sell until your tax rate is lower than it is now, perhaps after retirement. Better still, if you retire or move abroad and cease to be a UK resident, you can escape UK tax altogether by cashing in the holding after you have left the country.

Distributor status was introduced as a special concession. To qualify, funds must distribute at least 85 per cent of their income and this will be taxed in the hands of the investor at normal

income tax rates. They must also not engage in 'trading' – primarily, procedures designed to convert income into capital gains and thereby reduce the tax liability. Distributor status is only granted in retrospect, so funds that could be borderline tend to opt for accumulator status rather than risk their investors being faced with an unexpected tax position.

Distributor funds can be useful for non-taxpayers. Even for those who do pay tax, there is a small benefit compared with onshore funds as interest is paid gross, so there will be a short period of grace before you have to give the taxman what is due.

Where to find out more

Information on all the products mentioned in this chapter, with details of current offers and interest rates, can be found in the financial pages of newspapers (advertising and editorial) and in specialist magazines. *Money Facts*, a monthly publication, gives a guide to investment rates, including local authority bonds and offshore deposit accounts. It can be contacted on 0692 500765. Alternatively, you should consult an insurance broker or other professional adviser.

4

The Gilts Market

In recent years, the government has done a fair amount to encourage saving – with the introduction of personal equity plans and tax exempt special savings accounts. Yet the government itself frequently lives beyond its means by spending more than its revenues, hence the National Debt, which grows rather more often than it is reduced.

National Savings products, outlined in Chapter 2, are one form of borrowing by the government, but by far the biggest chunk is through gilt-edged securities, or gilts for short. These are issued regularly and come in a variety of types. Most have a lifespan of up to 20 years, though some last indefinitely, but although they cannot be cashed in before their maturity date, they can meanwhile be traded on the Stock Exchange.

Gilts are regarded as being one of the safest of all investments. This is not to say that you cannot make a loss on them – the prices fluctuate, so your capital is not guaranteed. But the promises made by the gilt itself – the interest payments and the redemption value – are as secure as you can get; the government has never yet been known to default.

Terminology

One of the off-putting things about gilts is the jargon. If you go along to a building society, the accounts may have fancy names, but the descriptions of 'instant access' or '90 days' notice' are usually pretty clear. In fact, the title of a gilt is descriptive of what it offers, but you need to be able to decipher the code. As an

THE SCOTS BOX

This old brassbound chest marked the beginning of one of the oldest charities in the land. Scots who came to London some 380 years ago in the train of James I and VI put regular contributions into it to help those among them who fell upon hard times. They called it the Scots Box. It became an institution, and in 1665 received a Royal Charter as **The Scottish Hospital of the Foundation of Charles II**. Over the centuries the name changed to the rather formal sounding **Royal Scottish Corporation**. The purpose, however, remained exactly the same: help for needy Scots in London and the maintenance of their self respect.

Any Londoner of Scottish extraction can, in effect, ring the Corporation's bell in Covent Garden and ask for help. It may be a youngster who has run away from home, is penniless and frightened. It could be a single parent stretched for funds, or a worker made redundant and trying to acquire new skills. More often though, the supplicant is elderly, perhaps unwell, struggling to remain independent. She, or he, will be visited regularly by one of a team of 10 Welfare Visitors who can arrange material help where necessary, and has time to talk and listen.

Times change, but human needs do not only remain but expand in need and variety. We need your help, please, to keep the Scots Box replenished.

The Royal Scottish Corporation

37 King Street, Covent Garden
London WC2E 8JS
Tel 071-240 3718
Fax 071-497 0184
Registered Charity No. 207326

example, let us suppose you are offered £100 nominal of Treasury $9\frac{1}{2}\%$ 1999.

To start with, 'nominal' refers to the face value of the gilt, which is the amount the government will repay at the date of redemption. This is also called the 'par value'. But between now and the redemption date, the price of the gilt will vary and may be above or below par. So your £100 nominal may cost you more or less than £100, but if you hold it for the rest of its lifespan, that is what you will get back. It follows that, at the time you buy, there is an in-built capital gain or loss if the gilt is held to redemption.

The name 'Treasury' can effectively be ignored. Some gilts, like 'War Loan', have names which reflect the original purpose of the borrowing, while most that are around today are called Treasury or Exchequer. Either way, the name has no relevance to the investment characteristics.

The percentage, $9\frac{1}{2}\%$ in this case, refers to the 'coupon', or the interest rate that will be paid on the gilt. The rate applies to the nominal value of the gilt, so £100 nominal at $9\frac{1}{2}\%$ will earn £9.50 interest a year. In practice, the true rate of return on your money will depend on the price you pay for the gilt. If you buy below the par value, you will be getting a higher rate than the one quoted. For example, if your £100 nominal costs you £98, the £9.50 interest works out at just under 9.7 per cent. This is known as the 'flat' or 'running' yield of the stock.

Finally, 1999 is the redemption date, when the nominal value will be repaid to whoever holds the gilt at that time. Some stocks are 'double-dated': they carry two redemption dates, for example, 2001–2004. This means that the government can choose to redeem the stock at any time between those dates, but no later than the second one. As a rule, if a stock is standing above its par value as redemption approaches, the earlier date is more likely; if it is below par, the later date.

Types of gilts

Conventional gilts are classified into four types, which are generally shown separately in newspaper price listings. Those with up to five years left to run before redemption are called 'short-dated' or 'shorts'; those with remaining lives of five to 15

An endowment policy which has a few years remaining is likely to provide an attractive lump-sum investment.

The market for the purchase of secondhand with-profits endowment policies has grown considerably in the past few years, likely to exceed £60 million in 1993. Endowment policies can be surrendered, but many policies, particularly those in force for more than five years, are likely to attract buyers at prices above the surrender value. The purchaser will acquire an investment in the first-class security offered by the leading life insurance companies, offering an attractive compound rate of interest.

By choosing policies which will mature on selected dates, the purchaser is able to create an investment portfolio geared to the occasions when the need for a capital sum may be anticipated. Future premiums will need to be paid, but the purchaser will have the opportunity of paying all subsequent premiums immediately to convert the policy to become fully paid. Policies sold at recent auctions have ranged in size from £2,000 to well over £100,000, maturing within two to 20 years.

Such secondhand policies can be bought at auction, where investors know they are paying the true market price. The only firm auctioning endowment policies is H E Foster & Cranfield who have been dealing in insurance policies since 1843. It holds auctions every two weeks at the Connaught Rooms, Great Queen Street, London WC2. Catalogues are available one week before each sale, and the firm offers advice to prospective purchasers.

years are called 'mediums'; 'longs' are those with more than 15 years to run; and half a dozen or so stocks are undated, which means there is no fixed redemption date.

The nearer a gilt is to its redemption date, the closer its price will get to the nominal value, in anticipation of the repayment due. So short-dated stocks should have the least volatile prices. Mediums and longs, on the other hand, may fluctuate substantially in either direction. Because of the difference in coupon, two stocks with the same nominal value and the same redemption date may have quite different prices on the market.

Undated stocks could in theory be redeemed at some point, but it seems very unlikely. The coupons are low, between 2.5 and 4 per cent, so there is no incentive for the government to redeem them, only to have to borrow new money at higher cost.

In addition to these various conventional gilts there is another category, index-linked stocks. With these, both the interest and the capital repayment value are adjusted in line with the Retail Price Index (RPI). In practice, the figure used is the level of the index eight months before payment is due, to ensure that the amount of payment is always known in advance. This is compared with the base index for the stock, which is the level of the RPI eight months before the stock was issued; the base index for each stock is shown in newspaper price listings.

The coupons on these stocks look lower than those for conventional gilts because the figure quoted is the unindexed amount, which is then multiplied up by the inflation factor. Like conventional stock, prices will vary and as the redemption date approaches will move towards the repayment value, but this will be the indexed value, not the £100 nominal.

Gilt prices

The prices of gilt stocks are listed in newspapers alongside other share prices, generally under the heading of 'British Funds'. Prices are quoted in pounds and fractions, which can look a bit bewildering; for example, a figure of 119 $\frac{3}{32}$ signals a price of £119.09. As a rule of thumb, $\frac{1}{32}$ of a pound is roughly 3p.

The prices listed are normally the mid-market prices that applied at the close of trading on the previous day. This will give

a reasonable guide, but prices are changing all the time; for an up-to-date figure you would need to consult a broker. You also need to remember that the actual buying and selling prices involve a spread – the buying price will be slightly above the mid-market figure quoted and the selling price slightly below it.

One other factor affecting the quoted price is the accumulated interest. Inevitably there is a time-lag involved in preparing and sending out interest payments and meanwhile stocks could change hands, so the rule is that payments are made to whoever was the registered holder 37 days before the interest payment falls due. At this point the stock becomes 'ex dividend', indicated in price quotations by the letters 'xd'. If you sell a stock that is ex dividend you will still receive the interest payment, but the part of it that relates to the period after you sold will be subtracted from the sale proceeds. Similarly, if you buy a stock ex dividend, this portion of interest will be deducted from the cost, to compensate for you not actually receiving it.

If you buy at other times, you will have to pay for the interest that has accumulated since the last payment date. For example, if you buy two months after the previous payment, your purchase includes two months' worth of interest and the value of this will be added to the price.

Aside from these factors, there are a number of influences on the general level of gilt prices, chief of which is interest rates. In simple terms, if bank interest rates are at 12 per cent, then a gilt with a coupon of 12 per cent should trade around its par value. If bank rates fall to 8 per cent, the gilt looks more attractive and this will drive the price up until the effective yield, based on the purchase price, comes into line with bank rates.

In practice, though, prices will reflect not only current interest rates but the market's expectations of future rates. Once you have bought a gilt, you have locked into a particular rate of return, so if general interest rates fall, you will be doing well. On top of this, a fall in interest rates will tend to mean a rise in gilt prices, so there will be a capital gain if you sell. Conversely, if interest rates are forecast to rise, the prospects are less attractive. Inflation will also affect the true value of both future income and capital value, so, again, prices will be influenced by the market's expectations.

The yield

As mentioned above, the flat yield on a gilt depends on the purchase price as well as the quoted coupon. It can be calculated by dividing the coupon by the price and multiplying by 100. This then represents the interest rate you will get on your investment. But the flat yield is not the whole story. The total return to be made from a gilt also depends on the change in the capital value between when you buy and when you sell or when the stock is redeemed.

If you hold the stock to redemption, you will make a known capital gain or loss depending on the price at which you bought it. Even if you stand to make a loss, this need not mean that stock is not worth buying. For one thing, if the maturity date is still some way off, the price may rise before then, allowing you to sell at a profit. Alternatively, if you hold on to the stock, the interest payments may be enough to outweigh the capital loss and still represent an attractive return.

This return can be judged from the redemption yield, which

takes into account the capital gain or loss as well as the flat yield. The calculation is complicated, but figures are included in newspaper listings and can also be obtained from stockbrokers, who have computer programs designed for the purpose. The figures assume that all interest payments are reinvested in the same stock at the same redemption yield.

A comparison between flat yields and redemption yields is shown in Table 4.1. Here, the high coupon short-dated stocks are standing above their par value and the redemption yield is therefore a lot lower than the flat yield, though still competitive with, say, bank and building society accounts. The low-coupon Funding 3½% stock, on the other hand, offers only a modest running income but a much higher redemption yield, as there is a sizeable capital gain to be made.

These figures are for gross yields. When tax is taken into account, the picture can change again, as the next section will explain.

Gilts and tax

Interest payments on gilts are made twice a year. If the stock is held on the Bank of England register, interest is paid net of basic rate tax, with the exception of 3½% War Loan which is paid gross. Stocks held on the National Savings Stock Register, accessible through post offices (see 'Buying and selling' below), also have interest paid gross. In either case, taxpayers will be liable for any unpaid amount. Non-taxpayers can reclaim any tax

Table 4.1 *Gross flat and redemption yields on gilts*

Stock	Price (£)	Flat yield (%)	Redemption yield (%)
Treasury 9% 1994	102.02xd	8.818	5.212
Treasury 14% 1996	112.22	12.424	6.207
Treasury 10.5% 1999	111.14xd	9.422	7.731
Funding 3.5% 1999/ 2004	75.26	4.617	6.828
Treasury 9% 2012	111.17	8.069	7.807

already deducted, but may find the National Savings route more convenient.

Special rules apply to interest that has accrued shortly before you buy or sell. Where accrued interest has been allowed for in the purchase price, that part of the subsequent interest payment will not normally be liable for tax. Conversely, when you sell, you will be charged tax on the amount of interest earned before the sale, calculated on a daily basis. However, these rules do not apply when your holdings of gilts have not recently been worth more than £5000. In this case, tax applies only to interest that has actually been paid; so if the sale price includes an allowance for, say, three months' accrued interest, the profit is treated as a capital gain. This is good news, as all capital gains made on gilts are free of either income or capital gains tax. (Equally, this means that losses cannot be used to offset gains elsewhere for capital gains tax purposes.)

These tax rules have an important consequence for higher rate taxpayers in particular. If you hold a gilt to maturity, your total return will be determined by the income stream, on which you pay tax, and any capital gain, which is tax free. Ideally, then, the more that comes from capital gain the better. This is illustrated in Table 4.2, which shows the net redemption yield for basic and higher rate taxpayers on a variety of stocks.

Table 4.2 *Net redemption yields on gilts*

Stock	Gross redemption yield (%)	Net redemption yield (%)	
		25% tax	40% tax
Treasury 12% 1995	5.295	2.407	0.678
Gas 3% 1990/95	5.342	4.579	4.121
Treasury 7.25% 1998	7.304	5.492	4.404
Treasury 14% 1998/2001	7.700	4.601	2.736
Funding 3.5% 1999/2004	6.828	5.796	5.179
Treasury 13.5% 2004/08	8.177	5.426	3.759
Treasury 5.5% 2008/12	7.538	5.936	4.983
Exchequer 12% 2013/17	7.999	5.659	4.233

Note: Yields based on later redemption dates where applicable.

Source: BZW, 25 April 1994

On the whole, taxpayers will do better from a low-coupon stock, if they plan to hold it to redemption. But if interest rates are high, and likely to fall in the future, there may be some mileage in a short-term holding of a high-coupon stock. It will give a good running yield, albeit taxed, plus the prospect of a capital gain if interest rates do indeed fall and gilt prices then rise, allowing the stock to be sold at a profit. However, this scenario involves a higher risk, since it is a gamble on a change in interest rates, and if rates are widely expected to fall, the market may already have built this into gilt prices.

Why buy gilts?

The majority of gilt dealing is done by institutions such as pension funds and insurance companies, but individual investors can also take part. In fact, the Bank of England has made particular overtures to the private investor: it published a free booklet to explain how gilts work; the investment limit for buying gilts through the National Savings Stock Register was raised from £10,000 to £25,000 and the register was expanded to include all existing stocks; the Bank then introduced a simplified application form, published in newspapers, for a new stock issue.

But should you be tempted? When interest rates are low, high-coupon gilts compare very favourably to bank and building society accounts as regards the running yield they offer. If income is your priority, gilts certainly have an appeal, but remember that high-coupon stocks are at a premium – the price is above the par value – so if you hold the stocks to redemption, the high income is achieved at the expense of a guaranteed capital loss.

For higher rate taxpayers, this is an extremely inefficient process, as the upside of high income will be reduced by tax, while the capital loss cannot be written off against gains elsewhere. Indeed, for any taxpayer, unless you have a very specific short-term need for income that outweighs any capital sacrifice, you should be guided by the net redemption yield, which reflects the total return.

This should be viewed in the context of future prospects from alternative investments. Any investment has an opportunity cost

EDITORIAL
Discount Services for private investors

From 1 January 1995 all financial intermediaries will be obliged by law to disclose in cash terms the exact amount of commission they earn when arranging any investment on behalf of their clients. Investors will therefore for the first time see just how much of their investment is eaten up in charges and commission. This important new change to the law will prompt investors to look around for a better deal when investing and to seek out those intermediaries who offer a lower-cost route into the investments they are interested in.

The purchase prices of unit trusts, PEPs, new issues of investment trusts, investment bonds and other lump sum investments are the same whether you go direct to the investment company or through an intermediary as the initial charging structure is identical.

Investors who need the minimum of advice or who make their own investment decisions should therefore always look around for a cheaper way of investing rather than going direct to the investment company itself.

There are several 'discount brokers' in the UK who specialise in giving discounts on most types of lump sum investments including unit trusts, PEPs, new issues of investment trusts, distribution bonds, with-profits bonds, guaranteed income bonds, single premium pensions, etc.

Initial costs of investing can be more than halved by dealing with the right intermediary. Instead of losing 5% – or more – of the sum invested, you can pay just 1% to invest in funds managed by Perpetual, Schroder, M&G and others. More and more management groups themselves are offering discounts and many independent financial advisors are able to negotiate additional discounts on behalf of their clients.

These discounts, whenever possible, are given as additional units thus enhancing the investment made. Where this is not possible the discount is given as a refund cheque payable approximately six weeks after the investment is made.

Discounts are also available on regular premium contracts such as endowments, pensions, life assurance, unit trust and PEP savings' schemes, etc.

The rate of discount depends upon the investment chosen and on the amount invested, but some typical examples are as follows:

PEPs, unit trusts, investment bonds – up to 4% discount

New Issues of Investment Trusts – up to 2% discount

Regular premium endowment and pension policies – 1% x the term of the policy

Most 'discount brokers' operate on an 'execution-only' basis where no advice is given, but there are some who not only give discounts but also offer free advice whenever requested.

'Buy your units through a discount broker to reduce the costs of investing'
Investors Chronicle – 18 March 1994

– by choosing one, you are giving up the chance of another. Of course, you can never be certain of getting the best, but you can consider probabilities. The lower the rates of interest and inflation, the more likely it is that they will rise in future. This will work against gilts in that the yield will become relatively less attractive, prices will fall, and the ultimate redemption value will be worth less in real terms.

Timing makes all the difference to a gilt investment. Ideally, they should be bought just as interest rates start to fall and sold just as they are about to rise – even though they may appear most attractive when interest rates are at their lowest. But much depends on your investment criteria. On a long-term comparison, gilts have consistently performed less well than equities, but for some investors the fixed income and capital return may carry more weight.

Conventional versus index-linked

If inflation is the enemy of investors, index-linking should be the saviour. The return offered is guaranteed to stay in line with inflation, while the capital value at maturity is also protected from erosion. The redemption value of a conventional gilt, on the other hand, may be worth a lot less by the time it matures.

While current interest rates are influenced by current inflation, index-linked gilts look to the future in that prices will be influenced by expectations about the trend of inflation. Lately, index-linked stocks have tended to outperform conventional gilts; with the economy moving out of recession, and in the run-up to the next general election, inflation could start to pick up again. In this scenario, index-linked gilts look more attractive, as the inflation protection will prove rewarding, while if interest rates rise alongside inflation, the prices of conventional gilts are likely to fall, so they have less appeal.

One method used by stockbrokers to judge the relative merits of index-linked and conventional gilts is to calculate the 'break-even inflation rate'. This involves matching the index-linked stock with a conventional issue with the same or similar maturity date. Using a computer, they then work out what rate of inflation between now and redemption would make the (monetary) returns from the two stocks equal. If inflation runs above the break-even rate, the index-linked stock will give a better return.

Of course, it is still a matter of judgement whether inflation is likely to be above or below the break-even rate during the period in question. The further away the redemption date, the harder this is to judge, as inflation is likely to go both up and down more than once meanwhile. But you can at least assess the chances in the light of past experience.

Table 4.3 shows some examples of break-even rates for a basic rate taxpayer. To put these in context, the inflation rate at the time of writing is 2.5 per cent; the January 1993 figure of 1.7 per cent was the lowest for many years, while in the worst days of 1980, the rate reached 21.9 per cent.

Buying and selling

There are three ways of buying gilts: direct from the Bank of England when there is a new issue; through a stockbroker; or through the National Savings Stock Register.

When a new stock is issued, prospectuses are published in newspapers and are also available from the Bank of England. Stocks are auctioned, which means institutions register the price they are prepared to bid and only the highest bidders will receive stock if the issue is over-subscribed. Private investors, however, can register a non-competitive bid and they will then receive stock

Table 4.3   *Break-even inflation rates*

Stock	Price (£)	Comparison stock	Break-even inflation rate (%)
2% 1996	198.14	Conversion 10% 1996	0.72
4.625% 1998	107.16xd	Treasury 7.25% 1998	3.10
2.5% 2003	165.16xd	Treasury 8% 2003	3.05
2% 2006	174.00	Treasury 7.75% 2006	3.00
2.5% 2013	134.20	Treasury 8% 2013	2.96

Note: Break-even rate applies at 25 per cent tax rate.

Source: BZW, 25 April 1994

at the average of the successful bid prices. Usually they are asked to pay the nominal value up-front and the Bank then makes a refund or asks for more money, depending on the average price set.

For recent issues, the Bank has provided shorter application forms as a way of encouraging private investors. The advantage of buying new stock in this way is that there is no commission on the purchase.

For existing stocks, the National Savings Stock Register offers the cheapest method of buying and selling for small sums. The costs are shown in Table 4.4. Aside from costs, there is the advantage that interest is paid gross, which means non-taxpayers avoid the effort of reclaiming tax paid; taxpayers will still have to pay what is due, but benefit from a grace period.

There is a maximum that you can invest in any one stock through the register of £25,000 a day, but there is no limit to the total amount you can hold on the register. New stocks bought through a prospectus can normally be registered with National Savings rather than the Bank of England by ticking a box on the application form, subject to a limit of £25,000 in nominal value. Stocks held on the National Savings register can only be sold

Table 4.4   *The cost of dealing in gilts through the Post Office*

Purchases

Cost of transaction	*Commission charged*
Not exceeding £250	£1
Over £250	£1 plus a further 50p for every additional £125 (or part)

Sales

Proceeds of sale	*Commission charged*
Less than £100	10p for every £10 (or part)
£100 to £250	£1
Over £250	£1 plus a further 50p for every additional £125 (or part)

Make a worthwhile investment

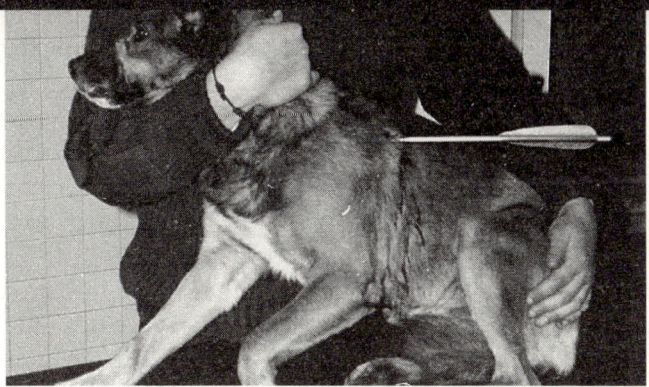

through it, while stocks held on the Bank of England register cannot be sold this way.

The drawback to buying and selling through National Savings is that it has to be done by post. While dealing will normally be carried out on the day instructions are received, you will not know until after the event what price applied.

The alternative is to deal through a stockbroker, which can be done by telephone at a known price. Commissions on gilt dealing are usually lower than for equities, but will still be subject to the broker's minimum, which can be £25 or more in London. Hence this is likely to prove an expensive route for small investments, especially as further commission will be payable when you come to sell.

One other route into the gilt market is through a collective investment such as an insurance company product or a unit trust. This gives you a stake in a portfolio of gilts for a much smaller outlay than buying your own collection, and with professional management as well, but, of course, there is none of the certainty you can get by buying stocks to hold to redemption.

Permanent interest bearing shares

Permanent interest bearing shares (PIBS) are issued by building societies as a means of raising permanent share capital. They are similar to gilts, in that they pay a fixed income, but the majority are irredeemable unless the issuing society is wound up. They can, however, be sold to a third party and are traded on the Stock Exchange.

Interest is paid twice a year and is paid net of basic rate tax, although non-taxpayers can reclaim it. Higher rate taxpayers will be liable for the extra amount. However, any profits made on the sale of shares are not liable for capital gains tax.

The interest rates are more attractive than those offered on the standard range of building society accounts, but there is, of course, a capital risk. Share prices move inversely to interest rates and are particularly sensitive to long-term rates. So, for example, if market rates move downwards, prices will rise, which reduces the effective yield as a percentage of the purchase price. This is illustrated in Table 4.5, which shows the prices at the time of

Table 4.5   *Examples of PIBS prices, coupons and yields*

Current price (pence)	Fixed coupon (gross)	Gross yield (%)
118.00	11.625	9.85
125.00	13.375	10.70
126.75	13.0	10.26
138.25	13.625	9.86
120.50	12.625	10.48
121.25	12.875	10.62

Source: BZW, 20 April 1994

writing on a selection of shares and the corresponding yields. All the shares were issued at an original price of 100p, but falling market interest rates since issue have driven up the price. Equally, if rates rise again in future, the share prices will fall, so, unlike building society accounts, these are investments you should review regularly.

Currently, there are some 16 PIBS available. As the table shows, the yields vary, reflecting the market's view of the issuing society. Shares can be bought and sold through stockbrokers, who may advise on which appears most attractive. The minimum investment is £1000, but most stockbrokers have a minimum commission, which can be around £25, making dealing expensive for small sums. PIBS are not normally liable to stamp duty.

Aside from the capital risk, there are other safety aspects. Interest payments are not guaranteed to be made if the board of the society decides payment would damage business interests or if interest has not been paid on shares and deposits. Also, PIBS are not covered by the building societies' investor compensation scheme, and if the issuing society were to go into liquidation, holders would be last in line for repayment, behind all depositors and ordinary shareholders. On the other hand, if the society is taken over by another, the PIBS will continue as the liability of the society making the take-over.

Where to find out more

Newspapers such as *The Daily Telegraph* and *The Financial Times* publish the prices of gilts on a daily basis, along with gross interest and redemption yields. Net redemption yields, break-even inflation figures and general advice on buying and selling can be obtained from a stockbroker. Stockbrokers can also provide information and advice on permanent interest bearing shares.

5

Equities

Equities could be said to come somewhere near the top of the investment tree. This is not because they necessarily demand a lot of money – privatisation issues have allowed people to own shares for a down-payment of just £100. But if you had only £100 to invest, the stock market would not normally be considered the ideal place to put it. Most investors come into equities only after they have built up more cautious funds elsewhere.

This chapter focuses mainly on the UK Stock Exchange. In fact, many of the points would apply in a similar way to overseas markets but, despite sophisticated communications technology, dealing in foreign shares tends to be both more expensive and more difficult. Unless you have a very large portfolio, it is more practical to invest abroad through pooled funds such as unit and investment trusts.

The Stock Exchange

The London Stock Exchange has its origins back in the eighteenth century, when people used to meet in coffee houses to exchange shares and arrange deals. It was formally constituted in 1802, in purpose-built premises on the same site as the current building, which was opened in 1973.

The exchange has two purposes: to act as a market for people wanting to buy and sell existing shares, and to raise money for companies by issuing new share capital. There are also two separate operations involved, jobbing and broking, corresponding to wholesale and retail functions. Jobbers are now known by the more descriptive name of market-makers; they make a market in shares by acting as primary buyers and sellers and holding stocks on their books. Brokers act as intermediaries between the market-makers and the end-clients, investors; they take orders from their clients and look for the best prices among the market-makers.

Trading used to take place physically on the Stock Exchange floor, but that came to an end with Big Bang, which reorganised the workings of the Exchange. Broking and jobbing firms were allowed to be taken over by companies, where previously they were partnerships, and both functions may now be carried out within a single company. They must, however, be kept separate, by means of a 'Chinese Wall'; this is to guard against any unscrupulous manoeuvring between them at the expense of the investor. If, for example, the broker knew that the market-maker wanted to get rid of some undesirable shares, he could connive at it by advising his clients to buy them.

Another effect of Big Bang was to remove the standard commission levels for buying and selling shares which were previously set by the Stock Exchange. Although some firms still roughly follow the old scales, there can now be wide differences. Much of the competition, though, is at the upper end and, for smaller investors, the general effect has been to increase costs. This is chiefly because brokers set a minimum commission, which can be as high as £40 for a London firm, making small transactions disproportionately expensive. Provincial brokers are generally cheaper, as they have lower overheads, and commission levels also vary according to the type of service provided.

Rolling settlement

The volume of shares traded has increased enormously since Big Bang. While prices are now posted on screens, dealing still involves a mass of paperwork and administrative logjams have not been uncommon, delaying the issue of certificates for shares bought and settlement for shares sold. The Stock Exchange planned to deal with this problem with the introduction of Taurus, a paperless dealing system which would have replaced certificates with electronic accounts, but after years of problems and delays it finally collapsed in March 1993.

The current proposal is for a rather less ambitious system called Crest. This is not expected to come into being until 1996 at the earliest, but the first step is being taken in July 1994 with the introduction of a ten-day 'rolling settlement' period.

The old settlement system was based on two- to three-week periods, known as 'accounts'. Settlement of transactions undertaken during any one account would normally take place on a fixed account day, some ten days after the end of the period. Meanwhile, investors could enjoy credit for shares bought, but would be waiting for the proceeds of sales.

Under the new system, settlement for both sales and purchases must take place no more than ten working days after the transaction date. This period is to be progressively reduced, first to five days, from around the start of 1995, and then to three days the year after.

The move to a ten-day period should present few problems. It does mean, however, that if you make a purchase and a sale within a short time, you will have to pay for the purchase before receiving the sale proceeds. Under the old system, the two transactions would have been netted out and you would only have paid, or received, the difference.

The move to five and then three days will be much more challenging. There will barely be time for a cheque to clear, let alone allow for postal delays, and if the investor's payment fails to arrive in time, the stockbroker will have to cover the amount. This means that some of the cheapest postal dealing services may disappear, while in other cases there is likely to be much wider use of nominee accounts.

These are accounts in the name of a nominee company, which hold shares on the investor's behalf while he remains the beneficial owner. They are already used in a number of situations, such as for discretionary broking services and personal equity plans. The advantage is that the broker can ensure in advance that there is sufficient money available in an account to cover any purchases. Also, since the shares are held by the nominee account, the stockbroker has security against which to advance money to cover short-term transactions.

Nominee accounts can be convenient, as all the paperwork can be handled by the broker. Against this, you may lose out on share perks, since the shares are not registered in your own name, and you will have to make arrangements with your broker if you want to receive copies of annual reports or go to shareholders' meetings. This may involve a cost, on top of any extra fee charged by the broker for running the nominee account.

Furthermore, nominee companies are not directly covered by the Financial Services Act, which means that investors are not automatically protected by the Investors' Compensation Scheme. The Association of Private Client Investment Managers and Stockbrokers has been lobbying the Securities and Investments Board for increased regulation in this area.

Hence rolling settlements may not be without some teething problems, but it is hoped that these can be sorted out by the time the system is fully implemented.

The Unlisted Securities Market

In addition to the main stock market, shares can also be quoted on the Unlisted Securities Market (USM). This can act as a first step for companies seeking to go public, as the requirements are less demanding than the main market, though some still move directly to a full listing.

For investors, USM shares generally carry more risk than the main market. This is partly because the companies are likely to be smaller and have less of a business track record on which their prospects can be judged, but also because the market itself attracts far fewer buyers and sellers – the institutions, which dominate trading, naturally prefer the main market where deals can be much larger. Hence it could prove harder to deal. But here, too, there are changes afoot. The USM is to disappear, though as yet there is no fixed date for this. The plan is to make it easier than it is now to get a full listing, but there is also a suggestion of setting up an Enterprise Market for very small companies. This would operate on an order matching system: instead of having market-makers acting as primary dealers, buyers and sellers would be directly matched with each other. This will add to the risk, as investors could end up being stuck with shares for which there is no willing buyer.

Market indices

Movements in the stock market are generally measured with reference to an index. For the UK market, there are two that are principally used: the FT–SE Actuaries All Share index and the FT-SE 100 index – known colloquially as 'Footsie'.

The All Share index does not in fact cover all shares quoted on the market, but the 850 or so that it does cover account for around 96 per cent of the total market capitalisation. Consequently, it gives the most representative overall picture.

The Footsie, which was begun at the start of 1984, covers the top 100 companies by size. The prices are calculated every minute during the trading day, so it gives immediate feedback to dealers on what is happening.

Although share price movements, and those of unit trusts, investment trusts and so on, are often measured in relation to the All Share or the Footsie, there are various other indices covering particular sectors, such as smaller companies or individual industries. These can be more relevant for judging the performance of an individual share or specialist trust. For example, smaller companies are unlikely to follow the same pattern as the large companies represented by the Footsie index; if the smaller companies sector is booming, a share that is performing only in line with the Footsie is probably doing relatively badly.

Private investors

Until quite recently, private investors were very much in decline in terms of their representation in the stock market. Meanwhile, the institutions saw a steady and substantial increase in the funds under their control and took on a heavily dominant position.

While there is still a heavy imbalance in favour of institutions, the private investor has staged a comeback. Currently, in 1994, there are about 10 million people who own shares, compared to around a quarter of that in the early 1980s. This is partly owing to an increase in inheritances following on from the growth in home ownership. People who already have a basic portfolio of investments and are then presented with a 'windfall' of, say, £50,000 to £100,000, are quite likely to give some thought to equities. Another factor has been the growth in company share option schemes for employees. But there is no doubt that a major influence has been the privatisation programme.

This is something of a mixed blessing. It has certainly brought about wider share ownership but, one could argue, of the wrong kind. Out of the 10 million shareholders, only a quarter or so hold shares in more than three companies and only some 300,000 are active dealers in shares. Many simply hang on to the few shares they bought, either for the incentives attached, or because they have virtually forgotten they have them.

Perhaps more dangerous was the reputation privatisation issues acquired as 'get rich quick' schemes. Priced to be enticing, the earlier issues in particular gave opportunities to make immediate attractive profits – and many buyers made the most of it, selling the shares as soon as they had the letters of allocation. While there is nothing wrong in making a quick profit, anyone who thought the principle could be extended to other shares, with the same degree – or lack – of risk, is likely to have been severely disappointed.

On a more positive note, privatisations have boosted the growth of dealing services aimed at smaller investors. A number of these simply deal without offering any advice, which may not be suitable for the stock market beginner, but they have contributed to the general opening up of the stock market to a wider circle of people and the more user-friendly approach now being adopted by stockbrokers. If privatisations have helped to dispel some of the fear and mystique that surrounded equities, that is a step in the right direction; the next stage is to learn a little more about the rest of the market.

Ordinary shares

To begin at the beginning, an ordinary share represents a stake in the ownership of a company. In theory, it also confers the right to have a say in how the company is run, at least to the extent of having a vote at the annual general meeting. In practice, of course, most private investors do not have enough shares for their vote to count for much and many do not even bother to go to the meeting; nevertheless, the right exists.

Shareholders are also entitled to a portion of the company's

Multiple Sclerosis. Stroke. Parkinson's Disease. Cerebral Palsy. Head Injuries. Arthritis. Cancer.

We could care more...

...if we had your support. BHHI has been caring for people who are chronically sick and disabled every day of the year for over 130 years.

Nursing, helping, promoting happiness and independence. Improving the quality of life. Of course, such care takes a great deal of money and, as a charity, we rely on legacies and donations from people like you.

Please remember BHHI in your will and help us now by sending a donation.

❏ Please send me your legacy leaflet
❏ My gift of £ _____ is enclosed
❏ I would like information on tax efficient giving

Name: _____

Address: _____

_____

Post Code: _____

Post today to:
Matron L. S. Kelly,
The British Home and Hospital for Incurables,
Crown Lane, Streatham, London SW16 3JB

Telephone: 081 670 8261

Regd Charity No. 206222

100 YEARS IN STREATHAM

BHHI
BRITISH HOME & HOSPITAL FOR INCURABLES

profits, paid out in the form of dividends. As a rule, some of the profits will be kept back to be reinvested in the company itself for future growth. The remainder are distributed at so much per share; the more shares you hold, the larger the total dividend.

In return for these rewards, you take on a risk. Should the worst happen and the company be forced into liquidation, the ordinary shareholder is last in line for getting any of his money back. As a rule, though, you can only lose as much as you put in – you will not be called upon to make good anyone else's losses. This is because companies listed on the Stock Exchange have limited liability – hence the term PLC, or public limited company.

An exception is if the shares have been issued partly paid, as several privatisation issues have. This means that at the time you buy the shares, you pay only part of their price, with subsequent calls being made for the rest of the money. In this case, if the company incurs debts it cannot meet, you could be required to pay over the outstanding balance on the shares you hold. The majority of shares, though, are dealt in on a fully paid basis, so your maximum loss is equal to your investment.

With luck, the worst case will not happen and the company will stay in business, but you still stand to lose a part of your investment if the share price falls. Equally, of course, you will make a profit if it rises. So what factors make a share price move?

The short answer is supply and demand for the shares. Quite simply, if demand outstrips supply – if there are more willing buyers than willing sellers – the price will move up; in the opposite case it will move down. So the next question is, what affects supply and demand?

In the first place, all shares are influenced by what might be termed national events: the general economy and the political situation. Increasingly, these days, they are also affected by international events; one country's exports are another's imports, so a recession in the latter country means they will buy less, restricting export growth in the former.

There are further influences at sector or industry level; again, there are trade factors, and also strikes, which can have a knock-on effect if the striking company or industry is a major supplier to another.

Then you come down to the particular company, and what drives demand here is quite simply the expectation of profit. For individual investors, the anticipated profit may be in the form of capital growth – the expectation that the share price will increase. But what lies behind such an increase is the profit made by the company, translated into rising dividends: it is the income potential that ultimately underpins the share price.

Anticipation also plays an important part in determining share prices. An obvious example is a general election, where the market may react in advance to what people think is the likely outcome. This is referred to as discounting an event – if it happens as expected, there will be little further movement, but if expectations are confounded, it could produce a violent swing.

But while it is perfectly in order to act on guesswork, it is illegal to engage in insider dealing, which amounts to taking advantage of unpublished information that may affect share prices.

Dividends

Dividends are generally paid twice a year, the first payment being the 'interim' dividend and the second the 'final' dividend, paid at the company's year-end. The amount is generally expressed in terms of pence per share, net of basic rate tax; this can be reclaimed by a non-taxpayer, while higher rate taxpayers must pay the difference.

As explained above, dividends underpin the share price and anticipation comes into play. Hence the price will often move ahead of the declaration and, if it fails to live up to expectations, the price can fall back, even though the dividend itself may have increased since the last declaration.

The yield on a share is the gross dividend divided by the share price. The average yield on UK shares is generally around 3 to 4 per cent; at the time of writing, with interest rates very low, this does not look so bad, but as a rule, shares do not produce high income. What they do offer is the prospect of growing income and, given inflation, this is a valuable asset.

Yields do, of course, vary, both between companies and between sectors. Broadly speaking, sectors with lower growth prospects will tend to have higher yields. For individual shares, the yield will obviously rise if the share price falls, while the dividend is maintained; the key question then is why the share price has fallen. It may be owing to 'technical' or short-term factors and, indeed, unit trusts in both the Income and Recovery sectors tend to look for just this type of share, which offers capital growth prospects and good income in the meantime. But it may be that profits, and dividends, are expected to fall in the future, so a share cannot be judged by its yield alone.

As mentioned, companies do not usually pay out all their profits as dividends, but retain some for future use. In this case, the dividend is said to be fully 'covered'. Equally, though, they could call upon these reserves to boost dividends in a year when earnings have been low, in which case the payment would be uncovered. Some degree of smoothing from year to year is perfectly acceptable, but a fully covered dividend is always more reassuring.

An alternative to cash dividends is a 'scrip' dividend, where the company offers the option of additional shares instead of money. In some cases, the value can be much higher, and if you are looking for cash, you can simply sell the extra shares. Of course, there will be dealing costs, but you may still come out ahead, and companies may also offer a buy-back scheme, which will cut the costs for small investors.

In principle, you cannot lose on this type of offer, but you do need to take care over the capital gains tax implications; if you have already used up the annual exempt allowance, you will be faced with a tax bill, although in the longer term it could reduce the liability on your remaining holdings in the shares. Scrip dividends are also treated by the Inland Revenue as having paid 20 per cent income tax which cannot be reclaimed. If you are in any doubt, you should seek independent advice.

Price/Earnings ratio

Besides the dividend, another means of judging shares is by the price/earnings ratio, or p/e for short. This is calculated as the share price divided by earnings per share and the result shows how many years it would take the company to earn enough to match the share price, if both remained unchanged.

In practice, the p/e ratio is used as a measure of the 'cheapness' of shares – the lower the ratio, the cheaper the share, relative to the company's earnings potential. But it has to be viewed in context. Average ratios vary between sectors, and are also affected by the economy in general – high inflation should lead to lower p/e ratios, since future dividends will be worth much less in real terms than the share price you have to pay now.

Also, while a high ratio means a share is relatively expensive, and should be viewed with caution, a low ratio is not always a reason to rush in and buy. It could be that the share price is low for good reason, because the market does not rate its prospects.

If you plan to invest overseas, you should bear in mind that p/e ratios may be on a quite different level to those in the UK. In fact, the UK has a relatively low average compared to markets worldwide, while Japan's is notoriously high.

How to buy and sell

It is no longer necessary to have a family stockbroker to gain access to the stock market. As mentioned above, the combination of Big Bang and privatisation issues has boosted the growth of new dealing services, often with low or no minimum investment requirement, while stockbrokers have been opening their doors to newcomers with a more obvious welcome than was once the case. Some larger companies have also become involved in share dealing services, particularly where they offer corporate personal equity plans that may include the shares of other companies.

Banks have also expanded the range of dealing services they offer. National Westminster, for example, has a computer-based 'Touchscreen' service that offers instant dealing. It was initially developed in response to privatisation issues but, at the time of writing, it can now be used to deal in 500 different shares and is available in nearly 300 branches across the country, for both customers and non-customers.

Several banks also provide postal and telephone dealing services, the latter generally confined to existing customers, while the former are open to anyone. For the most part, these are purely dealing services, though occasional advice may be given.

If you want more comprehensive advice, a bank may have its

FAR REACHING CHANGES IN STOCKBROKING PUT PRIVATE INVESTORS FIRMLY IN THE DRIVING SEAT

Gone are the days when you had to have a million pounds to invest, be a favoured client of a broker, or have inside track, in order to be taken seriously or to get the very best out of the stock market.

Private client stockbroking has been through a period of profound change. Investors now expect and demand better service and far better value for money. They are also offered much greater choice and should find things altogether more straightforward.

The growth of specialist, execution-only stockbrokers has played a critical role in this revolution. As well as the attraction of substantially lower commission, this newer breed of securities business usually offer the convenience of being open to everyone and just a telephone call away 7 days a week – some dealing services even offer 24 hour availability.

In addition to cost and convenience, a lot of attention has been paid to improving ease of access and quality of service. With ShareLink, for example, if you want you can deal on the very first call – no form, no fuss and no delay. You'll also get the same high standard of service and efficiency whether you are investing a few hundred or a million pounds.

Some brokers also give private investors direct access to overseas stock markets. You can obtain an up to the minute price, for example, quoted directly from the New York Stock Exchange, place a buy or sell order there and then and have the deal confirmed while you are still on the telephone, all in a matter of seconds. What's more, you could well pay less in commission than a US investor would be charged in the States by even one of the leading "discount brokers" there.

New style, centralised operations linked to modern systems and highly trained staff all give customers a consistently high quality of service, but one which still caters for individual requirements. The fact that some execution-only brokers get half their new customers from unsolicited recommendations is testament to the high degree of customer satisfaction they achieve.

Arguably, the most important change is the access many investors now have to a wide range of high quality information designed to make investment easier, more enjoyable and more productive. Along with an increasing amount of editorial coverage of personal financial affairs in top newspapers such as the Telegraph, the new leading light is ShareFinder. This is a publishing company recently set up by brokers ShareLink which probably offers the most comprehensive investment information anywhere.

Anybody can call ShareFinder and order reports on over 600 leading companies from just £4.95 each. Every report contains a wealth of up to date information, including a comprehensive survey of leading city research houses' current recommendations and their latest profit, dividend and yield forecasts. Comparisons against other companies in a sector, plus a complete 5 year history in chart and table format show, at a glance, how any particular company is really performing.

Such developments help take both the guesswork and "legwork" out of deciding which shares to buy and sell, and just as importantly, when to do so. They also put control and choice firmly with the investor, enabling him or her to take fuller advantage of the benefits direct stock market investment has always offered.

SHARELINK
is for people who deal
hundreds of times
a year.

Or just once in a
blue moon.

own associated stockbroker service, but you may be just as well off choosing a broker for yourself. The Association of Private Client Investment Managers and Stockbrokers (Apcims) produces a brochure that includes a directory of its members, outlining in brief the services they offer.

Another recent development is the New Issue Register which aims to give smaller investors the chance to participate in new share issues. Although these may be offered by stockbrokers, some issues may be placed only with institutions. The idea is that, by pooling resources, small investors will have the combined purchasing power to participate.

Investors joining the register pay an annual subscription of £75, initially charged only when they make their first investment. As well as getting access to new issues, they will also receive a quarterly newsletter. No advice is given on particular investments and members are encouraged to seek advice elsewhere.

The scheme's initiative was generally welcomed, but it has had mixed fortunes so far. Its success depends on companies that are placing new issues being willing to deal with it, and also on whether share allocations to members will be large enough to offer worthwhile profits after allowing for the membership fee. Nevertheless, the development is an indication of how private investors are starting to recapture their former role in the stock market.

Finding a broker

When it come to choosing a broker, the first step is to make sure what type of service you want. As regards share dealing, there are three options, as follows:

1. *Execution-only.* This is essentially for dealing only, with no advice given, although company reports or recommendations may be available. Some brokers may be prepared to accept 'limit' orders, under which you specify a maximum buying or minimum selling price; others may only be prepared to deal 'at best' – the best price that can be readily obtained on the market.
2. *Advisory.* This is offered by the majority of brokers and may cover individual share purchases and sales or provide a

comprehensive portfolio service. At the outset, the broker will discuss with you your needs and desires, without obligation; thereafter you will be consulted before any transaction can take place and you can also initiate consultations or deals.

3. *Discretionary.* In this case, you hand over all responsibility to the broker, although there will be an initial discussion to sort out your aims, attitude to risk and so on. You will also be kept informed of all transactions, as well as receiving regular valuations and reviews.

In addition to these dealing services, stockbrokers may also offer a comprehensive financial planning package. This would include, for example, advice on cash management, school fees planning, retirement planning, life assurance and tax planning.

One other facility is a nominee service, under which the broker (or a third party, such as a bank) will hold certificates on your behalf, in the name of the nominee company. This can save you having to get involved with any paperwork, as the broker will be able to handle it all, but it does mean you can miss out on any perks, because the shares will not be registered in your own name.

The majority of stockbrokers are regulated by the Securities and Futures Association, through which they are authorised on an individual basis to give advice. Clients are eligible for the Investors Compensation Scheme in the event of default, and brokers generally also carry professional indemnity insurance against fraud and negligence.

Costs

The stockbroker's charges will usually be in the form of commission on dealing, though where there are additional financial planning services there may be an annual fee. The level of commission charged will vary from firm to firm, but will generally depend on three factors:

1. *The type of service:* execution-only dealing is usually cheaper than advisory or discretionary facilities.
2. *The location of the broker:* provincial brokers are usually somewhat cheaper than their London counterparts by virtue of having lower overheads.
3. *The size of the deal:* the scale of charges reduces for larger transactions and there is usually a minimum charge at the bottom end.

On top of the commission, you will also be liable to stamp duty at 0.5 per cent. Examples of charges are shown in Table 5.1.

You may be able to deal within specified price limits, or at the best available price in the market that day. Once the order has been executed, you will receive a contract note from the broker, showing the price of the shares and the dealing costs. From July 1994, settlement will follow within ten working days of the transaction.

Shares in a portfolio

The minimum portfolio size specified by stockbrokers varies considerably, from firm to firm and depending on what type of service you want. Equally, different brokers will vary in their views on what constitutes a sensible minimum, regardless of what

Table 5.1 *The costs of buying shares*

£1000-worth	
Stockbroker's commission	£22.00
Stamp duty at 0.5%	5.00
Total	£27.00
£10,000-worth	
Stockbroker's commission	£133.50
Stamp duty at 0.5%	50.00
Total	£183.50
£25,000-worth	
Stockbroker's commission	£263.50
Stamp duty at 0.5%	125.00
Total	£388.50

they might be prepared to accept – some will say around £25,000, others anything up to £100,000.

Chiefly, it depends on your circumstances and the amount of risk you are prepared to accept. The points to bear in mind are first, that small deals cost relatively more than larger ones, as Table 5.1 shows, and second, that to achieve a spread of risk you should think in terms of holding 10 to 15 shares. If you were to put £5000 into each of 10 holdings, that would mean a portfolio of £50,000; if you then add in 'safety' money in alternative investments, you can begin to see why some advisers think in terms of six figures.

If you are only investing the odd few thousand, you will be restricted to the UK and only a small number of shares at that, whereas a unit trust, for instance, could give you a stake in a worldwide spread of holdings.

Having said that, there is nothing to stop you going directly into equities with any amount to invest. The so-called 'Super Sid' investor would usually be in the £5000 to £20,000 bracket and stockbrokers are generally prepared to accept smaller sums than they used to, particularly as they might now see only the equity portion of a larger portfolio, whereas in the past they tended to be given charge of all a client's investments. The only 'rule' is to appreciate the risks involved, and the same is true of speculation; as the saying goes, if you don't know whether you are a speculator or an investor, the stock market is an expensive place to find out.

There are, of course, a host of such sayings, many of them contradictory, and there is no guaranteed formula for investment success. If you plan to be a middle of the road, long-term investor, the best attributes are probably moderation and patience: don't expect to get rich overnight and don't hold out for even bigger profits at the risk of losing what you already have. Few people ever manage to buy at the very bottom of the market and sell at the very top; if you can come somewhere close, you should find ample rewards.

One other point on portfolio organisation is that it is worth considering using a personal equity plan for the first £6000, the maximum investment that is allowed per year in an ordinary plan (a further £3000 can be put into a single company plan). The advantage is that all income and capital gains arising from the investment are tax free. Against this have to be set the plan charges; for unit trust-based plans, there are usually no charges other than those on the trusts themselves, so if you are investing in trusts as well as equities, you may do better to use the PEP allowance for the former. PEPs are discussed in detail in Chapter 9.

Other ways to play the market

Warrants

Buying shares is not the only means of investing in the equity market. An alternative is to buy warrants, which may be available on the shares of trading companies and investment trusts.

A warrant conveys the right to buy a share in a company at some future time. The price is fixed at the outset and known as the 'exercise price', and the option may be taken up on specified 'exercise dates'. These may be a particular day, or a set of dates, each year up to a final date when the option lapses.

Buying the share would be worthwhile if the exercise price plus the original cost of the warrant add up to less than the current market price of the share, although if you plan to sell the share for a quick profit you would also have to take your sale costs into account. If there is no opportunity for profit, the right to buy need not be taken up, but the warrant will lapse without value once the final exercise date has passed.

Like shares, warrants are traded on the Stock Exchange so can be bought as investments in their own right with no intention of taking up the exercise rights. The price of a warrant is generally much lower than the price of its related share, but will move in line with it, giving you exposure to the share's fortunes for a lower outlay.

But, by the same token, warrants are much more volatile, and therefore riskier, than the shares themselves. If, for example, the share price rises by 50p, the warrant price will rise by a similar amount, but the lower starting-point means the proportionate rise will be much greater. Equally, the effect of any fall in the share price will be enhanced. This is called the 'gearing' on the warrant, which is measured as the share price divided by the warrant price.

A high level of gearing offers high potential rewards but also greater risk. The other factors involved are the remaining lifespan, up to the final exercise date, and the premium, which is the excess of the exercise price plus the cost of the warrant over the current market price of the share. The longer the lifespan, the higher the premium may be, as there is more time for the share price to rise high enough for the warrant to generate a profit.

Assuming the risk is acceptable, warrants can be suitable for higher rate taxpayers as they do not pay any dividends. Hence there will be no liability to income tax; profits will be taxed as capital gains, which can be offset by the annual £5800 exempt allowance.

Options

Futures and options contracts both come under the generic heading of derivatives – a family of financial instruments that allow a number of techniques, both to increase and decrease risk. But while futures are out of the price range of the ordinary investor, options can be very useful. They are traded through the London International Financial Futures and Options Exchange (Liffe) and there are currently some 40-odd stockbrokers who will deal in them on behalf of private clients. You can go to one of them for just this service alone, even if your main portfolio is handled by a different firm.

The options used by private investors are based on either individual shares or an index. In the former case, a standard contract covers 1000 shares in a particular company, while index options are based on the value of the FT-SE 100 index. In either case, there are two types of option: 'calls' and 'puts'.

Take the case of an equity option. Here, the buyer of a call option has the right to buy a quantity of shares, at a specified price, at any time between now and the expiry date, which can be up to nine months away. A put option confers a similar right to sell shares. The buyer of the option is not obliged to take it up, but if he chooses to, the seller must honour it; either way, the seller gets to keep the cost of the option, which is known as the 'premium'.

Suppose you expect a share price to rise. Instead of buying the share itself, you can buy a call option, which will cost a lot less. If the price does then rise – above the price specified in the option, plus the premium you paid for it – you have two choices. First, you can exercise the option, then sell the shares for a profit. Alternatively, you can sell the option, for a higher premium than you paid, making a smaller profit but for a much lower outlay than if you had bought the actual shares.

Put options can be used as insurance if you believe that the price of a share you hold will go down. If it does fall, you can exercise the option and thereby limit your losses. If the price rises instead, you can simply let the option lapse and perhaps recoup its cost by selling the shares at a profit.

You can also sell, or write, options, but unless you are prepared to take on a heavy risk you should only do so if you have the shares to sell or the money to buy. Suppose, for example, that you hold shares whose price looks likely to remain rather flat. You can then write a call option against them. If your predictions are correct, the buyer of the option will probably not want to exercise it, so you have gained the premium for no outlay. If the share price rises and the option is exercised, you will lose out on the price rise, but you still keep the premium, so you will be better off than if you had sold the shares at the original market price.

As with equities, dealing services in options can be on an execution-only, discretionary or advisory basis. For the beginner, an advisory service is probably best, as it allows you to build up a knowledge of the market. Commission scales tend to start somewhat higher than those on equities, but again, it will vary from firm to firm, so it is worth shopping around. A list of firms that deal in options can be obtained from Liffe.

One other possibility is to bet on the index, which can be done through a couple of organisations. The effect is similar to using an option, but losses are not automatically limited – you have to decide to close the bet if the index is moving against you. Winnings are also tax free, as the betting tax will be paid by the company and included in the quoted price spreads.

Other types of share

As well as ordinary shares there are other types that investors may consider.

Preference shares carry the entitlement to a fixed dividend each year. Most of them are 'cumulative', which means that if the dividend is missed one year, it would have to be made up later if the company resumes dividends on its ordinary shares. Preference shares also take priority over ordinary shares if the company is wound up. Currently, with interest rates at low levels, the income from preference shares looks attractive but, as with any shares, the capital value is not guaranteed.

Convertible stocks are securities which carry a fixed dividend plus the option to convert them into ordinary stock, at a set price, at some fixed time in the future. They also rank ahead of ordinary shares in the event of liquidation. Again, the yields look attractive when interest rates are low, and there is also the chance of making a profit from the conversion.

Debentures are loans to a company that are secured on a specific asset, such as property. The yield is fixed and there is a stated redemption date when the loan will be repaid.

Stock market terms

Most readers will no doubt have come across stock market

jargon, at least to some extent, but this is a reminder of the more common terms.

Bear: someone who believes the market will fall

Blue chip: companies regarded as high quality and the most safe – said to be named after the highest value chip in poker

Bull: someone who believes the market will rise

Nominee account: a facility whereby shares are held on behalf of an investor in a company's name

Partly-paid: an issue of shares on which only part of the price is paid up-front

Rights issue: the offer of new shares in a company to existing shareholders at a price below the current market price

Scrip issue: a free issue of shares to existing shareholders

Stag: someone who buys a new issue in the hope of selling immediately for a quick profit

Where to find out more

A directory of private client stockbrokers, listing their services, can be obtained from the Association of Private Client Investment Managers and Stockbrokers, 112 Middlesex Street, London E1 7HY; tel 071-247 7080.

A free information pack and a list of brokers dealing in traded options can be obtained from Liffe, Cannon Bridge, London EC4R 3XX; tel 071-623 0444.

Other useful telephone numbers are:

The Stock Exchange: 071-588 2355
The New Issues Register: 071-357 6608
The Securities and Futures Authority: 071-378 9000.

6

Unit Trusts and Offshore Funds (1)

Unit trusts, offshore funds, investment trusts and life assurance products all have a common characteristic: they pool investors' money into a large fund, so that smaller investors can participate in a broad spread of assets that they could never achieve by their own means. The concept was set out in the prospectus of the very first investment trust to be launched, in 1868, and it is still quoted by that trust in its literature today: 'We intend to provide the investor of moderate means with the same advantages as large capitalists in diminishing the risks ... by spreading investment over a number of stocks.'

The primary advantage of collective investments, as they are known, is this reduction of risk. If you hold only one share and it crashes, you lose everything, but if you have a stake in a portfolio, one failure will be cushioned by other successes. There are also other plus points which will emerge over the next few chapters, such as professional investment management, ready access to overseas markets and certain tax benefits – particularly through personal equity plans, which are discussed in Chapter 9.

Unit trust investments can start from as little as £500 for a lump sum and there is no set maximum. As mentioned in the last chapter, many people would consider £25,000 to be the working minimum for a direct investment into the stock market, but investors with up to £100,000 available may find that the range and scope of collective investments will amply satisfy their requirements. Larger investors may also find them useful to add an overseas content to their holdings, even where they are investing directly in UK equities.

The growth in the unit trust industry over the last decade has been substantial. In 1983 there were 91 companies, running 630 trusts, which had a total value of £11.7 billion. At the end of 1993, there were 156 companies, operating 1528 trusts, with a total value of funds under management of £95.5 billion. These trusts span a huge variety of geographical and industrial special-isations, from broad-based UK General funds to Asian Smaller Markets or International Technology. Investment choice is examined in the next chapter.

The size of companies, and the number of trusts they run, vary considerably: the top 10 alone account for over £42 billion of funds under management and the top 20 for some £59 billion, as shown in Table 6.1. Most companies are members of the Association of Unit Trusts and Investment Funds, which can supply a range of information and contact details.

Unit trust regulations

A unit trust is subject to a trust deed, which lays down the terms under which it operates, for example, where and how it will invest, the calculation of unit prices and the charges it may levy. The money in the fund is held on behalf of investors by trustees, generally a bank or insurance company, who are responsible for ensuring that the managers conform to the rules laid down in the trust deed.

The regulation and authorisation of unit trusts is in the hands of the Securities and Investments Board, which lays down rules on what investments are available to a unit trust. The bulk of the portfolio will normally be invested in quoted shares or gilts, but up to 10 per cent may be in unquoted securities, including up to 5 per cent in other unit trusts, and up to 5 per cent may be invested in warrants. Trusts may also make use of traded options and futures contracts for the purposes of efficient fund manage-ment, but these must be covered by holdings of cash or near cash, such as government securities.

To ensure that a trust preserves an adequate spread of risk – which, after all, is a prime objective – not more than 5 per cent of

Table 6.1   *Top 20 unit trust groups by funds under management*

Group	Funds under management £m
Standard Life	7595.5
M & G	6655.9
Schroder	5298.5
Gartmore	4287.9
Barclays Unicorn	3590.4
Mercury	3428.6
Allied Dunbar	3400.8
Save & Prosper	3214.3
Fidelity	2794.1
HSBC	2200.7
Perpetual	2161.3
Henderson	2072.1
Prudential Holborn	2052.4
TSB	2015.4
Hill Samuel	1548.7
Norwich Union	1428.0
Baring	1361.6
Abbey	1355.6
Legal & General	1286.4
Confederation	1286.3

Note: Figures as at December 1993.

Source: Association of Unit Trusts and Investment Funds

the portfolio can normally be held in the shares of any one company. However, provided the total of 5 per cent plus holdings does not itself exceed 40 per cent of the portfolio, an individual holding may go up to 10 per cent. This means that if one share suddenly shoots up in value, it will not have to be immediately sold. In practice, a trust would normally have upwards of 40 different holdings, depending on its size, so it is likely to be well within the limits.

The other main rule is that a trust cannot hold more than 10 per cent of any one company's issued share capital. This is to ensure that a trust does not build up a controlling stake in a company, which could undermine its basic objectives.

Charges

There are two types of charge levied by unit trust managers: the initial charge and the annual charge. The level of these will be specified in the trust deed and the managers cannot raise the charges above that level without getting permission from the unit holders. For this reason, the levels stipulated are sometimes higher than the charges that are actually applied; this gives the managers the flexibility to make an increase at a future date without the bother of seeking permission.

In recent years there has been a tendency for charges to rise, so trusts that have been in existence for many years may carry lower charges than those more recently launched, unless the managers have sought permission for an increase. These days, the typical initial charge is between 5 and 6 per cent. Some gilt trusts have a lower charge, around 3 per cent, and cash trusts also have a very small or zero charge, while the specialist overseas trusts tend to carry the highest fees.

Out of this initial charge, the managers pay commission to intermediaries who sell the trusts for them. The usual amount of commission is 3 per cent, with the rest of the charge going towards the managers' costs, such as advertising. But if you buy direct from the managers rather than through an intermediary, the 3 per cent allowed for commission will still be charged and simply kept by the managers. Sometimes, however, the managers may make a special discount offer. Introductory discounts, of 1 per cent or possibly more for large investments, are quite common during the launch period of new trusts.

The annual charge is commonly between 1 and 2 per cent, though again cash trusts generally have a lower charge, around 0.5 per cent, while specialist trusts are likely to be at the top end of the scale.

While it may seem best to go for trusts with the lowest charges, performance can be a more important factor in determining the investment return. Obviously, the higher the charges, the better the performance needs to be for the same result, but over longer periods, differences in performance - as the next chapter will show - can be more than large enough to wipe out the effects of a higher charge.

For Daniella, life is no longer a leap in the dark

Like any active youngster Daniella loves a rough and tumble now and again. It is one of the many reasons why she enjoys herself so much in the Ball Pool at her Nursery at Dorton House School, run by The Royal London Society for the Blind. Dorton House is one of the world's leading educational centres for blind and partially sighted children, and is just one of The RLSB's services providing education, training and employment for blind people of all ages.

The Society is 100% dependent on private donations, often in the form of bequests and legacies. The Royal London Society for the Blind produces a free booklet to take the confusion out of making A Will. For a copy, and a free RLSB lapel badge, please write to;

ROYAL LONDON SOCIETY
FOR THE BLIND
FREEPOST, 105 Salusbury Road,
 London NW6 1YA
Tel: 071-624 8844.
Fax:071-328 4353
Patron: Her Majesty The Queen
President: HRH The Duchess of Gloucester
Registered Charity No. 307892

Normally you should think of holding on to unit trusts for at least a medium-term period, say three to five years. If you buy and sell more frequently, the initial charge on each purchase could start to eat into your returns. However, if you do plan to be an active investor, this effect can be lessened by sticking with one management group.

Most managers offer a discount on switches between their own trusts, as an incentive to investors to keep their money within the group. The amount varies from 1 per cent to as much as 4 per cent, which means switching can be done at very little cost.

Bid and offer

If you look at unit trust prices in the newspaper you will see that there are two quoted, the 'offer' price and the 'bid' price. The offer is what you pay to buy units, while the bid is what you get when you sell. The difference between them is usually greater than the quoted initial charge of 5 to 6 per cent, because the calculations are based on complex rules laid down by the regulatory authorities.

To start with, a trust must have a creation price and a cancellation price. The creation price is based on the value of the shares in the trust's portfolio (valued at their offer price, which is the price at which they could be bought on the market), plus stockbroker's commission and stamp duty. To that is added any cash held by the trust plus accumulated income from dividends and interest payments, and the whole lot is then divided by the total number of units in existence.

The cancellation price is almost a mirror image, being the value of the shares held in the portfolio at their bid price, less the stockbroker's commission, plus cash and accumulated income, again divided by the total number of units.

The full offer price that the managers can charge when selling units then becomes the creation price plus the initial charge. The full bid price, which is the minimum at which the managers can buy back units, is equal to the cancellation price.

The difference between these two is called the full spread and can be as much as 10 or 11 per cent. In practice, of course, few people would be prepared to buy an investment that would

Table 6.2 *Price calculations*

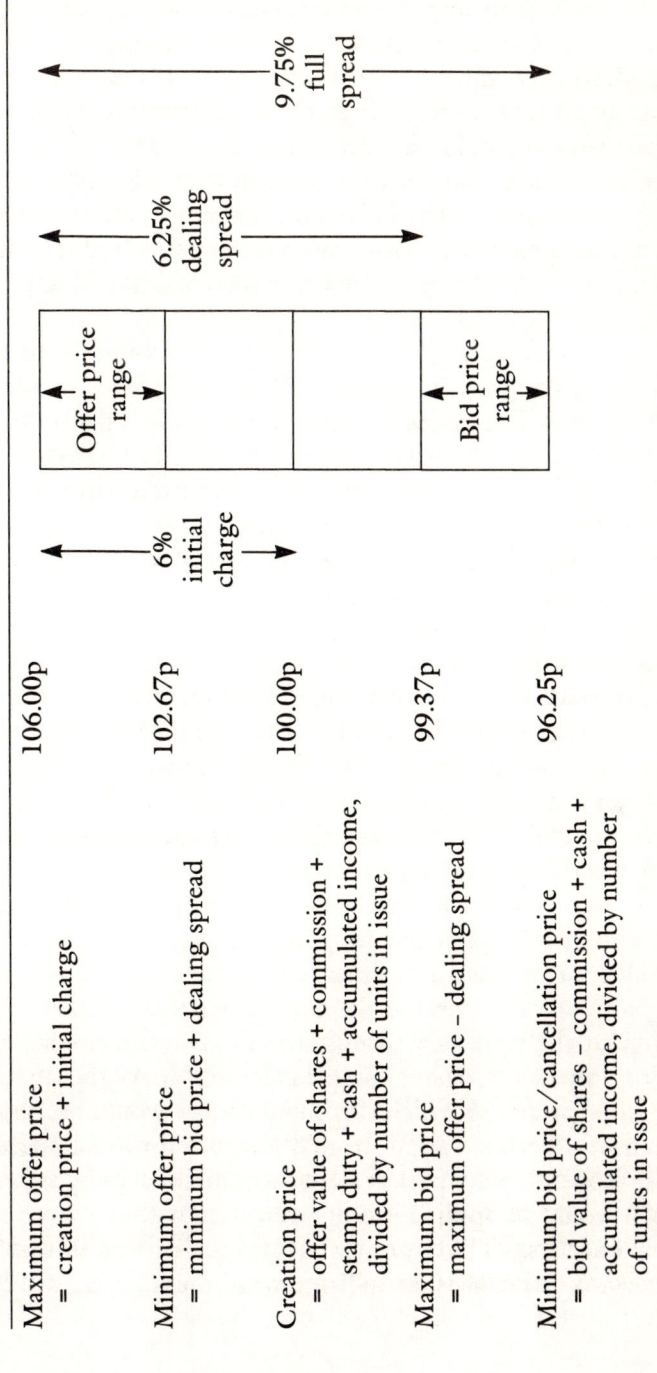

Maximum offer price = creation price + initial charge	106.00p
Minimum offer price = minimum bid price + dealing spread	102.67p
Creation price = offer value of shares + commission + stamp duty + cash + accumulated income, divided by number of units in issue	100.00p
Maximum bid price = maximum offer price – dealing spread	99.37p
Minimum bid price/cancellation price = bid value of shares – commission + cash + accumulated income, divided by number of units in issue	96.25p

9.75% full spread

6.25% dealing spread

6% initial charge

Offer price range

Bid price range

immediately drop 11 per cent in value, so the managers normally quote prices somewhere between the two extremes. The 'dealing' spread, which is the difference between the two quoted prices, is typically around 6 or 7 per cent. An illustration of the various prices is shown in Table 6.2.

When a trust is in demand, with new money coming in, the managers are likely to be buying more shares for the portfolio, so the quoted prices will move towards the top end of the range to reflect the costs of this. In this case the trust is said to be on an 'offer basis'.

Correspondingly, when more people are selling the trust than buying it, the managers may need to sell shares to meet the redemptions. The prices will then move towards the bottom end of the range and the trust is said to be on a 'bid basis'.

These price movements within the permitted range stem from the aim to be fair to all investors, particularly those who continue to hold units. For example, if sellers were given too high a price, it would dilute the value of the trust for the remaining unit holders.

As long as you buy and sell on roughly the same basis, it makes little difference where the prices are within the range. But if you buy when the trust is on an offer basis and sell when it is on a bid basis, you will effectively suffer the full spread.

Generally, managers will not move abruptly from one to the other, but will try to anticipate the trend of demand – whether the market is rising or falling – and move gradually over several days. But a very large order can force a sharper movement, so it is possible that the price can move against you quite suddenly.

The Securities and Investments Board has issued a green paper on proposals to liberalise the charging structure of unit trusts which, at the time of writing, is at the consultative stage. The major proposal is to have a single price in place of the current bid and offer prices, to which the initial charge would be added for purchases. Certain variations may also be allowed, in particular the option to replace part or all of the initial charge by an 'exit fee' which would be applied if units were sold within a given period from purchase. The argument in favour of this is that more money would be invested up front, while the trust can still recoup its costs if investors switch in and out quickly. Exit fees are already in use on some personal equity plans (see Chapter 9).

Different types of unit

Unit trusts may offer either or both of two types of unit: accumulation and distribution. Accumulation units are designed to reinvest any income earned by the trust with a corresponding increase in the unit price. Distribution, or income, units, instead pay out the income, usually twice a year, although some pay quarterly or annually.

The difference is simply a matter of convenience. Trusts that have the sole aim of producing capital growth, and those that invest in certain overseas markets, have a very low yield – in the case of Japan, it may be virtually zero. To pay out to every unit holder twice a year could cost more than the income itself, so it is easier to accumulate it into the fund. The managers will, however, send out information on the income that has been accumulated as investors will have to declare it for tax.

Distribution units are used by trusts that are designed for income or a combination of income and growth. Payments are made net of basic rate tax. Some trusts offer to reinvest the income in further units, but this will usually mean paying the initial charge each time. If you do not want the income, and there is a choice available, accumulation units should prove more cost-effective.

When you buy distribution units in a trust, the price will include an allowance for any income that has accrued since the last payment date. So when you receive the next distribution, part of it will represent the income earned since you invested, while the rest is in effect a return of the extra amount you paid for the units. For tax purposes, this portion – known as an 'equalisation payment' – counts as capital; it is not liable for income tax, but will be deducted from the purchase price in calculating any capital gains tax liability.

Funds of funds

A few years ago, a new type of unit trust was introduced, referred to as a 'fund of funds'. This is a kind of 'super trust' which invests across the range of the group's other trusts and thereby acts as a managed fund.

Initially, the concept attracted a fair degree of scepticism and even now only a third or so of the management groups offer such a trust. The advantage claimed is that it offers the equivalent of an investment management service for relatively small sums. For smaller investors, highly specialised trusts can be too risky, as performance is very volatile and timing – when to buy and sell – is crucial. Through the fund of funds, the investor can obtain a stake in these specialist trusts at lower risk, because the portfolio is spread over a range of trusts, and the manager makes the decisions on his behalf.

One drawback is that the fund of funds is limited by the other trusts run by the group. Obviously, it would not be worth while unless the range of trusts it can invest in is fairly broad. But even then it may not be possible to get the best mix, because the individual trusts have their own objectives which may not fit with the overview of the fund of funds. For example, the investment strategy of the Japan trust, which is focused solely on that market, might not be the best approach for the Japanese portion of the fund of funds, which takes a global view. And, of course, if the Japan trust happens to be performing badly, the fund of funds manager has the difficult choice of whether to invest in a poor fund or not to be in Japan at all.

So far, the performance of the funds of funds does not suggest that they have any particular advantage over ordinary international trusts, which also take a global view and are not limited in their investment choices.

Cash trusts

Cash, or money market, trusts are a more recent innovation, born out of uncertain stock market conditions. Unlike the normal run of unit trusts, cash trusts do not involve any risk to your capital, because they invest in fixed capital instruments. In most cases they carry no initial charge and the annual charge is generally only 0.5 per cent.

The aim is to provide a temporary refuge for investors who want to sell holdings in equity trusts when the stock market is falling. The managers benefit because the money stays with the group, while investors may also benefit because they will qualify for any switching discount the group offers if they later go back into an equity trust.

Cash trusts can also provide a higher income than bank or building society deposit accounts. By pooling investors' money into one large fund, the trust can secure top rates of interest on the money market, while the minimum individual investment is generally only £1000 or less. But one drawback is that there is currently no standardised method for calculating the yield on these trusts; companies may quote net or gross of expenses, and a simple or compound rate. A set formula is being considered, but meanwhile, investors should be wary of anything that looks substantially better than its rivals.

A couple of cash trusts provide a cheque-book facility for larger investments, so that you can have instant access to your money. Otherwise, if you want to sell, managers are obliged to issue a cheque within 24 hours of receiving the necessary documentation.

Index trusts

While most trusts are actively managed, index-tracking trusts take a passive line. The aim is to track the movement in one or another stock market index: there are index trusts based on the UK, the US, Europe, Japan, South East Asia and worldwide. One way of doing this is to buy holdings in every stock that is included in the index, but for the US, for example, this would be impossible, as there are just too many. Instead, the trust will aim for a representative sample in appropriate portions. Generally, trusts do not expect to be spot on every time, but will set a target margin of error.

Not surprisingly, the concept has both its supporters and its critics. On the downside, it does not seem much of an achievement simply to match the index, especially as investors will do slightly worse than that when charges are taken into account. It is also worth remembering that a tracker trust will follow the index downwards as well as upwards, while traditional trusts have the option to go partly into cash to avoid the worst of a fall.

However, supporters point out that many trusts consistently underperform their relevant index; over longer periods, the average performance of funds in any one sector may well be below the index for that market. So while an index trust is never likely to be top of its sector in the performance tables, it is never likely to be bottom either.

Futures and options trusts

These are a recent development in the unit trust world and as yet there are very few available. The use of futures and options contracts had previously been regarded as potentially too risky for unit trusts – some people felt that if high risk trusts were allowed, it would affect the general reputation unit trusts had of being relatively safe and thereby discourage investors altogether.

One type uses futures contracts to match the performance of an index. Buying futures is cheaper than buying each individual share, so most of the trust's money can be kept in cash, earning interest, which is paid out as income distributions. The trust tracks only the capital value of the index, ignoring share dividends, but with the interest, the total return should be roughly equivalent.

These are called 'bull' funds and are designed for investors who think the market will rise. There are also 'bear' funds, designed for those who think it will fall, which produce the exact opposite of the index movement: when it falls, the trust price rises by an equivalent amount.

Geared futures and options trusts involve higher risk with the potential for greater reward. For example, a 'two times geared' trust would give double exposure: if the index rises by 10 per cent, the trust price will rise by 20 per cent, but falls will also be doubled. However, as with any unit trust, your loss is limited to your initial investment.

A third type uses futures and options in a hedging role to reduce risk.

The effect is that when the market is falling, the value of the fund should fall by less than the index, so that losses are cut, while in a flat market returns should be enhanced. In rising markets, however, the fund may underperform the index, so some growth potential may be sacrificed in return for the protection against a fall.

The mechanics of futures and options contracts are described more fully in Chapter 5.

Warrant trusts

Spring 1994 saw the launch of the first unit trust to invest in warrants. These may be issued by trading companies, investment trusts and offshore companies and it is intended that the unit trust will hold a mix of all three.

The mechanics of warrants are explained in Chapter 5. The main point to bear in mind is that the price of a warrant is generally much less than that of its related share, but price movements of the two are broadly in line. This means that the proportionate movement in the warrant price will be much greater: if the share price rises, the gain on the warrant can be several times as much, but losses will be similarly magnified.

Because of this volatility, the unit trust should be considered a relatively high risk investment, although the risk is tempered to some extent by the spread of holdings and the facility to switch heavily into cash if the market is unattractive.

Unit trusts and tax

The income earned by a unit trust may be of two types, technically known as 'franked' and 'unfranked'. Income deriving from dividends on UK equities is franked, which means it is regarded as being tax paid and the trust has no further liability.

Other income, for example, from dividends on foreign shares or interest on cash deposits, is unfranked and the trust will have to pay corporation tax on it. In the 1993 Budget, the basic rate of income tax on dividends was reduced from 25 per cent to 20 per cent; during the 1993/4 tax year, trusts had to pay a transitional corporation tax rate of 22.5 per cent but from April 1994 the rate has dropped to 20 per cent.

Dividends from the unit trust are paid, or reinvested, net of basic rate tax and the investor receives a tax credit for the amount paid. Basic rate taxpayers have no further income tax liability, while non-taxpayers can reclaim the tax credit at the new rate of

20 per cent. Higher rate taxpayers, however, must pay the difference between the tax credit and their 40 per cent liability, in other words, 20 per cent.

As to capital gains tax, the unit trust has no liability on its dealings. Any profits you make when you sell may be liable, but only if your total profits from all relevant investments exceed the annual exempt allowance, which for the 1994/5 tax year is £5800.

Special facilities for the investor

Share exchange schemes
Unit trust groups run various schemes designed to encourage investors to buy their units. Most groups offer 'share exchange' schemes for people who want to sell direct holdings in shares to invest in unit trusts instead. This has become increasingly popular for privatisation issues.

There will always be a cost advantage to the investor. Occasionally the managers may want to keep your shares for their own trusts, in which case they may pay you the offer price for the shares, or a mid-market price, rather than the bid price less selling expenses which you would receive if you sold them privately. Otherwise, you will be paid the bid price but the managers will either bear the sale costs themselves or offer a discount.

Regular savings schemes
As well as accepting lump sums, many unit trust groups offer regular savings schemes, starting from a minimum of around £50 a month. As a rule there are no penalties for stopping or taking money out, and lump sums can also be added in at any time. Income would not normally be paid out, as the administration would be too complex, so trusts which offer accumulation units are preferable.

Even if you have a lump sum to invest, it can be better to 'drip-feed' it into a trust over a period rather than put it all in at once. This is due to a phenomenon known as pound-cost averaging. The argument is fairly straightforward: if you invest a bit at a time, you will benefit from times when the price falls because the same amount of money will buy more units. With a fluctuating price, the average cost of units over a period will be less than their average price. On the other hand, if you buy all at one go, the price could be at a peak or a trough, so timing becomes all-important – and few people can be confident of getting it right.

Table 6.3 gives an example of the mechanics of pound-cost averaging, using large price swings to clarify the effect.

Schemes for a regular income
Only a small number of trusts pay a monthly income, but many groups now offer monthly income portfolio schemes. Most trusts pay out dividends two or four times a year, so by packaging together three or six trusts with different distribution dates, a scheme can produce monthly payments.

The trusts in a package may not all pay out on the same day of every month and, more particularly, are not likely to pay the same amount. A refinement is to incorporate a deposit account in the scheme which will collect all the dividends and then pay out level amounts each month.

There are two drawbacks to packaged schemes offered by unit trust groups. First, you are restricted to the trusts of that group, which may not all perform well. Second, the trusts included in the package may not be ideal for your requirements. Several schemes include a gilt or fixed interest trust, which can boost the income level at the outset but provides little opportunity for capital growth and thereby rising income over time.

Table 6.3   *Pound-cost averaging*

Month of purchase	Unit price	Number of units bought for £50
1	100p	50
2	80p	63
3	125p	40
4	90p	56
5	85p	59
6	110p	45
Average price	98.3p	313 units bought for £300; average price paid: 95.8p

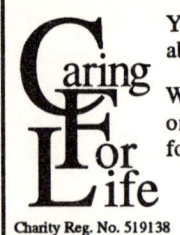

The alternative is to put together your own package, choosing the type of trusts you want from different groups. Several professional advisers run schemes of this type or can assemble one to match your particular needs. In some cases you can choose the level of income you want, but you need to remember that if you choose a level higher than the trusts are actually paying out, units would have to be cashed in to make up the difference. Over time this would make progressive inroads into your capital, so you would do better to settle for a lower income to start with and hope capital growth will boost it.

Keeping track of your investment

Generally, managers revalue at least once a day and prices are quoted in both *The Financial Times* and *The Daily Telegraph*. However, most groups now deal on a 'forward pricing' basis, which means that the deal is carried out at the price set by the next valuation. The remainder use 'historic pricing', which means the price used is that of the most recent valuation, but they must deal at a forward price if it is requested and will also move to forward pricing in certain circumstances, for example, if there is a large movement in the market.

So the prices published in newspapers are not necessarily what you will be quoted if you sell that day, but unless a very large deal has just gone through there is unlikely to be a substantial difference from one valuation to the next. *The Financial Times* indicates whether dealing is on a forward or historic basis, and also shows the cancellation price, so you can see whether a trust is on a bid or offer basis.

Another source of information is the manager's report on a trust, which is usually sent out to unit holders twice a year. Among other things, this will list details of the trust's holdings and any changes made since the previous report; it will also give a commentary on performance and how this ties in with the markets in which the trust invests. Although the information will be somewhat out of date by the time you receive it, it does provide a guide to the general strategy being followed.

How to invest

Investments can be made through an intermediary, such as a bank, stockbroker or financial adviser, or you can deal directly with the unit trust group by telephone or post. Advertisements in the national press may also carry a coupon form for buying units.

Initially you will receive a contract note, which gives details of the amount invested, the price and the number of units bought, and subsequently you will be sent the certificate. To sell, you can simply send the certificate to the group and a cheque will be issued within a few days.

Some professional advisers provide unit trust portfolio management services, usually for a minimum sum of £10,000 or so. These are looked at in Chapter 7.

Offshore funds

'Offshore' is a slightly misleading term, conjuring up visions of exotic islands where the very rich go to escape the rigours of taxation. Offshore funds can, indeed, be based in places such as Bermuda and the Cayman Islands, but the more prosaic definition is simply a location that is outside the UK mainland. The traditional bases for funds that might attract UK investors are Jersey, Guernsey and the Isle of Man, but the development of EU regulations has made Luxembourg a popular choice – the Channel Islands and the Isle of Man are outside the European Union (EU) – and more recently Dublin has established an offshore centre.

Offshore funds are collective investments but can take various forms; they may be open-ended, like unit trusts, or closed-ended, like investment trusts. The exact structure and legal framework will depend on where they are based.

Regulation

Moves to allow cross-border dealing in collective investments within the EU have resulted in an array of rules and jargon. For a start, European funds are often referred to by the French acronyms 'SICAV' and 'SICAF'. The former are open-ended funds, which means the size is unrestricted and will increase or decrease according to demand and supply; the latter are closed-ended, which means they have a fixed amount of capital.

Open-ended funds can apply for the status of UCITS (Undertakings for Collective Investment in Transferable Securities), which is granted by the regulatory authority in the country of origin. The main UCITS rules are drafted by the EU, but stipulations on how and where a fund may invest come under local regulations and may vary from country to country. At the time of writing, cash funds and funds of funds cannot qualify as UCITS, but the EU directive is being amended to encompass them. Once a fund has UCITS status, it can be freely marketed throughout member states, subject to marketing rules laid down by each individual country.

The Financial Times lists offshore funds as being one of three types: SIB recognised, Regulated and Other. The first category refers to funds that have been approved by the Securities and Investments Board, which means that they may be freely marketed in the UK, in the same way as unit trusts. Funds with UCITS status get this approval more or less automatically.

Funds based outside the EU can also apply for SIB recognition if their country of origin has 'designated territory' status. This is granted by the SIB to countries where the local regulations and compensation scheme arrangements are deemed to be of similar standard to those applying in the UK. From the investor's point of view, if a fund is SIB recognised, it is not too important where it is based, as it will be subject to much the same level of regulation as UK funds.

Regulated funds are those that are authorised under local regulations but have not obtained SIB recognition. This does not necessarily mean that they are less well regulated; it may simply be that the managers are not looking to attract UK investors or, in the case of European funds, that they wish to invest outside the limits of the UCITS rules. These funds can still be sold to UK investors, but only through private placements; they cannot use direct advertising or mailing.

Some countries allow funds to be set up and operated without coming under regulation. These are listed in *The Financial Times* under the heading of 'Other Offshore Funds' and are often aimed at institutional rather than private investors.

Taxation

For a UK investor, offshore funds are subject to one of two tax regimes. The fund may have 'distributor' status, in which case it must pay out at least 85 per cent of its income, which is paid gross but is subject to tax at the investor's normal rate. Any capital gains made on selling out of the fund will be liable to capital gains tax, subject to the usual annual exempt allowance.

Alternatively, the fund may be of the 'accumulator' type, which means all income is rolled up within the fund. No income tax is payable while you are invested, but when you come to sell, all gains are liable to income tax, whether they derive from income or capital growth.

Which of the two is preferable depends on your circumstances. If you are a higher rate taxpayer now, but expect to drop down to basic rate in future, then with an accumulator fund you can defer the tax bill to that point. Alternatively, if you are looking for capital growth, a distributor fund would mean a small tax bill each year, but the bulk of the return would be in capital gains, against which you have the annual tax-exempt allowance (£5800 for the 1994/5 tax year).

The problem with distributor status is that it is only granted for a year at a time, and in retrospect. Although the income distribution rule is fairly easy to comply with, there is another rule that bans 'trading'; this is designed to prevent funds cheating by turning income into capital gains, but the wording is rather vague and funds have occasionally been caught out. If you cash in your holding and distributor status is then refused, you can face an unexpected income tax bill.

A few years ago, when income tax went up to 60 per cent against a capital gains tax rate of 30 per cent, this was a severe penalty. Now that the two rates have been equalised, it is less drastic, but there is still a disadvantage because of the exempt allowance for capital gains tax.

Pros and cons

With so many onshore unit trusts and other funds available, the obvious question is, why look offshore? Originally these funds were primarily aimed at those who were non-resident for tax purposes and could therefore gain a tax advantage; there were few attractions for the UK investor. But the developments in EU regulations, combined with certain restrictions on UK-based unit trusts, have meant that a number of companies are now finding that an offshore base presents greater opportunities.

The major feature that is driving the UK unit trust companies to set up offshore is the facility to pay dividends gross. This is particularly attractive for funds that focus on producing income, such as bond funds and, in future, cash funds. Although the income is ultimately taxable in the hands of a UK investor, there may be cash flow advantages in gross payments, and for non-taxpayers it saves the trouble of reclaiming tax paid.

Another issue is investment flexibility: offshore funds can invest in areas that are not available to unit trusts, such as currencies and commodities. Even where the investments are of the same type, the restrictions may be fewer or non-existent. For example, a unit trust may invest only up to 10 per cent of its portfolio, in total, in countries that are not on the SIB's list of recognised stock exchanges. A Dublin-based UCITS fund, on the other hand, could put up to 10 per cent in each of these countries, and some may be wholly unrestricted.

A potential drawback is that, even if a fund is SIB recognised,

it does not come under the UK compensation scheme. In some cases, the local regulations may in fact offer a higher degree of protection, but some areas do not operate any compensation scheme. You should always check that the fund assets are held by an independent custodian and, for preference, stick to those run by a well-known name.

Offshore funds are often based on a single price, to which the front-end fee is added, rather than having a bid/offer spread like unit trusts, so they may be slightly cheaper to buy into. Annual charges, on the other hand, may be rather higher than for onshore trusts because, in addition to the management charge, the fund may have to meet the fees of the auditor and the custodian or trustee.

Umbrella funds

Umbrella funds, the first of which appeared in 1984, technically consist of a single overall fund which comprises several different sub-funds or share classes. One of the main advantages for some time was that investors could switch their holdings between the different sub-funds without being liable to capital gains tax, which would only arise when they sold out of the whole fund. Unfortunately, this loophole has since been closed and CGT now arises on all switches, just as it would if you moved from one unit trust to another run by the same group.

However, there may still be an advantage in cost terms, as the initial fee will be waived for switches between sub-funds. Some companies also run a parallel portfolio management service, which will look after your investments within the fund and make appropriate switches, but there is an extra charge for this. The main drawback of umbrella funds is that you are committing yourself to just one company, which may not have the best performing funds across the full range.

Another point to watch out for is whether the fund intends to apply for distributor status. This is granted to the umbrella fund as a unit, which means each separate sub-fund must comply with the regulations. If one fails, the fund as a whole fails, which has tax repercussions for the investor as outlined above.

How to invest

As mentioned, funds that have obtained SIB recognition can be freely marketed in the same way as unit trusts, but others can only advertise indirectly, by offering to send out a prospectus. In either case, but particularly the latter, it is probably worth while consulting a professional adviser.

Open-ended investment companies

While unit trusts with UCITS status can theoretically be sold throughout the EU, in practice they are not attractive to Europeans, who prefer the single price and the tax structure of a SICAV. As a result, several UK companies have set up offshore operations, mainly in Luxembourg and Dublin, to run SICAVs. But as SICAVs can be sold in the UK, and the range of funds offered generally parallels the groups' unit trusts, some are questioning whether there is a need to run two separate operations.

Obviously, it would be a considerable loss to the UK investment industry if management groups abandoned unit trusts in favour of offshore SICAVs. A solution that has been proposed is to allow SICAV-style funds, currently referred to as open-ended investment companies (OEICs), to be operated from and sold in the UK.

Proposals are still at the consultative stage, so no details are definite as yet, but OEICs seem likely to differ from unit trusts in two main ways. They will have a single price structure and there will be the option to roll up income within the fund, thereby deferring any income tax due to a later date, as with offshore accumulator funds. They will also differ in composition, being companies with a board of directors instead of trusts governed by trustees, and they may be more flexible in how and where they can invest.

If OEICs are allowed, the main beneficiaries will be the management groups, as they will be able to develop a single product range that can be sold throughout Europe, from a UK base instead of offshore. For the investor there will be little material gain over unit trusts – which may eventually come to be replaced altogether – although charges may be more flexible and this may also allow simplified umbrella funds.

Where to find out more

The Association of Unit Trusts and Investment Funds produces general performance figures and other statistical data, but does not offer advice or recommendation on individual trusts or management groups. It runs the Unit Trust Information Service, which can provide an introductory booklet, a unit trust user's handbook and a directory of trusts, and can be contacted on 081-207 1361 or by writing to 65 Kingsway, London WC2B 6TD. The groups themselves also have a range of literature on their own products.

The *Unit Trust Yearbook* is published annually by Financial Times Business Enterprises and contains details of both management groups and all unit trusts available.

Unit trust prices are quoted in daily newspapers such as *The Daily Telegraph* and *The Financial Times*; *The Financial Times* also publishes the prices of offshore funds.

7

Unit Trusts and Offshore Funds (2): The Investment Choice

In recent years there has been a degree of consolidation in the unit trust market, which has slightly reduced the number of companies operating in this field. Nevertheless, the number of trusts has continued to grow steadily, as Table 7.1 shows. With over 1500 available, it is difficult to know where to start, especially as many have similar aims and specialisations. The best way is probably to decide first what type of trust you are after, and

Table 7.1   *Authorised unit trusts*

Year	Number of trusts	Number of companies
1981	529	93
1982	553	99
1983	630	91
1984	687	102
1985	806	110
1986	964	121
1987	1137	139
1988	1255	153
1989	1379	162
1990	1407	154
1991	1400	157
1992	1456	151
1993	1528	156

Source: Association of Unit Trusts and Investment Funds

then to choose between the different management groups offering that type.

On the most basic approach, trusts can be divided into four types:

1. Trusts whose primary objective is to produce income;
2. Trusts whose primary objective is to produce capital growth, either with a general portfolio or specialising in a particular country or sector;
3. Trusts that aim to provide a mix between income and growth;
4. Cash trusts.

The first three of these groups may invest in the UK or overseas (or, in the case of international trusts, both). The fourth type is in a sense a sub-section of the first, since the aim is income, but cash trusts differ from others in that they do not involve any capital risk.

Unit trust categories

Looking in more detail, the Association of Unit Trusts and Investment Funds sets out 22 separate categories of trust for the purpose of making performance comparisons. These are grouped under eight headings, as follows.

UK funds
All trusts with at least 80 per cent of their investments in the UK.

UK General
Trusts with at least 80 per cent of their assets in UK equities, which aim to produce a combination of income and growth. These trusts must also aim to have a yield of between 80 and 110 per cent of the yield of the FT-SE-A All Share Index.

UK Equity Income
Trusts which invest at least 80 per cent of their assets in UK equities and which aim to have a yield of more than 110 per cent of the yield of the All Share Index.

UK Growth
Trusts which invest at least 80 per cent of their assets in UK equities and have a primary objective of achieving capital growth.

UK Smaller Companies
Trusts which invest at least 80 per cent of their assets in the shares of companies which form part of the Hoare Govett UK Smaller Companies Extended Index.

UK Gilt & Fixed Interest
Trusts which invest at least 80 per cent of their assets in UK gilts and fixed interest securities.

UK Balanced
Trusts which invest at least 80 per cent of their assets in the UK but have less than 80 per cent in either UK equities or UK gilts and fixed interest securities.

International
Trusts with a portfolio that is less than 80 per cent invested in any one geographical area (with the exception of the International Fixed Interest sector).

International Equity Income
Trusts which invest at least 80 per cent of their assets in equities and which aim to achieve a yield above 110 per cent of the yield of the FT-Actuaries World Index.

International Growth
Trusts which invest at least 80 per cent of their assets in equities and which have a primary objective of capital growth.

International Fixed Interest
Trusts which invest at least 80 per cent of their assets in fixed interest stocks. This includes all such trusts, regardless of whether they have more than 80 per cent in a particular geographic sector, unless it is the UK, in which case they come under the UK heading.

International Balanced
Trusts which have less than 80 per cent of their assets in either equities or fixed interest securities.

Japan
Trusts which invest at least 80 per cent of their assets in Japanese securities.

Far East

Including Japan
Trusts which invest at least 80 per cent of their assets in Far Eastern securities including a Japanese content that is less than 80 per cent.

Excluding Japan
Trusts which invest at least 80 per cent of their assets in Far Eastern securities but exclude any Japanese content.

Australasia
Trusts which invest at least 80 per cent of their assets in Australian or New Zealand securities.

North America
Trusts which invest at least 80 per cent of their assets in North American securities.

Europe
Trusts which invest at least 80 per cent of their assets in European securities, including the UK, but not exceeding 80 per cent in the UK.

Specialist
Trusts which invest their assets in a specialist area, regardless of any geographical specialisation they may also have.

Commodity & Energy
Trusts which invest at least 80 per cent of their assets in commodity or energy securities.

Objective Limited Risk Equity Fund

Investors often experience the proverbial conflicting emotions of a *fear of losses* and a *desire for profits*. While attractive stockmarket returns make equities a sensible part of any long term investment strategy, many potential equity investors are worried about risk of sudden, large, capital losses because of stockmarket volatility.

Objective Unit Trust Management calculates that investors in ordinary unit trusts are taking, perhaps unwittingly, a 1 in 4 chance of a capital loss of more than 5% over any six month period. The risk of a loss of more than 10% over the same period is 1 in 5, and a loss of more than 20%, roughly 1 in 20.

Until recently there have been very few investment products which directly address investors' conflicting emotions. Objective Unit Trust Management has now launched its **Limited Risk Equity Fund**, designed to be an ideal long term investment for investors who want both equity returns and a high degree of capital protection.

To calm fears, the fund is "rebased" twice a year to ensure that, even in the worst market conditions, the bid price of the fund cannot fall by more than 5% over any full six month period between rebasing dates. The rebasing consists of establishing a series of option positions which provide the necessary capital protection. This also "locks in" cumulative profits like a ratchet. This ingenious feature has the welcome effect of protecting not only the original investment from market falls, but also the successive profits made over time. The fund therefore offers firm, predictable protection from market crashes.

To satisfy the desire for profits, the fund will capture the "bulk" of both the capital and the income returns of the stockmarkets in which it invests. Objective calculates that the "bulk" means somewhere between 85% and 90%. This should enable the fund to compare well in rising markets with the returns of the average international balanced unit trust. Where the Objective fund really scores, however, is when there are sudden market falls. Whereas normal unit trusts will fall without limit, the Objective fund will stop at its minus 5% floor.

Objective have added other features to the fund to increase its appeal to cautious investors. Equity investment is spread across several global markets to make the fund less risky than one which invests in only one market. The mix will be roughly half in the UK and the other half divided equally across the US, Europe and Japan and the Far East.

The fund also makes income payments twice a year and it offers all the familiar benefits of a unit trust such as "instant access" to capital without penalty, daily prices published in the national press and simple dealing procedures.

Investors in the Objective Limited Risk Equity Fund can sleep easily at night in the knowledge that their capital is always protected and that as time rolls by, successive profits are also protected. Furthermore, owing to the fund's global investment spread, investors will have an excellent chance of capturing the benefits of strong economic growth, wherever and whenever it may occur in the world.

Financial & Property
Trusts which invest at least 80 per cent of their assets in financial or property securities.

Investment Trust Units
Trusts which are able to invest only in the shares of investment trust companies.

Fund of Funds
Trusts which are able to invest only in other authorised unit trust schemes.

Money Market
Trusts which invest at least 80 per cent of their assets in money market instruments.

Convertibles
Trusts which invest at least 60 per cent of their assets in convertible stocks.

In addition, there are exempt trusts and personal pension trusts. Neither are relevant to the ordinary investor; exempt trusts are available only to tax-exempt institutions, such as pension funds and charities, while personal pension trusts are for use only with pension contracts (see Chapter 11).

Table 7.2 shows some past performance results for each of the categories outlined above. These figures, which are compiled on a regular basis by the Association of Unit Trusts and Investment Funds, show the realisation value of £1000 invested over various time periods in the median fund in each sector – the middle one in the performance rankings, rather than the average.

Past performance, as the saying goes, is not necessarily a guide to the future; as the table demonstrates, different sectors may come to the fore over different periods. It is also important, in looking at figures of this type, to check exactly what they purport to show. Unit trusts are usually shown on an 'offer to bid' basis, which reflects the cash-in value if you had bought and sold on the respective dates. Alternatively, figures may be on an 'offer to offer' basis; this takes out the effect of the price spread and the initial charge, but can give an idea of what the manager has achieved. Statistics are also generally quoted with net income reinvested, which compounds the capital growth; if you are investing to earn income to spend, then obviously the capital return will be rather less.

Table 7.2 *Past performance of unit trusts*

| Sector | Value of £1000 invested in median fund | | |
	5 years	10 years	15 years
UK General	1594	3976	10,131
UK Equity Income	1566	4488	9937
UK Growth	1528	3592	8450
UK Smaller Companies	1339	3706	8792
UK Balanced	1477	3604	7054
UK Gilt & Fixed Interest	1485	2223	3998
International Growth	1650	2983	6862
International Income	1736	3351	—
International Balanced	1670	2132	—
International Fixed Interest	1553	2505	—
Fund of Funds	1566	—	—
Japan	1175	3509	8912
Far East: Including Japan	1843	4421	10,522
Far East: Excluding Japan	3260	4984	18,488
Australasia	1813	2023	3551
North America	1987	3069	6735
Europe	1891	4568	11,446
Commodity & Energy	1734	1741	5240
Financial & Property	1748	2843	7088
Investment Trust Units	1838	4326	11,254
Convertibles	1353	2550	2653
Money Market	1407	—	—
Building Society Higher Rate	1377	1993	3085
FT-SE-A All Share Index	738	4210	10,454

Note: A gap indicates that no trusts have been in existence that long. All figures are on an offer to bid basis, with net income reinvested. Figures as at 1 March 1994.

Source: Association of Unit Trusts and Investment Funds

Also shown in the table, for the purposes of comparison, are the results of £1000 invested in a building society higher interest account and the equivalent figures for the FT-SE-A All Share Index. Index comparisons should be treated with caution, as an index does not include dealing costs or the charges encountered with a trust. In the case of an overseas trust, there are also currency considerations; the return in sterling terms may vary significantly from the market trend shown by the index.

Investment aims

The first step in deciding where to put your money is to determine whether you are looking for income or capital growth. The two are not necessarily mutually exclusive; while trusts that go all out for capital growth will not produce any income to speak of, there are others that combine both objectives. Similarly, the strategies pursued by equity income trusts can often produce good growth, even where that is a secondary aim.

Income trusts

If you are looking for income, you need to bear in mind that investing in equities will not provide you with very high income at the outset. Even so-called 'high income' trusts may yield only around 5 per cent gross and, while at the time of writing this compares well with returns from a building society, just a short time ago it would have looked very meagre.

The advantage of investing in equities, however, is that they should produce some capital appreciation and a rising income over time, while a building society deposit will be static in value and the income will rise and fall with interest rates.

The income comparison is illustrated in Table 7.3, which shows the net annual income paid by an equity income trust and a building society higher rate account over a 10-year period. The building society provided higher income for the first three years, but was then overtaken by the trust, which would also have grown in capital value. The table also shows the gross annual income from the trust, which could be obtained by holding it in a personal equity plan, and this beats the building society after just two years.

Table 7.3 *Annual income from an equity income trust compared with a building society higher rate account*

£1000 invested 1 March 1984	Annual income		
Year	Unit trust net income (£)	Unit trust gross income (£)	Building society (£)
1	47	70	87
2	55	75	94
3	61	79	71
4	69	94	50
5	88	99	31
6	103	112	81
7	109	131	89
8	109	135	77
9	102	140	67
10	104	119	70

Note: Figures relate to the annual income paid by the average UK Equity Income fund and a building society seven-day notice account with a minimum balance of £2500, 1 March 1984–1 March 1994.

Source: Association of Unit Trusts and Investment Funds

It is possible to get a higher initial income from a unit trust by choosing one of the specialist types: those investing in gilts and fixed interest securities, convertibles or preference shares. These can offer a starting yield of around 6 to 8 per cent gross. But again, with these trusts there is much less potential for capital growth on the assets, hence the income return is less likely to improve over time.

In general, there is a limit to the amount of genuine income that can be produced, and to go above that level will entail some sacrifice of capital or capital growth potential. A couple of trusts launched in 1993 were specifically designed to convert future capital growth into current income, by the use of options. The trusts invest mainly in blue chip shares and special loan securities, which produce a reasonable base yield, and then also write options, on which a premium is earned. The premium boosts the level of income, but the effect of the options is that any capital growth above 4 or 5 per cent is given up.

Options are also used to limit falls in the capital value, but there is no capital guarantee and in certain market conditions there could be a progressive drop. Of course, this is true of any trust, but with these there is less chance of making it up again in future, since the capital growth potential is restricted. There is also no guarantee on the income and, at the time of writing, one trust has had to reduce the level it offers, from 10 per cent net to 9 per cent.

Even with equity trusts the yield can differ. As a rule, the higher the target yield, the greater the constraints on the manager and the more growth prospects may have to be sacrificed. So trusts with a more modest pay-out now may prove more rewarding in the long run.

But the pursuit of income can work to advantage on the growth side. The yield on a share moves broadly in inverse relationship to its price – if the price falls and the dividend remains the same, it will represent a higher yield. So it may then become an attractive holding for an income unit trust. If the share price subsequently recovers, it will bring a boost to the capital growth on the trust. Of course, as the price rises, the yield will fall, so the manager will sooner or later have to sell in favour of another higher yielding stock. But although he may then miss out on further growth prospects, he equally avoids the danger of hanging on too long and seeing the share price fall back again, so it can turn out to be a useful discipline.

To a large extent, then, if a trust has a good track record for its dividend payments, the capital performance should also be satisfactory. Although past results cannot be relied upon, a consistent dividend history is a fair indication of a manager's ability, as these trusts have a fairly broad range of investment possibilities and are therefore less dominated by market movements than a more specialised vehicle such as a commodity trust.

So the starting-point for choosing an income trust is to weigh up your needs for income today as against income in the future. If you are looking for immediate high income over a short time-span, a fixed interest or preference trust may be suitable. If you are prepared to settle for less now to have more in the future, then think about an equity-based trust or one with mixed holdings. In the latter case, check out the proportions held in ordinary shares as against preference shares or fixed interest securities; again, the higher the content of ordinary equities, the better should be the prospects of a rising income. Another important point is the level of annual management charge. This will be paid for out of the trust's income, so the higher the charge, the less will be left to distribute to unit holders.

If the trust is fairly new, you can only go by its portfolio structure and the charges. If it has a track record, you can also check the dividend history; ideally, payments should at least have kept pace with inflation. Finally, check the capital growth; although this may not be your top priority it will underpin the income return.

Overseas income trusts
The bulk of trusts focusing on income are invested in the UK, but there are a growing number based on overseas markets. Some of these invest in particular geographical areas, such as North America or Europe, while others are international in scope. These latter trusts are classified under two sector headings, equity income and fixed interest, which have the same characteristics as the equivalent UK trusts.

The overseas equity income trusts tend to have lower yields than their UK counterparts because the stock markets themselves have lower yields, and the management charge may also be higher, which will detract from the return. You should also bear in mind the currency factor, which can add to the degree of risk involved.

Special schemes
As mentioned in Chapter 6, there are a number of schemes available that are designed to produce a monthly income by packaging together trusts with different pay-out dates. If you are looking for regular income, a package has the advantage over an individual monthly-paying trust – of which there are around a dozen – that a spread of investments gives a spread of risk. There will, of course, be a higher minimum investment than for a single trust.

Set packages have the drawback that there may be little or no choice of which trusts are included, which means there may be a higher fixed interest content than you would like, and also commit you to one management group. The alternative is to put together your own package from among all the income trusts available. If you are prepared to manage with uneven payments, so much the better; aiming to get a similar level of payment on the same day each month will restrict the choice and may mean a sacrifice of overall performance.

General and balanced trusts

As mentioned, income and growth are not mutually exclusive targets, as there are a number of trusts which offer elements of both, either through a combination of higher and lower yielding equities, or through a mixture of equities with fixed interest securities.

General trusts, in particular, are often regarded as the plain vanilla of the industry, worthy but dull. Most groups have one, and some even have more than one, but they are rarely likely to be the subject of eye-catching advertisements. The yield is generally in the region of 3 per cent gross and they are expected to show steady, rather than spectacular, performance.

Balanced funds are those that mix equities with fixed interest stocks and have less than 80 per cent in either. The yield can be rather higher than on general funds, depending on the mix of holdings; the greater the proportion of fixed interest securities, the higher the yield but, as mentioned in the last section, this entails lower growth prospects. Most of these trusts, however, steer a middle course between the two in the same way as general trusts.

Although they may never top the performance listings, Table 7.4 shows that the returns are not to be scorned. Certain specialist sectors may well do better, but others will do a lot worse, so unless you have confidence in your powers of selection, or sufficient money to put together a range of specialist holdings, a general or balanced trust can be a good home for a first investment. Equally, if you are building up a portfolio, a general trust can form a stable core, from which you can venture into higher risk holdings.

Growth trusts

By far the majority of unit trusts available are designed to produce capital growth. They comprise a large variety of types, from broadly based international trusts to those specialising in a particular geographical area, such as the UK or Japan, and those concentrating on a particular industry or market sector. Given this huge range, it is impossible to make generalisations and not easy to set about making a choice. At any one time, different markets will be in the ascendancy, and the time-scale you have in mind for your investment will also have a bearing on where the best prospects lie. However, it is possible to narrow down the choice by considering the following alternatives.

UK versus overseas
Many UK investors naturally incline towards the home market, and there are arguments to support this. For one thing, the returns from a unit trust are in sterling, so if you invest in an

Table 7.4 *Past performance of General and Balanced funds*

Sector	Value of £1000 invested in median fund		
	5 years	10 years	15 years
UK General	1594	3976	10,131
UK Balanced	1477	3604	7054
International Balanced	1670	2132	—

Note: Figures are on an offer to bid basis, with net income reinvested, as at 1 March 1994.

Source: Association of Unit Trusts and Investment Funds

overseas trust you are exposed to a currency risk on top of the market risk. Some trusts aim to offset this by using 'hedging' techniques, but that in itself can have certain risks as well as costs.

Second, the stock market will respond to and reflect general factors in the economy, which may be appropriate since your other financial arrangements will be subject to similar influences. On the other hand, the major world economies move very much in line with each other anyway.

Also, any investment in a single market, even one the size of the UK, has limitations in terms of choice of stocks and spread of risk. If you are planning to build up a portfolio of any size, or you already have other UK investments, you should think of spreading your investments further afield for better balance.

International versus single country

If you decide to look abroad, you have the choice between single country trusts and those that maintain a global spread. Single country trusts range from those based on large markets, such as the US, to much more specialised types; for example, trusts focused on Switzerland or Thailand.

The same arguments apply to investing in a single overseas market as to investing in the UK: there is less spread of risk. This is particularly true in the smaller markets, where there may be a limited number of stocks available. There may also be problems or delays in buying and selling which can affect performance and add to the risk. For investors seeking to build an international portfolio, perhaps mainly through direct equity holdings, these trusts can offer convenient access to smaller markets; otherwise they give the chance of high rewards if you are prepared to accept high risk. The more cautious investor, on the other hand, will do better with an international trust or a selection of those based on the larger world markets.

General versus specialised

As well as trusts with a geographical specialisation, there are others which focus on a particular industry or market sector. These may operate on a global basis, such as an international technology trust, or within one particular market, such as a Japanese Smaller Companies trust.

Like trusts with a geographical specialisation, these carry a higher degree of risk than a general or international trust. But whereas you could build a collection of holdings in different countries, it would not be feasible to cover every type of industry. Hence the attraction is less to create a market balance among your investments than to inject a higher risk/higher reward element. Smaller companies, for example, are much more volatile than larger ones; they rise faster, but can also fall faster. Similarly, recovery and special situations trusts seek to take advantage of stocks that are under-priced; if the expected improvement occurs, all well and good, but it depends on how well the manager makes his selections. Industry-specific trusts can be even more dramatic; gold trusts, for example, had a phenomenal run in 1980, but subsequently spent a long period in the wilderness.

Management style

Once you have decided where to invest, you then face the choice of management group. Again, there are no easy answers: no one investment strategy is proved to be right or wrong. However, there are certain considerations which may help to sort out what accords with your own views or needs.

Active versus passive
Some managers take a very active approach, turning over the portfolio regularly in the search for value, while others operate on a longer term view. The former may have greater potential – if the manager gets it right – but the dealing costs will be higher and results may be more volatile.

Top down versus bottom up
This refers to the stock-picking approach of the manager. Some start from the top: country first (in the case of an international trust), then industry, then the specific share. Others build up from the bottom, choosing shares they think are attractive, with perhaps overall proportions for sectors or countries.

House style
Some management groups have an overall 'house style' within which the managers of individual trusts operate; this may be

simply a matter of the risk/reward approach they adopt or may go further, in that, for example, if particular industries are favoured at a given time, they are represented across the range of trusts. In other cases, each trust manager operates at a very individual level. A house style may impose constraints, but the individual approach could lead to a change of fortune, or at any rate of philosophy, if one manager leaves and another takes over.

Hedging and liquidity

Where a trust invests overseas, the returns – which are expressed in sterling, of course – will be affected by exchange rate movements as well as market trends. In some cases the manager may 'hedge' part of the portfolio to neutralise the currency effects; this can – if it works – protect against losses, although it also means missing out on favourable movements and there is a cost involved. Others take the view that if you buy the market, you also buy the currency, and that the two should not be artificially separated.

Similar views are taken on liquidity. Some managers will move out into cash if the market is falling, while others believe it is up to the investor to decide by staying in or selling out of the trust. Obviously, switching out and perhaps buying back in later would mean the investor faced a new front-end charge, but if the trust goes into cash and subsequently reinvests there will be dealing costs, and there could be a loss if the timing is not judged accurately.

Size of fund

There is a theory that a small trust will tend to outperform a larger one. This has some logic, in that a small trust is more flexible and can therefore respond more quickly to changes in the market – assuming the manager interprets the trend correctly. Large funds operating in a small market may also be hampered by a limited choice of stocks.

Small trusts will obviously tend to hold fewer stocks, but larger ones also vary in whether they are widespread or concentrated. The fewer the holdings in the portfolio, the higher the risk/reward ratio, as a gain or loss in any one holding will have a greater proportional influence.

Location

Some groups run their overseas trusts entirely from a UK base, while others have local offices in the major markets. Naturally there is much debate over which is better: the objective view from a distance or the 'feel' gained by being on the spot. In fact, those operating from the UK will normally make regular visits to the country and may also liaise with local brokers for information and – particularly in smaller markets – for dealing. Given the sophistication of global communications, one suspects there is not a great deal of difference, and certainly performance results do not point to either approach being consistently more successful.

New launches

One other theory on the relative merits of different trusts is that new launches will do well. This can depend on the reason for the launch and its timing. Some are 'bandwagon' products, investing in a market that is currently rising, in which case they are likely to look good to start with, particularly as they have new money to spend on the most attractive shares, while older trusts in the same market may be stuck with shares that have gone out of fashion.

The ideal timing, of course, is to launch just before a market goes up, to get the full benefit of the rise, but (aside from the difficulty of correctly predicting market movements) it is harder to attract money into a sector that is currently looking dull.

Are you an active investor?

One important question to consider before choosing a trust is whether you plan to monitor and alter your investment actively or simply want to invest and forget about it. In the latter case, you are likely to do best by sticking to fairly general trusts; the more specialist offerings are more volatile and need to be kept under supervision.

If you expect to be active and switch your holdings around between different trusts, this should influence your choice of management group. Of course, you are not bound to stick with the same group and there are drawbacks to doing so: no one group is going to top the performance tables with every trust it runs. But against that there is the advantage that switches from one trust to another within the same group attract a discount on the front-end charge, which can significantly cut the costs of active investment. So you should look for a group – or perhaps two or three – which have a wide range of funds and offer a good switching discount.

Portfolio management services

If you would like your investments to be actively managed, but lack the time or knowledge to do it yourself, there are a number of advisers who offer portfolio management services. These may be run on a discretionary or an advisory basis. In the first case, you would set out your basic aims, such as income or capital growth and the amount of risk you are prepared to accept, and the adviser would do the rest; you would be kept informed of changes to the portfolio and receive regular valuations, but would not be consulted on each deal.

With an advisory service, the adviser would consult you (and vice versa) before any change was made. The minimum for a discretionary service starts at about £10,000; for an advisory service it is likely to be higher, because of the extra work involved. Charging systems vary; the adviser may operate on the commissions he gets on each trust purchase, but it can be more efficient for both sides to rebate commission and charge an annual management fee.

Broker unit trusts

An alternative to a discretionary management service is a broker unit trust, offered by a number of professional advisers (not necessarily brokers). Often an adviser might be running a large number of individual portfolios on a discretionary basis and making similar investments and changes for each. By setting up a broker unit trust he can consolidate these portfolios into one fund, with a single transaction when he buys or sells, thus considerably reducing the administration.

The trust may invest directly into securities or through a range of unit trusts in a similar way to a fund of funds. In either case, it must have a defined investment objective and strategy and will be governed by the same regulations as an ordinary unit trust. Funds are normally valued daily and the prices are published in national newspapers.

The advantage for the investor is that his money is professionally managed, without the need for him to get involved in each transaction, but he still has access to the fund manager and a degree of personal service that he obviously would not get from the manager of an ordinary unit trust. There is, however, an extra layer of charges, as the adviser will charge a management fee, which needs to be weighed up against the 'added value' in terms of improved performance.

Offshore funds

For the UK investor, the appeal of offshore funds lies largely in the fact that they can offer investment in areas that are not open to onshore unit trusts, in particular, currencies and commodities.

Currency funds can be based on sterling or foreign currencies. Sterling funds can be deposit-based, offering the benefits of wholesale money market rates on short-term deposits, or invested in fixed interest securities, which gives the prospect of capital gains – or a combination of both. Foreign currency funds operate in a similar way, but have the added dimension of exchange rate movements against sterling, which can generate capital gains or losses.

Some companies offer a range of funds based on different individual currencies, with free switching between them. As a rule, though, single currency funds are high risk; markets move fast and timing is crucial to the end result. Unless you have a particular reason for wanting exposure to a certain currency, or have a large amount to invest that can be spread over several funds, you may be better off with a managed currency fund or a management service linked to a range of funds.

Commodity funds are also not for the faint-hearted. Where onshore unit trusts invest only in the shares of commodity-linked companies, offshore funds may additionally use commodity futures contracts or invest directly into the commodities themselves. The outlay required and the risk involved are rather less than if you undertook the same investments on your own behalf – you can only lose the money you put into the fund, whereas with direct investment you could be committed for further sums – but unless you are an inveterate gambler, this type of investment should only be considered within larger portfolios and then only for a small proportion.

Points to watch for with offshore funds are the level of charges, which may be smaller initially but larger annually than onshore funds, and the tax status. As explained in Chapter 6, offshore funds may have distributor or accumulator status. In the first case, at least 85 per cent of the fund's income must be distributed and will be taxed at the appropriate income tax rate in the hands of the investor, while capital gains will come under the standard CGT rules. In the second case, all income is rolled up within the fund and no tax is due while you remain invested, but when you sell out, all profits will be taxed as income at your highest rate.

With foreign currency funds, for example, most of the benefits come from capital gains, so distributor status is advantageous; when you sell, you can make use of the annual CGT exempt allowance before you need pay any tax. With sterling funds that generate interest, accumulator status allows the tax bill to be deferred, which will be a benefit if your tax rate is likely to fall in the future.

8

Investment Trusts

Investment trusts are not trusts, but companies. Their aim in life is to invest their capital somewhere else – in other company shares, in fixed interest securities and the like. Investors who buy investment trust shares are, therefore, getting a 'slice of the action' of a whole portfolio of shares for the price of one. In this respect, they are similar to unit trusts (with which they are often compared and contrasted) and certainly their basic reason for existing is identical: to provide the small investor with a spread of risk for a modest outlay.

This spread of risk is legally insisted upon by the fact that, to qualify for the tax treatment described below, investment trusts cannot invest more than 15 per cent of their assets in any one security, meaning a theoretical minimum portfolio of at least seven. In practice, trusts are likely to have anything between 40 and 200 holdings. The exceptions to this rule are the shares of other investment trust companies, which themselves will automatically provide a spread of risk. They must also distribute at least 85 per cent of the income they receive from their investments to their shareholders.

The taxation position
Investment trusts are similar to unit trusts in that liability to tax on any gains they make belongs to the shareholder, rather than the company itself. This means shareholders can realise up to £5800 of gains (in the 1994/5 tax year) before being liable to tax.

On the income side, dividends from other companies in which

PORTFOLIO MANAGEMENT IN YOUR OWN UK TAX HAVEN

It is often said that unit trusts are an expensive way to buy equities. This is certainly not the case, particularly if the unit trust group has low initial charges.

The main problem that unit trusts have is that they are obliged by Regulations to incorporate their costs in their pricing. In general, they have to show most (although not necessarily all) of their buying and selling costs up front and this makes them look more expensive than many other investments which, beware, only show half the picture.

Let us suppose you have £10,000 to invest in a broadly balanced portfolio offering a mixture of income and long term capital growth. You could choose an investment trust, a unit trust, a single premium insurance bond or even give the money to a stockbroker to manage.

Suppose someone was to suggest a vehicle which offered you the following advantages:

A minimum lump sum investment of only £3,000.

- **Low Charges:**
  A low initial charge, this would immediately work to your advantage in keeping your bid offer spread narrow. (The average unit trust front end charge is between 5% and 6% but it is now possible to find groups with charges as low as 1%. Your investment would have an annual charge of 1%-1.5% but, because it was directly invested in equities, it would involve no double charging. Your fund would probably not buy other investment or unit trusts but deal directly in quoted stocks and shares.

- **Capital Gains Tax Shelter:**
  Shares bought and sold within a unit trust umbrella are free of Capital Gains Tax. This means that your manager can move between UK and foreign equities/bonds and cash on your behalf without affecting your own personal liability to Capital Gains Tax. There is, however, a liability to Capital Gains Tax upon disposal of units in your fund but you are in control of this and can use your own exemptions at the time of disposal.

- **Minimal Paper Work:**
  Stocks and shares usually involve a snowstorm of paperwork – scrip issues, rights issues, dividend payments. Also you will receive schedules of income and Capital Gains from the various activity in your portfolio. With a unit trust, you will receive one certificate on purchase and two income distribution vouchers per year thereafter.

- **Spread of Risk:**
  It is difficult to spread risk adequately with a small portfolio of your own. With only £10,000 to invest, it is unlikely that you will hold more than a half a dozen stocks and shares. A balanced portfolio in a managed unit trust would offer you a spread of UK and international shares as well as fixed interest investments and also would be likely to hold assets in cash where appropriate.

- **Dealing at Institutional Rates:**
  The average stockbroker's commission for small bargains up to £5,000 can be as much as 1.65%. Some will make a minimum dealing charge of £25 per bargain. Deals within the majority of unit trusts are done at institutional rates of approximately 0.25%. On a portfolio of £10,000, this can result in savings of over £250 in a year.

- **Professional Day to Day Management:**
  With the average unit trust, you will have full time, day to day professional fund management, with an individual fund manager looking after the assets of the fund.

- **Quarterly Valuations and Reporting:**
  A number of these balanced managed unit trusts offer you quarterly reports and valuations – which show you the assets held in the fund. They are also likely to show you the movements in the portfolio and a summary of all that has happened over the previous quarter.

- **Personal Equity Plans:**
  Depending on the investment objectives of the fund chosen, a number of these unit trusts offer you the facility to put up to £6,000 per annum into a Personal Equity Plan. As the years go by and you convert additional money into the PEP, this obviously provides you with an added tax advantage as your assets within the PEP build up.

A unit trust is a cost effective and tax efficient investment vehicle that is already on your doorstep although most people fail to realise it.

There are plenty of specialised unit trusts which give you a broad spread of risk in specific markets, however, a limited number of unit trusts which offer balanced portfolio management and they are well worth considering for those seeking long term, low cost management of their assets. The recent move by one or two groups to reduce their initial charges makes investment into some unit trusts extremely cheap and this, taken with the points that I have outlined above, should make people consider carefully, before they invest, what the full range of benefits are before making their final investment decision.

Should you require advice on your investments, we recommend that you consult your stockbroker or other independent financial adviser. Please be aware that returns may go down as well as up and that you may not get back the amount that you originally invested. Existing tax levels and reliefs may change and the value of reliefs depends on personal circumstances.

By Richard Eliott Lockhart, Director, Murray Johnstone Limited.

MURRAY ACUMEN FUND

For the simple answer.... ....use your ACUMEN

We asked professional advisers what their headaches were in providing investment services to their clients. Mountains of paperwork, high charges and dealing costs, endless reporting, immediate capital gains tax liability, to name but a few.
We listened.
And then we designed the Murray Acumen Fund.

Murray Acumen Fund is a comprehensive investment service that gives you and your clients what they need such as:

○ Balanced investment and skilled management
○ Shelter from capital gains tax
○ Excellent reporting with minimal paperwork
○ Very low charges
○ Full PEP eligibility

For further details of how using our Acumen can give you and your clients more freedom and peace of mind, **FREEPHONE 0800 289 978.**

GOOD INVESTMENT COSTS LESS AT MURRAY JOHNSTONE

the trust invests are paid net of basic rate tax to the holders of the investment trust shares. Non-taxpayers can reclaim the tax; higher rate taxpayers will have to pay more.

Do investment trusts have a unique selling point? The answer is yes, they have several, some of which may be attractive to investors, others possibly offputting.

The share price and the discount

The major difference between investment trusts and unit trusts is that the former are 'closed-ended' funds of money while the latter are 'open-ended'. Unit trusts expand and contract according to the demand for them; if demand outstrips supply, new units are created; if supply exceeds demand, units are cancelled. Investment trusts, on the other hand, have a fixed number of shares.

This difference in structure has a practical effect on prices. The price of units in a unit trust is directly related to the value of its underlying investments, while the share price of an investment trust moves up and down according to the demand for it – just like the share prices of other quoted companies.

In fact, if you totted up the value of holdings in an investment trust's portfolio and divided by the number of shares in existence, the result (known as the net asset value) is almost certain to be different from the share price. Occasionally, the share price is higher, in which case it is said to be at a premium. More commonly, it is lower, which is described as a discount. At the time of writing, the average discount for all investment trusts was 6 per cent.

Why should the share price stand at a discount? One reason is technical. As a going concern, the investment trust's portfolio is valued at mid-market prices – halfway between bid and offer; but if it were to be liquidated or taken over, the valuation would move to the lower bid basis and there would also be professional costs involved in winding it up. However, the major part of the discount is explained by supply and demand. If the shares of a trust are in demand, the discount will narrow or the price may even move to a premium; if the trust is out of favour, the discount will widen.

There is some debate over whether the discount is a benefit or a drawback. The argument in its favour is that it means you are buying a stake in more shares than you are paying for. For example, if the discount stands at 10 per cent, then every £90 you invest in the trust effectively represents £100-worth of the shares in its portfolio. On the other hand, if the discount is still the same when you come to sell, you will lose the 10 per cent again.

The discount can be thought of as an extra layer of risk – or reward. At one level you have the opportunity to gain or lose with movements in the value of the underlying portfolio. On top of that, you will gain if the discount narrows between the time you buy and sell, and lose if it widens. Broadly speaking, if the market is rising and the value of the portfolio is going up, the trust is likely to be in greater demand and the discount will narrow. So you gain twice over. Conversely, when the market is falling, demand drops off, the discount widens and you lose twice over.

While you should be cautious about buying a trust that is already on a very low discount – the expectation being that it will widen – it would be wrong to place too much emphasis on the discount. The manager's ability to produce good performance is likely to be a much larger factor in the investment return.

One other point about the discount is that if it gets too large the trust can become vulnerable to a takeover. An institution can offer an attractive price to shareholders while still leaving plenty of scope to make profits for itself. A recent case was the Globe investment trust, which was standing at a 20 per cent discount when it was taken over by Coal Board Pension Funds.

In practice, though, discounts have narrowed considerably in recent years – only 10 years ago, discounts of 20 or 30 per cent were not uncommon. Savings schemes and personal equity plans have led to higher and more consistent demand from private investors, which has helped to bring discounts down and should continue to do so.

Gearing

The 'magnifying' effect of the discount is itself a form of gearing. But investment trusts can go one better than that: unlike unit trusts, they can borrow money to invest, alongside the share-holders' funds. If, for example, you can borrow money at 10 per cent, and invest it in something that goes up 50 per cent in a year, then you have magnified the profits. (Needless to say, if the stock you are investing in goes *down*, you will have magnified your losses.) An example of how gearing can work in your favour is shown in Table 8.1. In this case, the borrowing is in the form of a debenture stock.

Charges
Unlike unit trusts, investment trusts do not have an initial charge as such, though there are dealing costs when you buy shares just as there are with the shares of other companies. There is also an annual management charge, which tends to vary across the different categories: general trusts carry a charge of around 0.3 per cent of the asset value, while on specialist trusts it can be as much as 1 per cent. Newer launches have also tended to have higher charges than the older established trusts, but even so, they compare well with unit trusts.

Investment characteristics

The closed-ended structure of an investment trust, mentioned above, influences the management style as well as the share price.

Table 8.1 *Gearing on an investment trust*

Capital structure of trust:

4,000,000 5% debenture stock	£4,000,000
6,000,000 £1 ordinary shares	£6,000,000
	£10,000,000

Assume the portfolio doubles in value over five years and that the debenture stock is repaid at the end of that time. The effect is as follows:

	Year 1	Year 5
Value of portfolio	£10,000,000	£20,000,000
Less debenture stock	£4,000,000	£4,000,000
Assets attributable to 6,000,000 ordinary shares	£6,000,000	£16,000,000
Net asset value per ordinary share	£1	£2.67

Thus, while the portfolio has increased by 100 per cent, the assets attributable to each ordinary share have increased by 167 per cent (from £1 to £2.67).

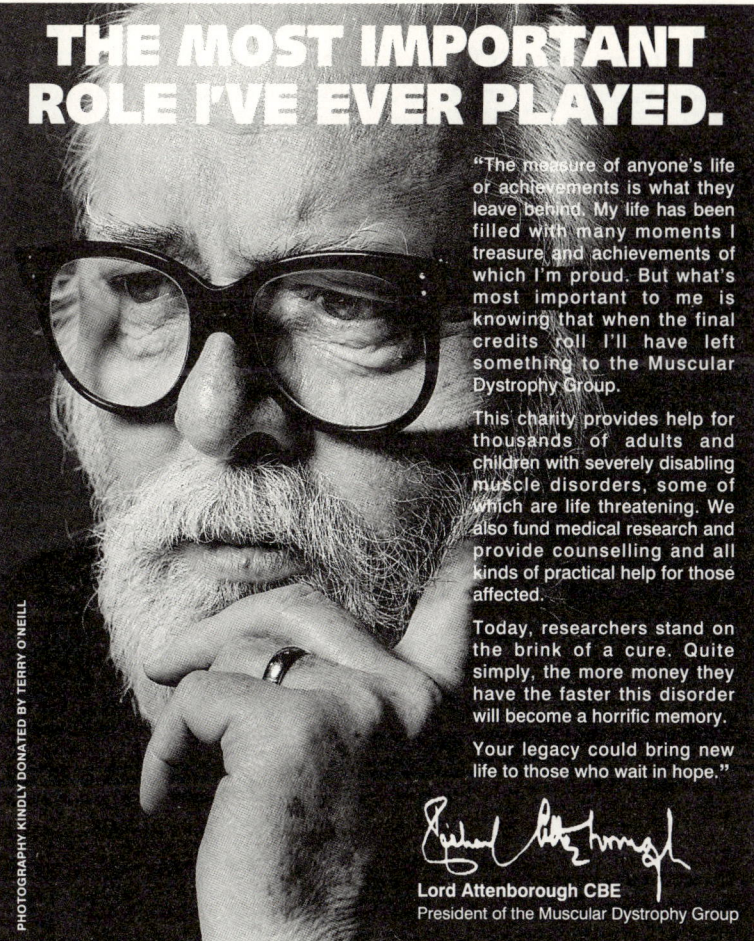

While the unit trust manager must accommodate new money coming in or demands for units to be redeemed, the investment trust manager is working with a fixed pool of assets, regardless of how shares are being bought or sold.

As with the discount, the closed fund has its supporters and its critics. In a rising market, new money attracted into a unit trust can be used to snap up good opportunities, while the investment trust manager may not be able to move so fast. But in a falling market, a unit trust may have to sell its better holdings to meet redemptions, while the investment trust is insulated.

This insulation allows the investment trust manager to make more speculative decisions. Indeed, investment trusts do not have the same restrictions on their holdings as unit trusts – they can invest in unquoted shares and the smaller stock markets around the world that are not yet approved for unit trusts. Obviously these can be more risky, but, with no redemptions to worry about, the manager can afford to take a long-term view.

Investment range

From the start, investment trusts had an international outlook. Many were set up in Scotland, which had a long history of looking abroad for opportunities. This is still reflected in today's trusts, which currently number around 300.

One of the problems in classifying investment trusts is that their investment scope is generally much more loosely defined than is the case with unit trusts. Another difficulty for investors is that the older trusts, in particular, often have names that have little to do with their aims: Scottish Mortgage, for instance, is an international general trust with no particular focus on either Scotland or mortgages.

Some guidance is given by the categorisation used by the Association of Investment Trust Companies (AITC). This divides trusts into 19 different sectors, as shown in Table 8.2. In most cases, the definition is that a trust has at least 80 per cent of its assets in the particular sector, but in the case of Smaller Companies the minimum is 50 per cent and for Venture and Development Capital, it is simply 'a significant proportion' in unquoted companies. International trusts have the broadest

Table 8.2 *Investment trust categories and average performance*

Comparative return to investor of £100 invested over various periods, adjusted to include income reinvested and exchange rate movements on overseas trusts

Sector	1 yr	3 yrs	5 yrs	10 yrs
International: General	129.5	179.4	223.8	525.6
International: Capital Growth	139.7	189.5	217.4	468.8
International: Income Growth	121.6	173.1	203.1	560.0
UK: General	134.1	183.3	171.8	396.2
UK: Capital Growth	156.3	185.7	209.8	659.7
UK: Income Growth	123.5	167.2	206.7	610.3
High Income	127.7	160.9	192.1	381.1
North America	120.7	215.1	251.8	402.6
Far East: Including Japan	158.4	209.8	196.5	543.1
Far East: Excluding Japan	149.7	260.3	336.0	—
Japan	169.7	166.6	167.9	426.1
Europe	140.5	160.7	226.3	433.6
Emerging Markets	163.8	334.6	209.4	—
Property	203.4	136.9	88.0	273.2
Closed-end funds	148.6	151.5	112.2	1248.9
Commodity & Energy	123.0	136.1	—	—
Smaller Companies	138.5	184.0	166.1	445.5
Venture & Development Capital	132.0	153.4	182.1	221.8
Split Capital*	—	—	—	—
FT-SE-A All Share Index	123.6	161.2	190.9	468.9
MSCI World Index (£)	119.3	163.3	159.0	421.9
Standard & Poors Composite (£)	103.1	175.1	214.2	387.3
Retail Price Index	102.5	108.5	127.3	162.7

Notes: Investment trust figures based on size-weighted average
* Performance figures not applicable.

Source: AITC, 28 February 1994

definition, of having less than 80 per cent of assets in any one geographical area, and split capital trusts are the most complicated type, with various different share classes.

The variation in scope between trusts within the same category means that performance comparisons are not necessarily on a like with like basis, but to give a general guide to investment returns,

Table 8.2 shows the average for each sector, plus a few key indices, over periods to the end of February 1994.

How to invest

Investment trust shares can be bought through a stockbroker, bank or other authorised dealer. When a new trust is launched, the company must publish a prospectus in at least one newspaper. In some cases, a full prospectus is published, including a coupon to apply for shares; otherwise there will be a contact address given from which you can obtain the full prospectus and an application form.

If you have only a small amount to invest, the minimum commission charged by stockbrokers would be disproportion-ately high and a much cheaper route is through a savings scheme, of which there are currently 41 available. The first scheme was launched in 1984 and the concept has proved highly successful at attracting private investors into investment trusts.

Despite the name, savings schemes can be used for lump sums as well as regular investments. The minimum can be as little as £20 a month or £250 for a lump sum. Dealing costs are very small – usually 1 per cent or less – because investors' money is pooled within the scheme to buy shares in bulk. In some cases this means that dealing takes place only once a month, so it is a good idea to find out when the deadline is. This and other information on savings schemes can be obtained from the AITC.

Share exchange schemes
As with unit trusts, several companies offer share exchange schemes through which you can swap holdings of equities for investment trust shares. The company will sell the shares on your behalf and may either bear the selling costs itself or offer a special discounted charge. The charge for buying into the investment trust will normally be at the low savings scheme rate, but may be waived altogether.

Keeping track of prices

Investment trust prices are published daily in newspapers such as *The Daily Telegraph* and *The Financial Times*. The Association of

Investment Trust Companies publishes a monthly information service, usually around the third week of the month. This gives two sets of performance figures: the total return on £100 invested as measured by the trust's net asset value – which gives an idea of what the manager has achieved in isolation from share price movements; and the share price total return on £100. In each case figures are over one, three, five and ten years. It also gives a host of statistical data, including the geographical spread of trusts, the total value of assets, the share price, the net asset value, the discount, the gearing potential, the gross yield and the annual growth in dividends as measured over five years. In addition there is information on savings schemes and personal equity plans and a contact list of names and addresses for the management groups.

Variations on a theme

Limited life trusts
Whatever the so-called 'advantages' of the discount, some companies have seen it as a drawback, and they have decided to get round it by offering 'limited life' trusts. These either have a fixed redemption date, at which point the company will be wound up and its assets realised at full market value, or a series of dates – perhaps once a year – at which shareholders have the option to vote for the winding-up of the company.

Either strategy has the advantage that the discount is unlikely to stray up too far; there can be a drawback, however, in that it means fund managers cannot be as far-sighted in their investment policy as they would with an ordinary investment trust.

Split capital trusts
Split capital trusts started out in the 1960s with the aim of accommodating two types of investor within the one trust: those who were seeking high and growing income, but had little or no interest in capital growth; and those seeking capital growth, with no desire for income. This was achieved by having two classes of share: income and capital. More recently the concept has been expanded and split capital trusts may now also include zero dividend preference shares, stepped preference shares and highly

geared ordinary shares. All split capital trusts have a fixed lifespan, although shares can be bought and sold at any time.

The original type of income shares offer high income during the life of the trust and a fixed redemption price when it is wound up. The nearer the trust is to its winding-up date, the nearer the share price is likely to get to its redemption value, but meanwhile it may stand above that, reflecting expectations of future income. So if you hold the shares to redemption there may be a capital loss.

A newer type of income share may get a proportion of the assets at winding-up, on top of the fixed redemption price, but only after other classes of share have taken their entitlements. In contrast, 'annuity income' shares have only a nominal redemption value, perhaps as little as 1p, so there is a built-in capital loss, but meanwhile they receive all the income generated from the trust's portfolio. Finally, highly geared ordinary shares, which are found in 'hybrid' trusts paired with zero preference shares, have no fixed redemption price but receive the surplus assets after the zeros have been paid off, and meanwhile receive all the trust's income.

Income shares are suitable for investors seeking high and rising income, particularly if they are non-taxpayers or can hold the shares tax-free within a personal equity plan. The highly geared ordinary shares are better suited to experienced investors who are prepared to accept a capital risk in return for potentially high rewards.

Capital shares normally receive no dividends during the life of the trust, but at winding-up they get all the remaining assets after the prior claims of preference and income shares have been met. There is thus a risk involved, but the chance of very good returns. Zero dividend preference shares, on the other hand, have a fixed redemption value and take top priority at winding-up. The return is not guaranteed, as the trust will have to generate sufficient assets to meet the liability, but the risk is very low.

Stepped preference shares offer a combination of income and capital returns, with a fixed redemption value and a fixed rate of annual dividend growth. As with zeros, the returns are not guaranteed, but the risk is small.

Split capital trusts offer a lot of potential for investors who have specific capital or income needs, or are prepared to take on

higher risk for potentially high returns. However, because of their complex structure it is important to be sure exactly what each type of share's entitlement is, and what the likelihood is of its being met – for example, what growth rate the trust will have to achieve between now and the winding-up date to repay the various classes of share.

Warrants
Around 110 trusts now have warrants available and new launches sometimes offer a free warrant for every so many shares you buy. A warrant is not itself a share, but gives you the right to buy a share at a fixed price at some point in the future.

The terms, which are set when the warrant is issued, specify the 'exercise price', at which the future share can be bought, and the 'exercise date', on which the option can be taken up. This may be a particular day, or a period between two dates, each year up to the final exercise date. There is no obligation to buy at any point and obviously it will only be worth while if the exercise price, plus the original price of the warrant, compares favourably with the current price of the share.

Of course, once the final expiry date has passed, the warrant becomes worthless. But during their life warrants can be bought and sold just like the shares themselves, so warrants can be bought as investments in their own right, with the intention of selling at a profit, rather than exercising the right to buy shares.

The warrant price is generally much lower than the share price, but its movements are proportionately greater. This is known as the gearing, the level of which is measured as the share price divided by the warrant price. The higher the gearing, the greater are the potential risks and rewards of the warrant. Two other features to look for in choosing a warrant are the premium – the amount by which the warrant price plus its exercise price exceeds the current price of the underlying share – and its remaining lifespan, up to the final exercise date. The longer the lifespan, the higher the acceptable premium: there will be more time for the share price to increase and represent a profit over the exercise price.

One other point to bear in mind is that warrants do not entitle the holder to any dividends. This means there will be no income tax liability, while capital gains will come within the annual £5800 capital gains tax allowance. The exceptions are subscription shares, which do pay an annual dividend, but currently there are only a couple of trusts which issue these.

Where to find out more

The primary source of information is the Association of Investment Trust Companies, Park House, 6th Floor, 16 Finsbury Circus, London EC2M 7JJ. The Association produces a free information pack which provides two general fact-sheets on investment trusts and the latest monthly information service, which includes statistical data on the trusts, performance figures and a list of contacts. In addition, it publishes free fact-sheets on choosing a trust, savings schemes, split capital trusts, warrants, investing for income, planning for school fees, investing for children and personal equity plans.

For more comprehensive information, the AITC publishes the *Investment Trust Directory*. The current (Spring 1994) edition costs £12.50 and is available from the above address. You can also subscribe to the monthly information service, either on a full monthly basis, at a cost of £28 a year, or quarterly, for £15 a year.

9

Personal Equity Plans

Personal equity plans (PEPs) were first announced in the 1986 Budget and came into being at the beginning of 1987. The aim was to encourage wider share ownership through tax advantages: all profits within a PEP were free of capital gains tax and all dividends, so long as they were reinvested in the plan, were free of income tax.

However, in the early days PEPs had little appeal to ordinary investors. A plan had to be held for a full calendar year to qualify for the tax benefits, but a more significant drawback was that the annual investment limit was only £2400. This meant that in practice the tax advantages were worth very little, particularly as few people pay capital gains tax anyway.

Another problem was that, for people who had no other equity investments, £2400 was too small an amount to get a proper spread of individual holdings and even packaged schemes had to be fairly basic to keep the administration charges at a reasonable level. Unit trusts and investment trusts, which can provide a wide spread for a small sum of money, could be included in plans, but only up to a limit of £420 or 25 per cent of the total investment.

So PEPs initially had little interest except for larger investors as a tax shelter for a small portion of their portfolios. But there was a surge in popularity in 1989, when the investment limit was increased to £4800 and in 1990, when it was raised again to £6000. By this time, the rule on holding a plan for a calendar year had been removed, and half the total limit could be put into qualifying unit and investment trusts. Further improvements followed: in 1991, single company PEPs were introduced, with a

SELF-SELECT PEPS–

THE FLEXIBLE, ECONOMIC ROUTE TO BETTER INVESTMENT PERFORMANCE

In a marketplace crowded with high profile, traditionally managed personal equity plans, a quiet revolution has been underway in the last few years as more and more investors discover the benefits and advantages offered by low-cost, self-select PEPS.

While there is little dispute that PEPs can form a useful part of a medium to long term personal investment strategy, much publicity has been given to the way high management charges can eat away at the tax benefits PEPs offer.

What's worse, high charges provide no guarantee of good investment performance. It is a sad fact that most managed funds fail to match overall stock market growth, and some fall disastrously short. According to figures from Micropal, over the 5 years from 1988 to 1992, only 6 out of 344 UK equity unit trusts actually beat the market, measured by the FTA-All Share Index. With income reinvested, £1,000 would have more than doubled if invested in the shares making up the FT Index. However, if you had been unfortunate enough to invest in the worst performing fund, your money would have shrunk by more than 50%!

So what's the solution? Self-select PEPs can help in a number of ways. Firstly they can offer the cheapest way to hold investment and get the full benefits of PEP.

Secondly, they provide the widest investment choice. With the ShareLink Premier PEP for example, you can invest in the shares of any UK quoted company, any investment trust or unit trust permitted by the government's PEP rules. So if you are happy selecting which shares or funds to by and sell, you can benefit from your own expertise.

Increasing numbers of investors are also taking advantage of the special concession allowing the transfer of shares directly into a PEP, whether from a company share save scheme or a new issue.

Once you have made an investment decision, a self-select PEP allows you to change whenever you consider it advantageous to do so. You can even hold cash within the PEP and earn gross interest. With other types of PEP you normally have to transfer to another PEP manager and possibly incur punitive "exit" charges if you want to change, or close the PEP and lose your tax free allowances.

If you're looking for somebody to manage your investments, there are funds which aim to track stock market performance, as measured by a specific indicator such as FTA-All Share Index of FTSE 100. One of the benefits of such index funds is that you can get consistently good performance, year after year.

Index Funds can be purchased within a self-select PEP. In the case of the ShareLink PEP, you have UK and European Index Funds and it's simple and economical to mix and match these and any other investments, as and when you want.

You Will Be Grinning From Ear To Ear

Once You Discover The Benefits Of The ShareLink Premier PEP

Whether you're already a regular stockmarket investor or a beginner; looking for tax free income or tax free capital growth; have as little as £30 a month, or as much as £9,000 to invest - the Premier PEP has it all.

For further information or a brochure either call:

021 200 4545

Or complete and return the coupon below to:

ShareLink PEP Unit , FREEPOST BM 4549, Birmingham B3 2BR.

Name _____

Address_____

Post Code _____ Tel. No. _____

ShareLink Limited is a member of the Securities and Futures Authority, the London Stock Exchange and an Inland Revenue Approved PEP Plan Manager.

MK133

separate investment limit of £3000, and the scope of plans was widened from UK shares to those quoted in EU countries; and in 1992, the £3000 ceiling was removed from qualifying unit and investment trusts, allowing the full £6000 to be invested in these vehicles.

PEP rules

The investment limits apply to a tax year, rather than a calendar year, and for 1994/5 they remain at £6000 for a general PEP plus a further £3000 in a single company PEP. Plans can be taken out by anyone over 18, and husbands and wives each have their own investment allowance. All profits made within a plan are free of capital gains tax and dividends can now be paid out to the investor free of income tax as well as accumulated tax-free within the plan.

Following the 1993 Budget, the income tax 'rebate' on dividends earned within a PEP dropped from 25 per cent to 20 per cent. This was because the income tax rate charged on dividends was reduced to 20 per cent, so the amount that could be reclaimed fell accordingly.

For basic rate taxpayers, this has had the effect of making PEPs a little less worth while than before. If you hold shares or trusts within a PEP, you are saving only 20 per cent in tax on the dividends, compared with holding the same investments directly. So where the PEP involves extra charges, the benefits may be marginal or even completely outweighed.

Conversely, for higher rate taxpayers, the PEP advantage is slightly greater than before. If you hold shares directly, you receive dividends together with a tax credit that can be set against your income tax liability. For basic rate taxpayers, this tax credit exactly matches the liability, but higher rate taxpayers have to pay the difference between the value of the tax credit and their tax rate of 40 per cent. As the tax credit is now worth only 20 per cent instead of 25 per cent, the extra tax due has gone up from 15 per cent to 20 per cent. So there is a greater benefit to be had from holding investments free of tax within a PEP.

PEPs may invest in authorised shares, unit trusts, investment trusts or any combination of these. Shares must be quoted in an

EU country, while to be fully qualifying, unit trusts and investment trusts must be at least 50 per cent invested in EU shares. Trusts which do not qualify under this rule can still be included in PEPs, but only up to a limit of £1500.

PEPs must be run by a registered scheme manager and you are restricted to one scheme manager a year for a general PEP, although if you have a single company PEP as well, that can be with a different manager. There is also nothing to stop you choosing another manager in subsequent years. Plan managers include banks, building societies, unit trust groups, investment trust companies, stockbrokers and independent financial advisers.

There are now nearly 900 different PEPs generally available, as well as plans run by some institutions specifically for their own clients. These can be divided into five different categories.

Types of plan

Managed PEPs

Managed PEPs are the largest category and the easiest option, particularly if you are making your first foray into the stock market. Essentially, all you need do is hand over your money and the plan manager will make all the investment decisions on your behalf. Some plans invest only in shares, others only in unit or investment trusts and others again in a combination of these.

The minimum for a lump-sum investment can be as little as £500, though some managers will only accept the full £6000. On the whole, plans that include shares are likely to require a larger investment than those based only on unit or investment trusts.

They may also involve higher charges. Some plans carry an initial charge as well as an annual management fee, and on top of these there are dealing charges for buying and selling shares and investment trusts, plus the standard initial and annual charges on any unit trusts included – though a few managers will rebate part of the initial charge or pass on any discounts they negotiate.

PEPs offered by unit trust groups generally have no plan charges other than those on the trusts themselves. Both these and plans run by investment trust companies normally allow the investor to choose which trusts are included, but, of course, the choice is restricted to their own range. Also, now that the investment allowance for trusts is the full £6000, few of these managers offer a facility to include shares, so if you want a plan with a mix of holdings you may find more choice with a stockbroker or independent adviser.

Advisory PEPs

Advisory PEPs are available from stockbrokers, investment managers and independent advisers. They generally offer a completely free choice of investments and the final decision is up to the plan holder, but the manager will offer advice on what to buy and sell and when. This type of plan is best suited to investors who already have a fair knowledge of the market but still prefer to have some guidance.

As with the managed share PEPs, there are likely to be initial and annual plan fees, as well as the charges arising on the investments themselves. If you plan to buy and sell actively, the dealing charge is the most important; this can vary from as little as 0.5 per cent to as much as 1.9 per cent. Several managers also have a minimum charge, which makes it expensive to deal in small amounts.

Obviously, the quality of advice is important, but so is the quantity. If you intend to invest actively, you need to be sure you can get advice when you need it, otherwise good opportunities could slip by. You also need to check who takes the initiative – whether it is up to you to request advice or whether the manager will contact you if he thinks the time is right to buy or sell.

Self-select PEPs

As mentioned, PEPs must always be operated by an authorised plan manager. The nearest you can get to a do-it-yourself PEP, under which the investor takes all the decisions, is a self-select plan. These plans are run mainly by stockbrokers and, while in principle any qualifying investment can be selected, the main emphasis tends to be on shares.

The minimum investment can be as little as £250. But because you are buying your own individual holdings, rather than a stake in a managed pool of money, these plans are better suited to larger investments, which will enable a reasonable spread of shares to be bought.

The prime advantage of self-select PEPs is, of course, that you are not restricted to any one range of unit or investment trusts, or a manager's selection of shares. However, not all self-select plans offer a completely free choice. A few have restrictions on the shares that may be bought, although the limits are generally quite broad – for instance, shares included in the FT-SE 100 Index or the FT-SE-A All Share Index. More importantly, some exclude unit trusts or investment trusts or both, so you should check before you buy that the plan will meet your particular requirements.

Perhaps surprisingly, self-select PEPs can be more expensive than managed plans. Although you are not paying for any management expertise, there are still set-up and continuing administrative costs which will be met through initial and annual charges. More significantly, there will be dealing charges each time you buy and sell. In a managed plan these are kept to a minimum because the manager is dealing in very large sums on behalf of all the plan holders pooled together; with a self-select plan you have to meet all the costs yourself.

This is another reason why these plans are not suitable for small investments. A number of managers have a minimum dealing charge which can be as much as £30 or £40, so it is uneconomic for small sums. Aside from that, dealing charges can vary enormously, from as low as 0.5 per cent up to 2 per cent of the transaction value. The more actively you intend to run your plan, the more these dealing charges will mount up and eat into any profits you are making.

Since the investment performance is entirely down to your own efforts, charges are the major factor in choosing a plan, but you should also check the services offered and the quality of administration, in particular the speed of response when you give the manager instructions to buy or sell your holdings. If you spot a good investment opportunity that needs immediate action, it will be no good if the manager takes a week to respond, so you need to be sure you can get ready access to give instructions and that they will be carried out without delay.

Because the onus is entirely on the investor, these plans are

suitable only for the more experienced, with a fair slice of capital to invest and the time to keep track of market movements. If you are already investing in equities on your own account, then the charges become less important – you would face them anyway – and the plan can be used as a convenient trading service, with the manager taking care of all the paperwork.

Corporate PEPs

Corporate PEPs are set up by companies, through an authorised plan manager such as a bank, building society or stockbroker, to allow their shares to be held in the tax-free environment of a PEP. They are usually aimed chiefly at the company's own employees and existing shareholders but are available to anyone. A wide range of corporate PEPs is now available, generally based on large companies such as British Gas, BAA and ICI.

A few plans offer the investor a choice of company or specify a minimum holding in one company, after which the investor can choose any quoted shares for the rest of the portfolio. For the most part, though, shareholdings are confined to the one company, so these plans are pretty inflexible. Under PEP rules, corporate PEPs come under the 'general' category, which means you can invest up to £6000, but you cannot take out another general PEP in the same year, so it is very much a case of having all your eggs in one basket.

Of course, you are not committed for all time, only for the current tax year; thereafter you can take out a more balanced plan, or you may already have one from previous years. So if you hold a large chunk of shares in one company, and you have no other current PEPs, it may be worth putting your holdings into a corporate PEP for the tax advantages.

Shares that you already hold cannot be transferred directly into a PEP except within six weeks of buying a new issue. What you can do, however, is a 'bed and breakfast' operation, which means selling your shares and then buying them back again within the PEP. All PEP investments must be made in cash, so you have to wait a while for settlement from the sale before you can reinvest; this does not affect the operation, but the longer the delay, the more chance there is that the share price could move against you.

Once the shares are inside the PEP the investment will be free

of any income and capital gains tax, but beware that the tax gains are not eaten up in plan charges. Many plans have no, or only a small, initial charge, while the annual charge is usually 0.5 per cent, but can be up to twice that. For a basic rate taxpayer this could outweigh the savings.

Single company PEPs
Single company PEPs are similar to corporate PEPs in that they are based on the shares of a single company. This means that they are usually inflexible, but they have the advantage that they carry their own separate investment allowance, of £3000 a year, and can be held in addition to a general PEP.

There are three types of single company PEP: those that are based on one particular company, those where the choice of share is at the manager's discretion and those offering the investor a choice of share. The first type operate very much like corporate PEPs and are likely to have particular appeal to employees of the company who are participating in a share scheme.

Holding the shares within a PEP will bring the usual income and capital gains tax exemptions. But unlike general and corporate PEPs, shares that are already held can be transferred directly into a PEP providing that they have been acquired through an employee share scheme and that the transfer takes place within 90 days.

Non-employees can also invest in this type of PEP, either directly or, if they already hold shares in the company, by using a bed and breakfast transaction. One advantage is that the charges are generally low, with only a nominal or possibly no initial charge and annual fees of around 0.5 per cent.

'Managed' single company PEPs are almost a contradiction in terms, since there is little management involved in a portfolio that consists of a single company's shares. Of course, the manager may decide to switch from one company to another if it appears to give better prospects; there is also the argument that to pick a single share that will perform well can be a harder task than managing a portfolio where a few wrong choices will be compensated by a few right ones. Even so, the charges on these plans can be quite high – as much as 5 per cent at the outset and up to 1.5 per cent as an annual management fee. In some cases, a discount is offered on the initial charge if you also take out a general PEP with the same manager. Otherwise, there may be better value in the corporate style plan, if there is one available for the share that interests you, or a self-select plan.

Some self-select plans offer a completely free choice of share, while others provide a list for investors to pick from. Again, it is important to check the charges. These tend to be fairly low – one or two plans have no charges other than the dealing costs on the share – but the initial charge can be as high as 4 per cent, which is a hefty sum when you are making your own share selection. Similarly, annual charges vary from none to as much as 1.5 per cent.

Corporate-style single company PEPs generally offer a monthly savings facility and the minimum for lump sums can be as low as £300. Managed and self-select plans are mainly geared to lump-sum investments, from £500 to the full £3000.

Single company PEPs have most appeal for those who have a large amount of money to invest and want to maximise their tax allowances, or for employees acquiring shares in their own company. For the average investor, putting £3000 into the shares of just one company carries a high level of risk, even with the tax advantages, and a general PEP should certainly be considered first.

Choosing a PEP

The first step in choosing a PEP is to decide on the type of plan that you want. Broadly speaking, advisory and self-select PEPs are for the more experienced investor, corporate and single company PEPs are for the specialist, while managed PEPs suit a range of types, from the more cautious seeking the safer spread offered by unit and investment trusts to the more adventurous seeking to invest in equities but preferring to leave the decisions to a professional. Once you have decided on the type that suits you best, there are various other considerations which may help to narrow the field.

Growth versus income
This distinction applies chiefly to managed PEPs. With advisory and self-select plans, you can simply pick the investments that match your requirements, and corporate and single company plans can also encompass either strategy, depending on the particular share chosen. However, it is worth checking on the plan's procedure for dealing with dividends. If you are looking for a regular income, you may want to receive the dividends as they are paid, so check that this is possible, without an exorbitant charge being levied. Conversely, if you are looking primarily for growth, you are better off with a plan that will reinvest the dividends automatically without a new set of initial or dealing charges.

Managed PEPs may also offer a choice between income and growth objectives, but some are specifically set up for one or the other. It is sometimes said that smaller investors will get more benefit from an income PEP, primarily for tax reasons: few people pay capital gains tax anyway, and over the shorter term, the income tax benefits will be more visible and immediate.

However, the choice depends very much on your investment aims and any other holdings you have in addition to the PEP. For instance, if you require a measure of income, then it will usually make sense to hold income-producing investments within a PEP, to benefit from the tax shelter, particularly if your other investments are not large enough to make capital gains tax a concern. Beware, however, of simply choosing the PEP showing the highest current yield. Often this will be achieved only at the expense of opportunities for capital growth and increasing income in the future, which can prove much more valuable.

If you are not looking for income, but simply want to accumulate capital for future use, then a growth PEP may be more suitable. Even if capital gains tax is not a problem today, the regime could change in the future, and over the medium to long term you can build up a sizeable sum in a PEP which would then be protected against any such changes. Growth PEPs can also be useful to meet specific financial needs in the future, such as paying for school or higher education fees, or boosting retirement income.

Charges and services

Charges on the plan are obviously an important factor as they will eat up a portion of the profits made. As mentioned, unit trust PEPs generally add nothing to the underlying charges on the trusts held, but with share PEPs in particular, there is a danger that the additional running costs of the plan could outweigh the tax gains.

In the past couple of years, a number of unit trust and investment trust plan managers have reduced or abolished the initial charge on their plans. In most cases, this has been combined with the introduction of an 'exit' fee if you take your money out, which applies on a reducing scale for the first three to five years.

If you keep up the plan beyond the exit fee period it can be very attractive, as the initial charge may be only 2 per cent or less, instead of the usual 5-6 per cent. But if you need to take your money out suddenly, you can face a penalty of up to 4.5 per cent. In almost all cases this is based on the current value of the plan, so if it has grown since the outset the total charge will be more

"The people involved with IT give incredible value for money..."
Baroness Chalker, Minister for Overseas Development, on visiting
Intermediate Technology, August 1993

Intermediate Technology (IT) is a charity, founded in 1965 by Dr Fritz Schumacher, author of the best-seller *Small is Beautiful*. IT works with communities in the Third World, concentrating on long term development rather than short term emergency relief.

By sharing skills and training, IT gives people access to a choice of technologies which are appropriate to local needs, which make the best use of local skills and resources, which create jobs and incomes, and are sustainable and environmentally responsible. Communities are then less dependent on expensive imports.

IT works in partnership with local organisations in nine countries overseas. From hundreds of different projects the following are just two examples:
– In Sri Lanka and Kenya, improved stoves, which save fuel, provide local potters with employment and reduce the risk of chest and eye diseases caused by excessive smoke.
– In South India, work with fishermen on the development of new boat designs, where traditional materials like mango trees have become scarce and expensive, so helping to preserve their livelihoods and independence.

A donation or legacy to Intermediate Technology is a sound investment in the future of the global family.

than if you had paid a normal up-front fee.

The plan managers argue that PEPs should be viewed as a medium- to long-term investment. With a lower initial fee, more money is invested at the outset, which should lead to higher returns. But over longer periods, the recurring annual management fee can have a greater impact on returns, so you should check that this has not been bumped up to compensate for a lower initial charge.

On top of initial, annual and dealing fees, there are a number of others that can crop up. A few plans make a charge for collecting or paying out dividends. A more common extra is a charge for investors to attend shareholders' meetings, where they are entitled to do so. This can be as much as £100 a time, which is a substantial sum if you hold five or six shares and want to go to all the meetings.

Charges may also reflect the services provided. Commonly, statements and valuations of the plan holdings will be sent out half-yearly, but it may be more frequent and there may also be newsletters and reports. Most important is the quality of administration and this can only be tested by experience. It is now possible to transfer from one PEP manager to another, so you should not be afraid to vote with your feet if you are not satisfied with the service you are getting, but again there may be a charge made to transfer out, in or both.

Past performance

Corporate PEPs, and single company plans where the same holding is maintained, can be judged by the track record of the company concerned but managed PEPs, and particularly those investing in shares, are so diverse that comparisons would not be on a like-with-like basis.

With unit trusts and investment trusts, you can check the track records of individual trusts and of the management group generally. As the saying goes, past performance is not necessarily a guide to the future, and today's league leaders are not always the heroes of tomorrow, but a consistent past record is a reasonable indication of potential. Other points to consider are the overall investment philosophy of the plan manager; whether the attitude to risk broadly accords with your own; how actively the plan will

be managed; and the degree of commitment to PEPs – whether they are viewed as an important part of a company's business or just a sideline.

PEP facilities

Share exchange

A number of PEP managers offer share exchange schemes through which you can convert existing holdings of shares into a PEP investment in different shares, unit trusts or investment trusts. This is particularly useful if you have small holdings, such as privatisation issues, that would be expensive to sell through normal channels, as the charges are usually low and in some cases the scheme is free.

Apart from newly issued shares or those recently acquired through an employee share scheme, which can be directly transferred into a PEP, all investments must be made in cash, so there may be a short delay before the sale is settled and the proceeds can be reinvested.

PEP mortgages

A number of lenders will now accept a PEP as a repayment vehicle for a mortgage in place of the more standard endowment and pension contracts. They can offer greater flexibility, but, of course, there is no guarantee of the eventual proceeds, so lenders may be quite fussy over the plans they will approve. As a rule they will expect you to make regular savings into the PEP, rather than occasional lump sums.

Keeping track of your investment

Prices of unit trusts, investment trusts and shares are quoted in newspapers such as *The Daily Telegraph* and *The Financial Times*. This can give you a general idea of how your investments are performing, although the actual value of the PEP may be affected by additional charges. More accurate information will be given in the statements and valuations sent out by the plan manager, usually at half-yearly intervals, and they may also provide reports on the companies or trusts included in the plan, plus newsletters or commentaries on the investment strategy.

Where to find out more

Chase de Vere publishes the *PEP Guide*, which currently lists around 870 plans from some 200 managers. Listings include the investment aim of the plan, the minimum investments accepted, the various charges and facilities such as share exchange. There is also a quarterly supplement which gives performance figures and annualised growth rates for qualifying and non-qualifying unit and investment trusts and companies that currently make up the FT-SE 100 Share Index. The *PEP Guide* costs £9.95 and can be obtained from Chase de Vere, 63 Lincoln's Inn Fields, London WC2A 3JX, telephone 071-404 5766.

On the second Saturday of every month, *The Daily Telegraph* publishes a performance table covering all the major unit trust and investment trust PEPs, showing performance over one, three and five years. There are also regular articles on PEPs in the personal finance pages.

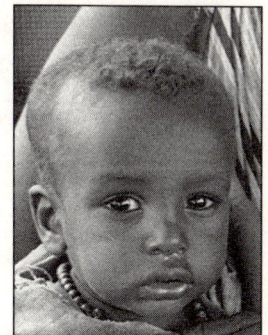

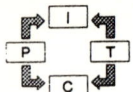

THE BENEFITS OF USING BROKERS IN THE SECOND HAND ENDOWMENT POLICY MARKET

From an Investor's point of view, the second hand endowment policy market has two categories of participant, the so called Market Makers trading as principal, and genuine Brokers trading as agents and serving the market, to the benefit of both buyers and sellers of policies.

A broker solicits his sellers and purchasers of policies directly from the public and the financial industry at large, and attends to the entire completion process involved with a transaction. Brokers are officially regulated by Fimbra.

A broker's *modus operandi* differs from that of a market maker because the latter trades for his own account, whilst the broker trades only as a negotiator, matching buyers and sellers. Market makers execute two segregated transactions when they move a policy from a seller through to a buyer. Initially, they would acquire a policy as cheaply as possible for their own account and then, completely separately, sell the policy at the highest achievable price.

A broker concludes only one transaction between a seller and a buyer, negotiating prices acceptable to both parties, and taking a "brokerage" or commission from the differential. In this respect a broker can offer both parties a deal better reflecting the prevailing conditions in the market. Unfortunately associations or groups of own account traders could benefit from, and run the risk of, cartel price rigging.

Brokers depend on the continued goodwill of all their clients and cannot afford to favour one above another. Some market makers service one or more key end users, like the endowment funds. This highlights a subtle twin risk with serious implications for the buyer or investor dealing with a market maker, and which cannot exist with brokered deals.

A market maker can withhold, in his portfolio and for his own benefit, policies which show above average potential, releasing them only when the holding profit potential has been realised. Similarly, and in particular, where the market maker has a major fund behind him, he might tend to offer the less attractive and more risky policies to the general public, channelling the best choices directly to his fund. The interests of the individual investor may be compromised by both these risks.

Because a broker does not trade for his own account, the investor purchasing policies avoids these risks by dealing through a broker in the same way as he would when purchasing stocks or shares on a recognised exchange.

10

Life Assurance and Friendly Society Investments

Within the last generation, life assurance companies have become sizeable players in the savings market. This is not to say that they have abandoned their traditional role of supplying straight-forward protection products such as term assurance, or the savings-plus-protection vehicles such as endowment plans. In fact, this range has been expanding, with the introduction of the likes of critical illness insurance and long-term care plans.

But the fact remains that insurance is generally sold rather than bought, so to maintain a healthy flow of new business, insurance companies have been broadening their horizons in the invest-ment field. Many have associated unit trust companies, but they are also competing for lump-sum investments with their own products.

This chapter looks at the main types on offer. Single premium bonds are a version of collective investments, like unit and investment trusts, that provide smaller investors with a stake in a large portfolio of assets, thereby spreading risk. Annuities are income-producing vehicles and are also put to use in 'hybrid' plans, which aim to produce a fixed level of income plus the prospect of capital growth. They therefore offer greater oppor-tunities than fixed capital investments such as building society accounts, but with a measure of capital risk.

Second-hand endowments are policies which have been sold by their original holders and provide a lump-sum route into what is traditionally a regular savings product. Finally, the chapter looks

Latin America: The next big investment opportunity

One of the recent trends in the investment industry has been the launch of a number of funds investing in Latin America. This trend may be surprising to those people who cling to memories of Latin America as a series of Banana Republics, with military dictatorships saddled with debt and inflation rates that make even West Indian cricket scores look small!

But the face of Latin America has changed dramatically from those dark days. The 80s are now known as the 'Lost Decade' and the world's investment community is now looking for Latin America to be the next big investment opportunity. Why?

As usual, in the end, it all boils down to the growth in the underlying economies: Latin America's are forecast to grow by 4.4% p.a. from 1995 to 1998 – compared with 2.7% in the UK and 2.4% in the US. Ultimately you are likely to receive superior rates of stock market growth where you have superior rates of economic growth.

The strength of Latin America's economies can be put down to the combination of a variety of factors. Many of these have resulted from the dramatic political change which has happened in most of the countries: Military juntas are now a thing of the past and have been replaced by elected governments which have introduced numerous economic and social reforms.

Most notably these reforms have led to many countries successfully bringing their crippling inflation rates under control. For example between 1989 and 1993 Argentina's inflation fell from around 5000% to just over 7%, Peru's from 2775% to 39% and Chile (which has been relatively more economically advanced) from 21% to 12%.

Brazil remains the principal exception – with 50% inflation each month. However, they are soon to introduce their 'Cardoso Plan' which is widely expected to succeed and in the process free up a large amount of the productive capacity currently engaged in overcoming that rampant inflation. To show you the benefit this process can have on the economy, I quote an example Save & Prosper's Investment Director recently came across during a visit to a super-efficient Brazilian retailer, which reported that 20 to 30% of their workforce is currently employed simply to stay ahead of inflation – marking up prices etc.

The economic and social reforms have also helped establish an educated and affluent middle class. This in turn creates political stability and also an atmosphere in which free enterprise and private investment can flourish.

The healthier business environment has hardly passed foreign investors by as they focus on a huge burgeoning potential market place. As a result foreign money has been flowing into the region. For instance, Mexico has attracted $35 bn of foreign investment in only 3 years and BMW has just announced its intention to open a plant there.

At the same time, the region's debt burden has been substantially reduced by the cuts in interest rates we have seen around the world in the 90s and also by banks writing off substantial amounts of their outstanding debts. Leading US broker, J P Morgan, now estimate that the average interest payments on foreign debt as a proportion of export earnings fell from 39% to 17% from 1982-1984 to 1991-93.

Inevitably there will be teething problems in the development of the region which means there is likely to be stock market volatility along the way. However, for those prepared to accept what could be a bumpy ride, I am sure the long-term rewards will be there. All people who are building a portfolio of investments aiming for capital growth should consider having a small exposure to this region – "the next big investment opportunity".

Mike Ryder Richardson
Director, Save & Prosper Securities Ltd

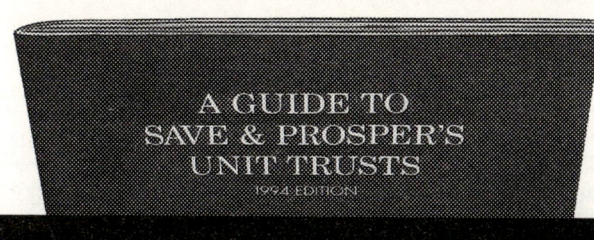

**THE ONE GUIDE
NO SERIOUS UNIT TRUST INVESTOR
CAN AFFORD TO BE WITHOUT.**

If you're considering investing in a unit trust, you'll certainly want to know about Save & Prosper's. After all, we're one of the UK's largest unit trust groups.

And where better to look than the new Guide to Save & Prosper's Unit Trusts? The 1994 edition is now out. In its 44 pages you'll find information on all the funds we currently offer.

For your free copy just ring our free Moneyline.

CALL FREE 0800 282 101
9.00 a.m. – 6.00 p.m. ● 7 DAYS A WEEK

To: **Save & Prosper Group Limited, FREEPOST, Romford RM1 1BR.**
Please send me my free copy of 'A Guide to Save & Prosper's Unit Trusts'.

Surname   Forenames

Name (Mr/Mrs/Miss) _____

Address _____

Postcode _____

Home Tel (STD)   No.   Work Tel (STD)   No.

So that we may call and offer further information.

**SAVE &
PROSPER**

422/16/DT

■ THE INVESTMENT HOUSE ■
A member of IMRO and Lautro.

at friendly societies, which have similarities with life assurance companies but certain tax advantages.

Single premium bonds

Single premium bonds – so-called because they are based on a one-off contribution – offer a broad investment choice and a spread of risk for sums starting at around £1000. Although technically they include an element of life assurance, it is relatively small – often it is simply the current bid value of the bond. This means that the investment potential is maximised rather than money being siphoned off to pay for life cover.

The bonds can be invested in a wide range of underlying funds operated by the company. These are similar to the various categories of unit trusts; for example, there are equity funds covering the UK, North America, Europe, Japan and the Far East, as well as broadly based international funds. There are also types that are not found among unit trusts, such as managed funds, with profits funds, currency funds and, to a large extent, property funds.

Managed funds invest in a mixture of equities, fixed interest securities and property, thus giving the widest possible spread of assets and risk. For this reason, they are the most popular, appealing both to very conservative investors and to those who prefer to leave all the investment decisions to a professional. There can, however, be considerable differences between one managed fund and the next, depending on the investment strategy adopted.

Essentially, there are two types: those which have a more or less set division between equities, fixed interest and property, which are sometimes called 'three-way' or balanced funds; and those where the manager takes a more active role in determining the proportions. A fairly recent trend is to offer more than one managed fund with differing degrees of risk; for example, Adventurous, Balanced and Cautious (or Conservative). The Adventurous fund will have a higher proportion in equities, which carry the highest risk/reward prospects, while the Cautious fund will lean more towards fixed interest securities.

In theory, a more actively managed fund should produce a

better return by responding to changes in market conditions, but equally there is more scope for wrong decisions. The three-way fund, on the other hand, is likely to produce steadier, if unexciting, returns. Some examples of the past performance of managed funds are shown in Table 10.1.

In the late 1980s and early 1990s, property funds were in the doldrums, thanks to the sliding fortunes of the property market, and many shrank considerably in size. But from mid-1993 performance started to improve, as demand increased with the upturn in the economy. At the time of writing, expectations are for steady, if not spectacular, growth in both the commercial and residential sectors.

The drawback of property funds is that they are unwieldy – property cannot always be sold readily, so the portfolio cannot easily be adjusted to changing market conditions. Managers also reserve the right to delay making repayments to investors for up to six months, to avoid having to sell at a loss to raise cash quickly. In practice, this has only ever been imposed on funds invested in residential property, while the bulk focus on commercial property. Smaller funds are often invested instead in the shares of property companies, which are more tradeable, although the returns are subject to different influences.

With profits funds, like managed funds, are invested in a mix of assets, but instead of the value of your holding depending on the value of investments in the underlying fund, with profits funds work by adding bonuses. The bonus rate is declared annually and depends on the investment profits made by the fund, but a part of these is usually held in reserve to boost rates in bad years. So there

Table 10.1   *Past performance of managed funds*

Percentage increase in fund value over different periods

	1 year	3 years	5 years
Best	47.38	122.20	148.02
Average	14.82	38.84	50.79
Worst	3.72	14.37	2.09

Note: Figures to 1 April 1994, on an offer-to-offer price basis.

Source: Micropal

Choose a Chartered Accountant for Independent Advice

An Independent Adviser

One of the main problems encountered when choosing an investment is where to go for advice. There are two types of adviser "tied" or "independent". A "tied" adviser acts on behalf of a particular company, and will only recommend a product picked from the range of those offered by that particular company.

Chartered accountants are independent advisers. They will act on your behalf in recommending a product picked from the ranges of all companies that make up the market place. They may receive commission from the company that issues the life policy or units to you. If so, they will notify you of the amount and terms of this commission and you will also be given details of the company paying it.

Chartered Accountants and the Investor

Some 6,000 firms of chartered accountants are authorised by The Institute of Chartered Accountants in England and Wales under the Financial Services Act to carry on investment business, and this is shown on their letterhead. Depending on their category of authorisation, they can advise on investments, arrange deals in investments and undertake the management of investments.

The institute monitors the firms' compliance with detailed regulations on the conduct of investment business, requiring the firm to:

★ Explain the main features of the product it is recommending to you.
★ Help you to understand the risks and costs there will be, as well as the future benefits you could gain from the product.
★ Tell you whether you have a right to change your mind before you commit yourself to buying the product and inform you of any costs you may incur by doing so.

Good advice is good value

★ The way money is invested can have a major impact on a person's tax liability and general financial position.
★ Life assurance and provision made for retirement should be seen as part of a total financial package.
★ Chartered accountants are required to advise their clients with independence and objectivity, and always to act in the client's best interest.
★ You may be surprised at how little such advice costs. Many chartered accountants will give you an initial consultation free of charge: all will discuss the charges with you beforehand.

For independent financial advice on personal and family finances, consult a firm of chartered accountants authorised by The Institute of Chartered Accountants in England and Wales to carry on investment business.
To find a firm in your area look in the Yellow Pages or the Thomson Local Directory.

MAKE THE MOST OF YOUR MONEY WITH A CHARTERED ACCOUNTANT

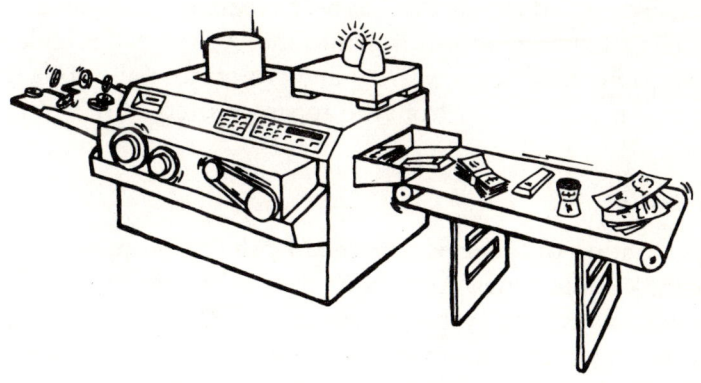

The fees charged will be based on the time spent and your chartered accountant will be happy to discuss the fees in advance. To find a chartered accountant look in the Yellow Pages, the Thomson Local Directory or contact your local District Society of Chartered Accountants, who are listed in the telephone directory.

The Institute of Chartered Accountants in England and Wales  PO Box 433, Moorgate Place, London EC2P 2BJ, Telephone 071 920 8100.

should be a 'smoothing' effect on market fluctuations, which reduces the risk. Some companies set a minimum guaranteed bonus rate and there may also be a terminal bonus, although this is not guaranteed.

Companies also reserve the right to make a 'market value adjustment' when money is paid out or switched to another fund. This would arise if the actual investment performance has not matched up to the value that has been credited, and is designed to protect continuing investors in the fund. Although this is likely to apply only in the early years – and is not normally applied on death – it does detract from the apparent safety of these funds.

Taxation

The taxation of bonds is governed by the rules applying to life assurance companies. As regards the underlying fund, this will pay tax on investment income and is also subject to capital gains tax on profits from the disposal of assets, hence the fund will set aside a reserve against future liabilities. The tax paid by the fund cannot be reclaimed, which is a major drawback for non-taxpayers.

Basic rate taxpayers have no tax worries on their own score – their liabilities are covered by what the fund has already paid. For higher rate taxpayers, however, it is a different – and rather complex – story. To start with the good news, up to 5 per cent of the original investment can be withdrawn from the bond, free of tax, each year for 20 years – this counts as being a return of capital. If the allowance is not used every year, it can be carried over, so if, for instance, you take nothing out in the first year, you have 10 per cent to play with in the second, and so on. The bad news comes at the end, when you cash in the investment. Tax is then assessed by a procedure known as 'top-slicing'. First, the total profit made from the bond is calculated, taking into account any withdrawals that have already been made, and the resulting amount is divided by the number of years for which the bond has been held. This figure is then added to your income for the year in which you cash in the bond to determine if you are liable to higher rate tax. If so, the higher rate will be applied to the whole of the profit made, and you will have to pay the difference between that and the basic rate tax which has already been paid.

There are two ways to mitigate the tax bill. If you can, you should put off cashing in the bond until a year when you are a basic rate taxpayer – after retirement, perhaps. Then you will have no further liability. You should also opt for the bond to be split into separate segments, each of which is effectively a policy in its own right; some companies do this automatically, others may do it on demand. The advantage is that, if you want to withdraw more than the 5 per cent allowance, you can cash in all of one segment, which gets more favourable tax treatment than making a partial withdrawal above the limit.

Bonds versus unit trusts

Bonds and unit trusts have certain similar characteristics – both offer low-cost access to pooled funds and charges are comparable. Hence there has long been debate about their respective merits for investors.

One drawback of bonds is that capital gains tax is paid by the life assurance company on profits within the bond. With unit trusts, the capital gains tax liability falls on the investor, which means it only arises when you cash in and then you can make use of the annual exempt allowance, currently £5800 for the 1994/5 tax year.

Against this, the returns from a bond are treated as having had basic rate tax already paid, whereas in practice the charge incurred by the insurance company may be well below 25 per cent. Hence the returns may be higher than could be achieved on unit trusts. There is also the annual 5 per cent tax-free withdrawal allowance, which is useful for higher rate taxpayers. If you can cash in at a time when you are subject only to basic rate, and if you are also already using your capital gains tax allowance on other investments, bonds can be tax-efficient.

However, unit trusts can be held within a personal equity plan, which offers complete exemption from both income and capital gains tax for investments of up to £6000 a year. If you have not already used this allowance, it should be a prime consideration.

The other main attraction of bonds is the facility to switch between different underlying funds at low cost and without any tax liability. If you move from one unit trust to another, there may be a capital gains tax liability and you will have to pay a new front-end charge; even with a discount offered for staying with the same management group, this is likely to be at least 2 per cent. Bonds generally offer one or more free switches per year, after which there is a small charge of perhaps 0.5 per cent. Of course, you are restricted by the range of funds offered by the company, and it is unlikely that any single company will top the investment tables across the board.

For different investors' needs and circumstances, one or other product is likely to have the edge, so it is a good idea to seek advice before you commit yourself.

Variations on the bond theme

Guaranteed equity bonds

Guaranteed equity investments are a fairly recent innovation, born out of the disillusion with the stock market of many smaller investors after the 1987 crash. At first sight, they seem to be the perfect investment: they guarantee to return a high percentage of any increase in a given stock market index over the investment period, or your original capital if the index should fall.

However, you need to check the small print to be quite sure what you are being promised, as there are a number of variations on the theme. The investment period is commonly five years; if you take your money out before then, you normally forfeit the guarantee and there may be early surrender penalties as well. So if the market starts falling just before the end of the period, you could lose all the gains made up to then. Some products have a periodic 'lock-in' facility, whereby gains to date are consolidated into the guarantee; while others average the index value over the last 6 or 12 months, to protect against a last-minute fall.

In several cases, the guarantee applies only to the capital growth in the index, which means the income from share dividends is sacrificed. Over longer periods, this can be quite a lot to give up.

The message is that guarantees only come at a price, but these bonds can be attractive for short periods if you are nervous of stock market movements. For larger sums, though – say,

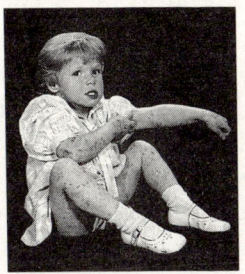
£10,000 upwards – you could put together your own package to offset risk, so it is worth taking independent advice.

High income bonds

These are another fairly recent idea, stemming in this case from the plunge in interest rates during 1993 which was a severe blow to building society investors dependent on income.

The bonds generally run for five years, during which time they offer a guaranteed level of income – recently, this has tended to be between 8 and 10 per cent a year. They also offer a guarantee on the capital return at the end of the term; this varies a little from bond to bond, but is commonly such that the total return, including all the income received, will be not less than the original investment.

The bonds use quite sophisticated derivative instruments to provide the guarantees, but in essence what happens is this. Part of the original capital is siphoned off to provide the ongoing income, while the rest is invested with the hope that, over the five years, it will grow enough to replace the full original sum, in addition to the income paid, or perhaps even show a profit.

In other words, capital is being sacrificed up-front to provide income, but there is the potential for it to be replaced through investment growth and in the worst case, if the stock market falls, there is a guarantee that you will get back your original investment less the income you have already been paid.

The bonds have attracted a fair amount of criticism, focusing on the concepts of 'income' and 'guarantee'. First, it is argued that the payments made are not truly income, because they are made from capital. Second, the capital guarantee has been called misleading, as it provides for a return of your initial investment *including* the income already paid, not in addition to it. As a result, the regulatory body Lautro has laid down strict rules on how the bonds should be described in advertisements and product literature and the warnings that should be given.

Certainly you should make sure you know exactly what you are being promised. If the stock market falls, and you get back only the minimum amount guaranteed, you will effectively have lost out on the interest you could have earned meanwhile from a building society account, which would also have preserved your capital intact.

But if, say, you need a 10 per cent annual return to live on, and a building society account is paying only 5 per cent, you would need to draw on your capital anyway. The advantage of a bond in this case is that there is the opportunity for capital growth to replace what you spend, whereas with a building society your capital would simply dwindle.

What you should check is the required annual rate of return on the bond to get back your original capital in addition to the income paid. This will vary from bond to bond, depending on the exact structure and the economic conditions at the time the derivatives are bought, plus the level of income offered. The greater the income, the higher the rate of growth required to pay back all the capital, so there is a trade-off between the income you receive and the chance of getting back your full investment or showing a profit.

Another point to bear in mind is that the money is generally locked in for the full term: withdrawals may be banned completely or very restricted, possibly invalidating the guarantees.

Distribution bonds

These are bonds designed to pay out the dividends accumulated by the underlying fund, so that investors can receive an income without cashing in holdings. They tend to focus on UK equities and gilts, which offer higher dividends than overseas securities.

The income is free of tax for basic rate taxpayers, and also for higher rate payers as long as it is within the 5 per cent annual allowance. But they share with other bonds the drawback that the fund itself is liable to capital gains tax and income tax, which cannot be reclaimed by those not liable.

Personalised bonds

These are bonds which allow you to have your own choice of investments held within the medium of a bond. They are designed for sizeable investments – around £50,000 upwards – which would normally be managed by a stockbroker. Personalised bonds enjoyed some popularity when the top tax rate was 60 per cent, as the bond environment offers tax protection for investment income. Now that tax rates have fallen, this market has gone quiet, but there are still a few offers available.

Broker bonds

Broker bonds are offered by a number of independent financial advisers, not necessarily insurance brokers as the name suggests. They had their origin in the early 1980s, when advisers who managed bond funds on behalf of clients used the power of proxy to make block switches instead of making the same move individually for each client.

Broker bonds have moved on a long way since then. The concept is that clients' money is pooled into one fund, which the adviser will manage, moving it between underlying funds to make the most of current market conditions. These funds can be 'fettered', meaning they are invested with just one life company, or 'unfettered', which means they can be invested across a number of companies, depending on where the adviser sees the best prospects. The latter are more common and offer greater scope for the adviser to give added value, compared with an individual bond.

The advantages of a broker bond are that you have your investment professionally managed, without being required to approve every move, but still have access to the person doing the managing, which would not be the case if, say, you simply put your money into a life company's managed fund. In return, you will be faced with an extra layer of charges levied by the adviser.

So will performance justify the extra cost? Anyone offering a broker bond must be authorised to do so, and life companies are responsible both for vetting the advisers in the first place and for monitoring their performance. There are, however, no rules on what action should be taken if an adviser fails to achieve performance bench-marks, so you should always satisfy yourself as to the adviser's track record.

Annuities

Annuities are a means of transforming capital into income. The basic concept is simple: you pay a lump sum to a life assurance company and in return you get an income, at a predetermined level, for the rest of your life. A basic annuity is irrevocable; once you have given up your capital, you cannot have it back.

Annuities operate rather like a mirror image of life assurance. Instead of paying out a lump sum when you die, they pay an income until you die. So the older you are, the fewer payments are anticipated and the higher the rate will be. For this reason, annuities are not normally suitable for anyone under about 65; the income offered would be too low to justify giving up the capital for good.

The income from an annuity is taxable, but only in part. A portion of it is treated as being a return of your original capital, and is therefore tax-free, while the rest will be taxed as income at your normal rate. The capital element is determined by scales laid down by the Inland Revenue, based on your age; the older you are, the shorter the likely payment period, so a higher proportion of the return will be treated as capital. However, new scales were brought in at the beginning of 1992 – previously they were based on mortality tables that were around 40 years old, when life expectancy was lower than it is today. The new scales reduced the capital element for any given age, making the after-tax return rather less attractive than before. Examples of current rates are shown in Table 10.2.

One exception to this tax rule is an annuity bought with money from a pension fund. This is known as a 'compulsory purchase annuity', because you are obliged to buy it (though you may still have a choice of companies to buy it from), and it is wholly taxable as income. Ordinary annuities that you buy voluntarily are called 'purchased life annuities'.

Variations of annuities

The main failing of a basic annuity is that it dies with you. To take an extreme example, if you handed over £100,000 and died the very next day, your estate would be £100,000 the poorer and the insurance company equally the richer. For insurance companies,

Table 10.2 *Annuity rates*

Purchase price £10,000	Gross annuity	Capital content	Net annuity
Male, aged 65, single life, no guarantee	1081.56	570.00	953.67
Male aged 65, single life, guaranteed 5 years	1047.36	564.00	926.52
Male aged 75, single life, no guarantee	1506.00	911.04	1357.26
Male aged 75, single life, guaranteed 5 years	1389.60	871.08	1259.97
Male 65, female 60, joint life, no guarantee	802.08	366.00	693.06
Male 65, female 60, joint life, guaranteed 5 years	802.08	366.00	693.06

Note: All rates are based on level annuities payable monthly in arrears, without proportion or capital protection. Net rates based on 25 per cent tax.

Source: Annuity Direct, March 1994

premature deaths make up for clients who live unexpectedly long, but for your heirs it could be a serious blow.

There are several ways of overcoming this problem. First, the annuity can be guaranteed for a certain period, such as five or ten years. Payments will then be continued for that time, regardless of whether you die sooner. In practice, if the annuity-holder dies, the insurance company may offer his heirs the option of commuting remaining payments to a lump sum.

Second, if you are married but have no other dependants, you could opt for a joint life, second death annuity. As the name implies, this will continue paying income until the death of the second partner.

Third, you can ensure that you (or your estate) at least get back the original outlay through a capital protected annuity. If at your death the income payments so far are less than the purchase price, the insurance company will pay over the difference. All of these options cost money, in that the rate will be reduced, as can be seen in Table 10.2. Rates for women will be lower again, as they have a longer life expectancy.

Annuity rates are also affected by how often the income is paid, whether it is paid in advance or in arrears, and with or without proportion. The latter refers to the position if you die between payment dates – whether or not a proportion of the next payment is made. Obviously, it hardly matters if payments are monthly, but for annual income it could be useful. If you have no heirs and are in no immediate hurry for money, an annuity payable yearly in arrears, without proportion and with no guarantees, would give the best possible rate.

Another drawback of the basic annuity is that the income is fixed for life and therefore vulnerable to inflation. It is possible instead to have an increasing annuity, under which payments rise each year, either by a fixed percentage or in line with, say, the Retail Price Index. Two further, much less common, options are with profits and unit-linked annuities, where the income is linked to an investment fund. This means it is dependent on the fortunes of the stock market, so while the long-term trend should be upwards, it can fluctuate year to year. Both this and the increasing annuity will give a lower income at the outset than the plain level type.

Hybrid plans

One variety not mentioned above is the temporary annuity, which pays out for a fixed period of time rather than for life. These have little application by themselves, but are often used in packaged schemes offered by life companies. Sometimes called 'hybrid' or 'back to back' plans, these combine different products with the aim of providing a reasonable level of income plus the prospect of capital growth.

Plans fall into two types. With one, the lump-sum investment is used to buy a ten-year annuity; payments from this are used to fund the premiums for a ten-year endowment policy, while the surplus provides a running income. At the end of the ten years, the maturing endowment should provide a return of the original capital. With the second type, part of the original lump sum buys a temporary annuity to provide income, while the rest is put into an investment such as a bond, unit trust or personal equity plan, again designed to return at least the original capital at the end of the term.

Some of the packages around now are quite sophisticated. With the second type, for example, you may be able to choose the level of income you want, either by adjusting the amount put into the annuity or by taking additional income from the second investment. But there are two important questions to ask. First, what return would there be if you die during the term? The annuity will normally die with you, so the return may be less than you invested. Second, what rate of growth is needed from the investment to return the original sum, and how realistic is this? Remember that the higher the income you take, the less money will be left to build up capital.

One other point is that the package will usually combine products from the same company, which may not be good for both annuities and investments. You might get a better deal by putting together your own combination from different companies.

Second-hand endowments

These are with profits endowment policies which have been sold by their original holder before maturity owing to a change of circumstances. They can be bought either through auctions or through 'market-makers' – firms which buy up policies to sell on to investors. When you buy a policy the details stay the same – it is still based on the life of the original owner – but you take over responsibility for paying the remaining premiums due. These can usually be commuted to a lump-sum payment, but this is not always beneficial; the discount offered may be negligible and the policy will become non-qualifying in status, which means there may be a tax liability on the maturity proceeds.

While policy auctions have been around for decades, market-makers are a fairly new phenomenon. The market, however, is expanding fast, as selling a policy can give a much better return than the surrender value. For the investor, a second-hand policy can be attractive if you need a lump sum at a specific time in the future; for example, to meet school fees or for retirement.

Policies will normally have run for around two-thirds or more of their total term, so in addition to the basic sum assured they will have built up bonuses which, once they have been allocated, are guaranteed to be paid at maturity. In some cases, the value of the sum assured plus bonuses can be as much as the purchase price, so your profit then depends on the level of bonuses allocated during the remainder of the term and the amount of the remaining premiums.

The price is determined by the current value of the policy, its original term and the period remaining, the future premiums and the seller's mark-up. Sellers usually quote an anticipated rate of return at maturity, but whether this will be achieved or not depends on the future pattern of bonus rates. The recent trend

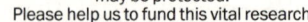
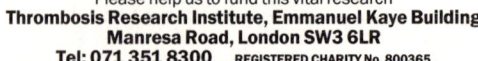

has been downward, and since most policies bought have fairly short terms to run – between three and ten years – it is not likely that they will pick up again significantly.

Unless you already have some experience in this area, you would be wise not to buy at auction. Like car auctions, they can offer bargains, but you could equally end up paying over the odds if you lack the specialised knowledge. Similarly, policies issued by 'top name' insurance companies offer the safest prospects though they may not be the cheapest. It is usually worth taking some professional advice.

Friendly societies

Friendly societies have been around for a couple of centuries. In some respects their operations resemble those of insurance companies, but on a smaller scale, as they have been subject to tight restrictions on their activities. However, the Friendly Societies Act 1992 has opened the way for expansion and most societies incorporated in 1993. This means that they may own assets directly instead of through trustees and may set up subsidiary companies that can manage unit trust schemes and personal equity plans or do insurance broking. They are also due to be brought under the Policyholders' Protection Act, which has not previously applied to friendly societies.

The societies' chief advantage over insurance companies is that they can issue tax-exempt policies, which invest in funds that are free of income and capital gains tax and pay the proceeds tax-free to the investor. These are ten-year plans designed for regular savings, but many offer a lump-sum version, using an annuity from which payments are drip-fed into the plan over its term.

The bad news is that the maximum premium for these plans is only £18 a month or £200 a year. Using the annuity method, this would translate to a lump sum of about £1750, though the exact figure will depend on current rates. You can also have only one such plan, although children can also take out plans, so a family of four could invest lump sums totalling £7000. One other point to bear in mind is that if you surrender a plan before it has run for at least three-quarters of its term, the return is restricted by law to the premiums already paid. Thereafter, normal surrender values will apply.

11

Retirement Planning

Pension planning can be as complex as any other investment described in this book, and twice as important. Once you retire, your income will very largely depend on the investments you have built up during your working life and a pension can be the core element. It may seem out of place in a book devoted to lump-sum investment, as pension planning is (or should be) chiefly a matter of regular saving. But there are three good reasons why it should have a prominent place in any investment strategy.

1. Very few people have the maximum possible pension provision. In fact, it is estimated that fewer than 2 per cent of members of company-run pension schemes will retire on the maximum two-thirds of final salary that is allowed by the Inland Revenue. This can arise because the company scheme is not geared to producing maximum benefits, or because the employee does not put in a sufficient number of years of service. Most people, indeed, are likely to end up with a far lower pension than they expect or imagine.

2. Pensions are extremely tax-efficient as an investment. All contributions, to whatever type of plan, qualify for tax relief at the highest rate of income tax you pay and the funds in which they are invested are themselves free of all income and capital gains tax. In addition, when you retire, you can take part of the proceeds as a cash lump sum, tax-free; the exact proportion depends on the type of pension you have and when it dates from.

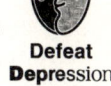
3.   There has been a host of developments in pensions legislation in recent years, aimed at improving private provision and, alongside that, reducing the burden on the State. As a result there are now greater opportunities to make your own pension arrangements, through lump-sum investments as well as regular savings.

Personal pensions

Personal pensions, which came on the scene in July 1988, are arguably the most important development of recent times. They are open to anyone who has earnings that are not already covered by a company pension scheme. That includes not only the self-employed, but also those who have freelance earnings in addition to a main job – or, indeed, in addition to a current pension. Moreover, employees have the choice of opting out of a company scheme and taking a personal pension instead.

On the face of it, this is not an attractive choice. For a start, if you take a personal pension, all the costs fall on you – both the charges of the plan and the payments into it. Your employer may make a contribution to it, but there is no obligation for him to do so.

Then there are the benefits to consider. Most large company schemes operate on a 'final salary' basis; this means that the pension is equivalent to a proportion of your salary at the time of leaving the company, typically one-sixtieth per year of service. Should runaway inflation suddenly double your salary, or investment performance not measure up to expectations, that is

LOOKING TO THE FUTURE

A key component in retirement planning, is ensuring your will is up to date and accurately reflects your wishes for the disposing of your estate.

As time goes by, personal and financial circumstances change and it is easy to ignore what could be the key document in your financial portfolio.

Partnership with solicitors

Help the Aged have been working with solicitors in providing information on the importance of combining the will making process with a review of future needs, as people enter their retirement years. Planning includes decisions about housing choices; the financial implications of long term health care; enduring power of attorney regulations and a myriad of associated topics.

In 1993, the Charity prepared a Counselling Guide for Solicitors and has backed this up with information services including leaflets, covering the main subjects associated with growing older. Solicitors who specialise in counselling older people can be identified from a window sticker on the window or door – *"This practice specialises in counselling elderly people, with the co-operation of Help the Aged."* If you are older yourself, or have a relative or friend about to retire or already enjoying their leisure years, then a solicitor who is aware of the specialised information required and available, is invaluable.

Be prepared

To prepare for a visit to the solicitor, with all the required data, for the making or changing of a will, can save time and money. Included in Help the Aged's Wills Guide is an insert "Preparing to Make or Change Your Will – Solicitor's Checklist". If you contact the Charity for a Will Information Pack, the Checklist is included along with another useful document "Record of Personal Assets". This booklet ensures that you can notify your relatives and friends of the whereabouts of personal papers and information.

The address where you can obtain the "Will Information Pack", including the inserts, is detailed below. Alternatively, please complete the coupon in our advertisement or send a letter if you do not wish to deface the book.

Thinking of others

Finally, when organising your finances, why not consider leaving a legacy to Help the Aged? Remember all gifts to charity are currently free of Inheritance Tax. You can be sure your money will be gratefully received and carefully allocated to assist needy, elderly people instead of the government taking it.

The plight of many of our older citizens is often quite distressing. For instance, did you realise that one in six elderly people in the UK live alone and many never receive any visitors? A sad statistic and with three million elderly people experiencing mobility problems, improving their lives is a formidable, but important task.

Help the Aged distributed by way of aid in 1992/93, £28.8 million. All of this money came from donations and legacies, so any help you can give would help us face the many challenges ahead.

The address for more information about our work and those important Wills Guide documents is:-

The Legacy Department,
Help the Aged
St James's Walk,
Clerkenwell Green,
London EC1R 0BE

and ask for our Will Information Pack

the company's problem. With a personal pension, all the risk is on your head: you will only get what you put in and the investment growth it achieves.

On top of this, a company scheme will normally offer additional benefits: life assurance, should you die before retirement, which can be up to four times your annual salary; a widow's or widower's pension, of up to two-thirds of your own prospective pension; and guaranteed or discretionary increases in your pension once it is being paid. In fact, from a date yet to be specified at the time of writing, it will be compulsory for final salary schemes to provide increases in line with the Retail Price Index up to 5 per cent.

Under the rules, employees who opt for a personal pension are still eligible to have life assurance through a company scheme, but again, there is no obligation on the employer to provide this. If you decide to go it alone, you will have to think in terms of paying for all these benefits yourself.

So why consider a personal pension? The most important reason is job mobility. If you leave a company, your pension entitlement is based on your years of service to that point and your final salary at the time of leaving. Since the beginning of 1985, companies have had to revalue these preserved rights by the lesser of the inflation rate and 5 per cent, which means so-called 'frozen' pensions have been somewhat thawed. But higher rates of inflation, or promotional salary increases, can still make this entitlement look pretty feeble.

Alternatively, you can take a transfer value out of the scheme to put into a new company scheme or a private arrangement. However, transfer values are usually conservatively assessed, so each time you move you are likely to lose out. In contrast, a personal pension can be continued intact across any number of job changes, so, for younger people in particular, it can be a much more stable means of building up benefits.

There are limits on the contributions you are allowed to make to a personal pension, which start at 17.5 per cent of annual earnings for those under 35 and increase with age to a maximum of 40 per cent. There is also an overall earnings cap on the calculation, which for the 1994/5 tax year stands at £76,800. However, if you do not use the full contribution allowance in one

year, the rest can be carried forward for up to six years. So if you find yourself with windfall cash, you may be able to tuck away a sizeable lump sum by picking up unused allowance from past years.

Types of plan

Personal pensions are available from insurance companies and unit trust groups and offer a variety of investment choices: with profits, unit-linked, deposit-style and unit trusts. Deposit-type plans offer maximum security with the lowest growth prospects, and are suitable mainly for those very close to retirement who need to know their capital is safe. With profits plans invest in a mix of assets and aim to smooth out fluctuations, thereby offering a balance between risk and reward. Unit-linked and unit trust plans provide direct exposure to the equity market through a range of funds, which themselves offer different levels of risk and growth prospects. Broadly speaking, the further you are from retirement, the more risk you can afford to take, in return for the likelihood of higher growth.

One other type of plan, which first appeared in 1990, is the self-invested personal pension. This is a 'do-it-yourself' option that gives you a free choice of all allowable investments, which include equities, unit trusts and investment trusts, insurance company funds, deposit accounts and commercial property. These plans are geared towards larger investors, and would not normally be cost-effective for lump sums of less than about £20,000. The attractions are that you are not tied to the investment fortunes of one company and there is generally a fixed fee structure which is economical for very sizeable sums.

Contracting out of SERPS

If you are a member of a company pension arrangement, you cannot normally have a personal pension as well. The one exception to this rule is that you can have a 'rebate-only' plan for the purpose of contracting out of the State Earnings Related Pension Scheme (SERPS). In return for giving up your rights under SERPS, you receive a rebate of part of your, and your employer's, National Insurance contributions and this money can be invested in a special personal pension.

As things stand, contracting out is not a lifetime decision – you can decide for each tax year. The main criterion is your age. The current consensus seems to be that men under 40 and women under 35 should opt out of SERPS, while men over 45 and women over 40 should stay in or return if they are currently contracted out. Between these ages is a grey area where the benefits of opting out depend partly on personal preference and partly on the personal pension plan charges. If the plan has an initial set-up fee, for instance, it may not be worth taking out for just a year or two.

It also seems possible that the rebate system will be significantly changed when it is next reviewed in April 1996. Because people are living longer, the ratio of working people to pensioners is progressively falling and the State will no longer be able to afford SERPS if everyone opts back in at a certain age. From the 1993/4 tax year, the government introduced an extra 1 per cent rebate for those over 30 contracting out via a personal pension and this may herald a move to a scale of age-related rebates in future. A fully age-related system would mean there was no inherent advantage on either side and the decision would be purely personal.

Meanwhile, an important point to remember is that a plan based only on the National Insurance rebates is not going to produce an adequate pension. So if you are not also in a company pension scheme, you should be making further contributions of your own.

Additional contributions

As mentioned, you cannot make contributions to a personal pension if you are a member of a company scheme. You can, however, make extra payments through an Additional Voluntary Contributions (AVC) scheme. This can be an in-house scheme provided by your employer, or a free-standing plan operated by an insurance company.

Why should you do this? The answer is that a company scheme can fall short of the ideal for a number of reasons: it may offer less than the standard one-sixtieth per year of service; the final salary assessment may not include extras such as bonuses and overtime payments; it may not provide the maximum possible death benefits or spouse's pension. Most of all, if you change jobs, you will not clock up the necessary number of years of service, and benefits from previous employment may be partly or wholly frozen.

The choice between in-house and free-standing schemes depends on your circumstances. Briefly, an in-house scheme is convenient, as payments are usually deducted directly from salary and the employer will bear the plan charges; but a free-standing scheme can offer a wider investment choice and is yours to take from job to job.

Members of company pension schemes can put in up to 15 per cent of earnings a year, tax-free. Compulsory contributions are normally around 5 to 6 per cent, so there is plenty of scope for making AVCs. However, while it is possible to have a single premium plan – to which you can make one-off payments as and when you can afford it – the allowance cannot be carried forward from year to year, so there is less scope for large lump-sum payments than there is with a personal pension.

An alternative route to building up savings for retirement is a personal equity plan. Unlike a pension, there is no tax relief on the money going in, but there is greater flexibility: the investment limits are generally higher; you can get the money out whenever you like; and all the proceeds can be taken as cash, whereas an AVC can only be used to provide income. The two are not mutually exclusive: to maximise savings, you can have a PEP in addition to an AVC.

How much to save

The chief drawback of pensions is that you cannot draw on the money until you reach a minimum age – 50 for personal pensions and normally 60 for company schemes. Other investments may be difficult to convert into cash, but a pension is by nature non-negotiable. Hence most of us contribute only grudgingly – on average, around 4–5 per cent of earnings.

A glance at Table 11.1 shows how inadequate this can be. Even

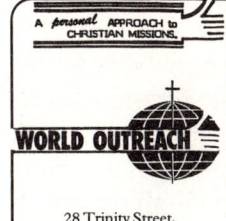
contributing at 10 per cent a year, starting at age 30, will not produce the maximum allowance of two-thirds final salary at 65. This is based on a fairly conservative assumption for investment growth, but the truth is that the danger of over-funding is pretty remote, while under-provision is extremely common.

Table 11.1 *How much should you put into a pension plan?*

The columns show what level of pension (expressed as a percentage of final salary) can be expected, assuming that contributions of 10 per cent of salary are made each year

Age now	Pension[a] at age 65	
	Male	Female[b]
	%	%
30	58.9	53.4
35	47.6	43.2
40	39.5	35.8
45	28.7	26.0
50	20.6	18.7
55	14.7	13.3

[a] These figures assume a 2 per cent 'real' growth rate on the pension fund, and that pension contributions keep pace with salary increases, i.e. they are always 10 per cent of salary. They also assume that all the fund is taken as a pension, rather than a proportion as a lump sum.
[b] The figures for women are lower at all ages because pension rates are lower for women (they live longer).

Source: Allied Dunbar

On top of that, you may not want to soldier on to the age of 65. If you retire early, not only will you have accumulated fewer rights from a company scheme, say $^{35}\!/_{60}$ths instead of $^{40}\!/_{60}$ths, but most schemes also levy a penalty, often up to 6 per cent a year. Hence there is all the more reason to plan now for your future leisure.

The good news is that pension plans are becoming much more flexible. Many insurance company products will allow you to switch without penalty from, say, a free-standing AVC to a personal pension, if your employment circumstances change, and contributions can be made in the form of occasional lump sums instead of, or in addition to, regular savings. So there is no excuse for not acting!

Where to find out more

The financial pages of newspapers run frequent articles on pension issues, as do specialist magazines. For specific suggestions on your own circumstances, you should think of consulting a financial adviser.

There are also a number of bodies which can offer certain types of information and help. The Occupational Pensions Advisory Service can advise on the rights of members of company schemes and can be contacted on 071-233 8080. To track down pension entitlements you may have from past employment, contact the Pensions Register, on 091-225 6237. If you have any disputes that you cannot resolve with your pension provider, there is the Pensions Ombudsman's Bureau or, for aspects of personal pensions, the Insurance Ombudsman's Bureau, both on 071-928 4488.

12

Tangibles and Other Investments

This chapter looks at alternative investments which do not fit into any of the categories covered so far. Chief among these are 'tangibles' which, as the name implies, are physical objects rather than financial instruments. They can be highly specialised – rarity is often a key factor in their value – and may therefore require a high degree of expertise. Hence investors should be prepared either to do considerable research on their own part, or to put their trust in an expert. Tangibles also tend to be less liquid than financial investments, partly because there is not always a ready market, and partly because of indivisibility – you can sell a small parcel of shares, but you cannot sell one arm of an antique chair.

Tangibles

Tangibles are extremely wide-ranging and can be categorised in a number of ways, but a broad breakdown can be made as follows.

Objects of intrinsic value
This would include items such as precious metals and gemstones whose value is determined more or less by objective criteria rather than any artistic or cultural merit. For this reason, they can be easier to get to grips with, though an understanding of the market is still useful.

Arts and crafts
This group covers items such as paintings and antiques, ranging from furniture to silver or porcelain. Specialist knowledge is

Since the personal computer revolution started 10 years ago, private investors have been one of the groups of people able to benefit dramatically from this new technology. One of the first into the field was FairShares Software. By using this newly available software investors have found new freedom to manage their own affairs.

FairShares enables them to track a wide range of investments and dealings, and help analyse market information and other pertinent data. Shares, unit trusts, gilts, bonds, PEPs, traded options, Tessas and deposit accounts can all be tracked and FairShares will tell you what has been purchased, how much and when. There is no limit to the number of portfolios you can enter on the software.

The program can set price alert levels, keep a cash account for automatic re-investment of dividends, distribution splits as well as automatically calculating dealing costs. It does the hard work that stockbrokers used to do. And without any loss of accuracy, it takes the drudgery out of successful investment.

No longer do investors have to rely on financial advisors on when to buy and sell their shares. FairShares provides a number of indicators as used by the professionals to time their transactions. Nor do they need expensive accountants to sort out their capital gains tax calculations. FairShares displays all the information they need. It even provides a detailed calculation sheet to show how the tax was calculated. Instead of telephoning their stockbroker to get regular reports on the state of their holdings investors can value their portfolios at the touch of a key. Rather than having to pore over hundreds of figures trying to make sense of a company's situation the investor can simply switch to a graphical view of a wide selection of information.

The key to FairShares' success has been to offer sophistication and flexibility without compromising user-friendliness. It has virtually put a stockbroker on everyone's desk. With the latest release in the popular Windows environment FairShares has become more flexible and easier to use than ever. And that the prices have always reflected real value-for-money is a firm policy of the company.

If you want to take charge of your own financial affairs you will find FairShares a most suitable tool.

Jules Lewicki

more or less essential and some objects may need particular storage conditions. Security and insurance are also important considerations; it is worth checking out specialist art insurers, who can offer better rates with fewer specifications on security measures than the big general companies.

Collections
Collectable items range from those with recognised markets and dealers, such as stamps and coins, to the more esoteric, such as matchboxes and beer mats. The latter, of course, are usually collected for pleasure rather than financial gain, but even in the former case, enthusiasm for the subject is often the key to financial success; the essence of a good collection is that the items have been hand-picked, rather than simply thrown together, so that the sum is greater than the parts.

Other items
Tangibles that do not come into the above categories include, for example, jewellery, exotic rugs and classic cars. Like collectables, these are often bought for pleasure rather than investment gain; for the latter purpose, specialist knowledge or advice is desirable, as the most aesthetic objects are not necessarily the most financially rewarding.

Although there is such a wide variation in types, tangibles do have some common characteristics, which should be borne in mind if you are buying primarily for investment purposes.

1. They produce no income, which can be an advantage to higher rate taxpayers, but meanwhile they involve running costs for storage and insurance. Hence the prospects for capital gain should be enough to finance this ongoing 'deficit' as well as producing a profit.

2. While some tangibles such as gold and precious stones have intrinsic worth, in many cases the price depends on current supply and demand rather than 'face' value. This in turn may be influenced by fashion as much as market trends, as well as economic factors such as inflation which detract from financial alternatives.

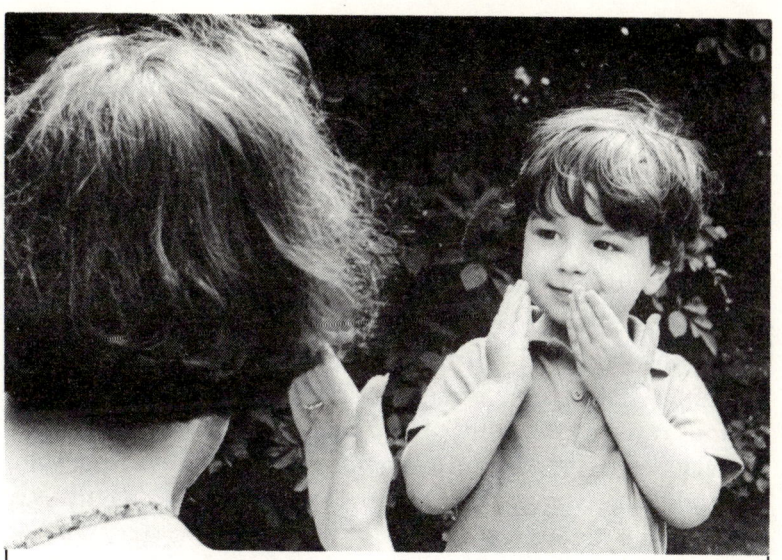

Christopher is learning to say 'Thank you'.

There is nothing out of the ordinary about Christopher except that he will grow up understanding sign language. For Mum is profoundly deaf and this is the only way they will ever be able to talk to each other.

Helping families like Christopher's is just part of the work of the RAD among hundreds of people who are deaf, or who in addition to deafness suffer from other disabilities as well. We help meet their spiritual and social needs, we help with a multitude of practical problems, we provide Centres and help set up Clubs. We hold regular Sign-Language services in a number of dioceses. We give pastoral care. We provide translators in the Courts. Our work is wide-ranging and, quite literally, 'Hands on'.

But we need a hand too, and inevitably we need money most of all. Please help deaf people with your legacy!

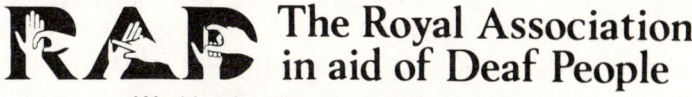

RAD The Royal Association in aid of Deaf People

Working hand in hand with deaf people

27 Old Oak Road, London, W3 7HN.   *Tel: 081-743 6187*   *Registered Charity 207358*

3. Some items, especially collectables, may not be freely market-able, so money invested should be truly 'spare' capital that you will not need access to in an emergency.

4. Because the markets are often limited, with little competition, dealing costs or mark-ups may be high, so you need to invest over a longer term before there is an appreciable profit.

Precious metals

As alternative investments go, precious metals have a certain glamour, but investors should not get too carried away with the glitter. Investment value and beauty are two very different characteristics; jewellery, for example, may have increasing value but should not be considered purely for investment purposes, because the retail mark-ups are high and the cost of the workmanship involved can outweigh the intrinsic value of the metal.

Both gold and platinum can be bought in the form of bars and coins. Gold is the more popular choice with investors; while platinum is much rarer, and is underpinned to some extent by industrial demand, it does not have the same history as gold of being seen as the ultimate store of value and haven in troubled times.

In the UK, the one-ounce gold Britannia coin is minted for investment purposes. Other options are the South African Krugerrand and the Canadian Maple Leaf; there are also sovereigns, which are smaller, but these are not always available singly – a minimum purchase might be 20 coins.

An important point to bear in mind is that if you buy coins in this country they will be subject to VAT at (currently) 17.5 per cent. This can be avoided by buying offshore, usually in the Channel Islands, and this can be arranged through a high street bank. On top of the price of the coin, you will also have to pay a dealing charge and transportation costs, including insurance while the coins are in transit.

To continue to avoid VAT, the coins will need to be held offshore, which the bank will do for you. This is also convenient in terms of security, but it does of course mean further charges, for both storage and insurance. Together these would currently

come to around £60 a year upwards, depending on the number of coins and their value. Furthermore, any urge to see your treasure should be resisted, as this can incur yet another charge, on top of your own travelling costs.

Given that there are these various running costs, and no income being generated, gold is only attractive if there are good prospects of capital growth. In fact, the last great 'gold rush' was in 1980 and the metal has spent much of the time since in the doldrums. The increasing sophistication of 'hedging' instruments such as futures and options has meant that gold is no longer the prime refuge from inflation that it once was. While the trend now seems to be upwards, it is still a high risk investment, as there are many factors of influence.

As an alternative, you can buy shares in gold mining companies, either directly or through a unit trust. These are also volatile and tend to move ahead of the price of gold itself, so by the time an upswing becomes apparent, shares are likely to be already expensive. Offshore funds are another possibility; these may invest in shares, physical gold or gold futures, so will respond to different market factors.

There are also both onshore and offshore commodity funds, the former investing only in shares of associated companies, while the latter can include direct investment; these may include some exposure to gold, but within a spread of holdings which can reduce the risk. Finally, you can buy gold options, but these are not currently traded in London, so the dealing cost is relatively high.

Diamonds

Diamonds share some of the characteristics of gold: a hard-headed approach is needed, and jewellery should be ruled out for purely investment purposes, because too much of the cost relates to the settings and there is also the fashion element which can affect the value. Again, it is best to buy and store the stones offshore, which a dealer can arrange for you, but there will be storage and insurance costs.

Diamonds offer rather more scope than gold to pick and choose what you want, because there are a wide range of grades.

Stones are categorised by the 'four Cs': cut, colour, clarity and carat (in other words, weight). Each of these may be good, bad or somewhere in between, so there are various possible permutations which will influence the current price and the future prospects.

The conventional rule is that investment stones should be at the upper end of the scale in each category, as quality stones are more likely to hold their value, but you need to take expert advice in the light of how much you want to invest and how long for. It may be, for instance, that several lesser stones will suit you better than a single one of very high quality, as it would give you greater flexibility in selling; but depending on supply and demand in the market, lower quality stones may be less readily marketable.

Like gold, diamonds used to prosper in times of high inflation, but have been less talked of in recent years. As well as market influences, they are subject to investment fads, so can experience sudden booms when prices reach unrealistic levels, as happened in the late 1970s, but can equally undergo long periods of disinterest.

Wine

Wine drinking has enjoyed increasing popularity in this country in recent years, leading to a growing interest in fine wines and corresponding opportunities for investment. Getting it right, though, can be tricky, as there are fashions in types, as well as acknowledged good and bad vintages.

The most popular wines among investors are claret and port.

At Wood Green, caring is just the beginning ....

This is Buster. He is one of the lucky ones.

We receive thousands of animals whose families have had to give them up because their domestic circumstances have changed (Buster's owner had to go into a home but many are from house repossession) or because of personal tragedy.

Nearly all our cats and dogs, including Buster, are rehomed and go on to live happy and fulfilled lives. To help prevent further problems, we offer pet counselling, training and home visits to ensure that all our animals have the best possible chance.

We even offer to record your wishes for their future should anything happen to you - free! (Pet Alert Scheme) and of course we also run the National Pet Register.

All this costs money and to continue this valuable work, we would be grateful for a donation of any size or just to be able to send details on the Shelter and our various schemes. For more information or to send a donation, please contact us at :

Heydon, Near Royston,
Hertfordshire SG8 8PN.

Tel : 0763 838329
Fax : 0763 838318

WOOD GREEN ANIMAL SHELTERS

REGISTERED CHARITY 298348. A COMPANY LIMITED BY GUARANTEE (NO. 2073930)

WOOD GREEN ANIMAL SHELTERS

The Shelter was founded in 1924 in London and now has four sites in the UK. Every year we receive around 15,000 domestic and wild animals and in over 80% of cases, these animals are found new homes. Others, particularly the farm and exotic animals, become permanent residents whilst wild animals are returned to the wild whenever possible.

The Shelter offers excellent medical facilities and also provides extensive courses on Veterinary Nursing through the College of Animal Welfare which was founded by Wood Green Animal Shelters in 1989 and is based at King's Bush Farm at Godmanchester.

The College is housed in a purpose built complex which includes lecture rooms, Olympic size arena, restaurant and catering facilities. As well as offering excellent education courses, the complex is also used by the Riding for the Disabled Association and other charity events. It is self funded by providing commercial facilities to local companies and other animal organisations.

Wood Green Animal Shelters is widely considered to be the most progressive animal charity in Europe and advises governments on many aspects of animal care. It also visits schools, clubs and other organisations interested in promoting good animal care.

The Shelter is wholly dependent on public support and welcomes visitors to all of its sites especially King's Bush Farm, Godmanchester in Cambridgeshire where visitors will find an excellent restaurant, pet care shop and plenty of interesting animals including Vietnamese pot bellied pigs, llamas, horses, donkeys, goats, birds and of course, cats and dogs for re-homing. All visitors are welcome!

Wood Green is also the home of the National Pet Register . It is a fully computerised database which contains the details of hundreds of thousands of pets and their keepers. Animals whose details are contained in the National pet Register have a unique and individual identification which allows us to reunite lost or stayed pets with their owners in 100% of cases.

The Emergency Pet Alert Scheme, which is free, is a record of wishes in the event of death or permanent incapacity. Details held on our files are confidential and include the name and number of the person or organisation to whom the pet is to be entrusted. It is designed to give peace of mind to everyone, especially the elderly and those living alone. We also have information on legacies, fund-raising, deeds of covenant and the Shelters themselves.

For more information, please contact us at Heydon, Near Royston, Hertfordshire SG8 8PN. Telephone 0763 838329 or fax 0763 838318.

As these take some years to mature, prices and prospects will depend on the time-scale on which you are prepared to invest. If you are willing to tie up your capital for ten years, say, you can go for a fairly young wine and wait for it to reach its prime; if you are taking only a five-year view, you may need to look at something older, which will be more expensive.

The minimum investment could be as low as £200, depending on what you choose. Remember, though, that you need proper storage conditions, which may require a certain outlay.

There are numerous books available on wine, as well as occasional press articles, and Christie's and Sotheby's both hold regular auctions.

Forestry

One of the main attractions of an investment in forestry is that it attracts substantial tax concessions. For a start, commercial timber that is growing is free from both income and capital gains tax. The 1992 Budget also doubled the business property relief from inheritance tax, from 50 per cent to a full 100 per cent, on commercial woodland. This applies after the first two years of ownership and means that, on the investor's subsequent death, there will be no liability to inheritance tax. With the tax rate currently at 40 per cent for assets outside the nil rate band of £150,000 (except property inherited by a spouse, which is exempt from tax), this represents a considerable saving.

The condition is that the woodland must be run as a commercial enterprise, which may mean you have to employ a qualified manager. The other drawback is that you can no longer claim tax relief on plantation expenses under Schedule D, as this has been phased out. This has removed the attraction of the traditional route into forestry, which was to buy bare land and plant it, offsetting the costs against other income for tax purposes, and then passing on the forest to your heirs as a long-term investment.

During the first 25 years of its life, a plantation incurs a good deal of expense in management and tending, while producing no return, as the trees are too young to be felled. Although the tax relief has been replaced by the Woodland Grant Scheme, this does not offer the same degree of financial support during the maturing phase, hence investors are turning away from new or young plantations towards those that are already mature enough to offer some felling opportunities and thus produce an income from the start. As a result, good quality woodlands of an appropriate age are moving into short supply.

The current outlook for forestry as an investment is good, with timber prices on the increase. But while it is possible to buy part shares through a management company, it has to be remembered that this is essentially a large-scale, long-term investment rather than one of quick returns and in many cases, the tax advantages are a significant part of the appeal.

Theatre productions

You do not have to be rich to become an 'angel' – a sponsor of a theatre production – but you do have to be sanguine about losing money. There have been some notable successes, but for many productions, even commercial viability is a stiff target. By the time the initial cost and the running expenses have been met, ticket sales have to be very good for you to make a return – many shows fail to make enough even to recoup the original investment.

As well as being philosophical about losses, you need to be hard-headed in your choice of show or producer. Worthy causes are generally not the money-spinners; what matters is not what the critics say, but what the audiences think. The recommended approach is to back a successful producer, rather than choosing an individual production.

The Society of London Theatres operates a scheme on behalf of its members to put investors in touch with producers looking for backers. Another scheme is run by the Theatre Investment Fund.

Information can be obtained from:

The Society of London Theatres
Telephone 071-836 0971

Theatre Investment Fund
Telephone 071-287 2144

Enterprise Investment Scheme

The Enterprise Investment Scheme (EIS) was announced in the 1993 Autumn Budget as the successor to the Business Expansion Scheme, which was phased out at the end of 1993. Dubbed 'Son of BES', it has the same aim of encouraging investment in small, unquoted companies.

The scheme differs from its predecessor in certain respects. The maximum you can invest each year is £100,000, as against £40,000 for the BES, but income tax relief on the investment is limited to 20 per cent. This makes the scheme less attractive for higher rate taxpayers, who could get a full 40 per cent relief from BES investments.

For investments made between 6 April and 5 October, the tax relief on half the amount can be carried back to the previous tax year, up to a maximum of £15,000. Providing the shares are held for at least five years, any gains made on selling will be completely free of capital gains tax and there will also be income and capital gains tax relief available on losses.

The scheme specifically excludes investments in private rented housing. This had become a particularly popular area under the BES, with many schemes based on assured tenancies and offering fixed exit prices underwritten by financial institutions such as banks. With this possibility removed, EIS projects are likely to carry a higher degree of risk.

The scheme rules may also prove tighter than those which applied to the BES, which had tended to drift away from the original aim of raising finance for high risk new ventures. Hence prospective investors will need to be careful that any scheme they choose will comply with the requirements, as otherwise they stand to lose the entitlement to tax relief. At the time of writing, however, no EIS projects have yet been launched, so the rules have not been tested.

Enterprise zone trusts

Enterprise zone trusts are based on enterprise zones, which are government-designated development areas around the country that attract special tax reliefs for construction. The trusts offer investors a stake in a portfolio of commercial properties, which should generate an annual income from rents.

Investments can be made during a trust's subscription period, with a normal minimum of £5000 and no maximum. Tax relief is available at your highest rate, but applies only to the portion of money used to buy or build properties, not to acquire the land. The Inland Revenue decides for each trust what proportion relates to land and is therefore disallowed for tax relief; on average, this is about 10 per cent, although it could be up to 30 per cent.

Besides the tax relief, a further attraction is that investments can be funded by borrowing that is itself tax efficient. You can borrow up to 70 per cent of your gross investment and interest on this loan will be set against the income earned for tax purposes. Hence you will need to provide very little, if any, money up front, while the income tax bill on your returns will be substantially reduced.

The income comes from rent on the properties, which is

distributed to investors, less an amount to cover the scheme's costs. Several trusts offer a guarantee for an initial period, which will provide a set return if no tenants are found or if the rent drops below a certain level.

But these guarantees should be treated with caution. For one thing, the payments are fully taxable and no tax relief is given against them for interest on money you borrow to invest. Second, the value of the guarantee depends on the financial strength of the guarantor; there have been cases where schemes have collapsed. Third, the guarantee period is generally no more than five years and income thereafter will depend entirely on the rent received, which in turn will depend on the quality and location of the properties.

Enterprise zone investments also represent a long-term commitment, as tax relief is normally clawed back if investors pull out within 25 years. The exception is that, after seven years, the trust may sell a lesser interest in its properties, thereby raising capital which can be distributed to investors.

While returns can look attractive, with current yields of up to 10 or 11 per cent on the net investment, enterprise zone trusts should be viewed as high risk. The administrative costs can be high and the potential for capital appreciation is becoming more limited, as many zones are nearing the end of their 10-year life and the shortage of new investment opportunities is driving up prices. Hence it is well worth seeking advice from a specialist.

Lloyd's of London

Becoming a member of the Lloyd's insurance market has never been for the faint-hearted. The losses of recent years have only served to emphasise this: in 1989 they amounted to a record £2.06 billion. 'Names', as they are known, have had more than their fingers burned and the market has suffered considerable turmoil.

The primary feature of the market has always been that members have unlimited liability. To become a member, you must have minimum assets of £250,000 and this excludes the value of property which is your main residence. But in the event of losses, all your assets can be at stake, including your home and

furniture. Underwriting profits and losses for any given year are not finally assessed for three years so, in the event of a disaster, there can be a long wait to discover the total extent of the damage.

There are currently around 17,600 Names, operating in 179 syndicates. The standard procedure for joining has been that, in addition to showing you had sufficient assets, you had to be supported by two existing members and satisfy the committee that you were suitable.

But the recent upheavals brought a radical rethink, as the market needed to put aside its difficulties and attract new money. In October 1993, Lloyd's members voted to allow limited companies to invest, to provide a back-up for underwriting syndicates. This has spawned a number of investment trusts, which provide a means for private investors to participate for as little as £1000.

The trusts invest primarily in equities, gilts, bonds or some mix of these. As with ordinary investment trusts, the shares can be bought and sold on the stock market and some of the trusts qualify as holdings for a personal equity plan. But in addition the trusts will use their portfolios to underwrite Lloyd's syndicates, which they may do to a limit of twice the capital involved.

In theory, then, investors' money will work twice over. The underlying portfolio will generate dividends, and offer the potential for capital appreciation, in the ordinary way. On top of that, a proportion of any underwriting profits will be passed on to the shareholder. However, because Lloyd's accounts take three years to complete, these profits would only come through in dividends in the fourth year from launch, which means 1997.

The downside is that there are also two ways of losing money. The underlying portfolio may fall in value, while any underwriting losses that are sustained will have to be met by selling assets. But the risk is mitigated by the fact that there will be a time limit on claims for the contracts underwritten, which is not the case for existing Names, and also because, with limited liability, you can never lose more than you invest.

Nevertheless, these are still high-risk vehicles and opinions vary widely on the future prospects of the Lloyd's market. Some people reckon that the massive withdrawal of capital after recent losses means that demand for new insurance exceeds supply, which will drive up premiums and offer high profits. Others believe the bad run will continue or get worse.

The most important factor for the trusts is getting access to good syndicates. In this respect, smaller trusts may be more successful, as they can afford to be more selective. Involvement in a larger number of syndicates may appear to spread risk, but after a certain point the benefits diminish, as there is a lack of choice and monitoring becomes more difficult.

Costs are also a consideration. Fees and commission have to be paid to Lloyd's, Lloyd's members' agents and other advisers to the trust, as well as the trust manager, all of which will reduce the returns for investors.

So even if you are prepared for the risks – which means being prepared to lose your entire investment – picking a trust is not straightforward. One way around this is a 'fund of funds': at the time of writing, one such vehicle has been launched, which will invest in a selection of all the Lloyd's trusts available. Otherwise, you should certainly consider taking professional advice.

A free guide to investing in the Lloyd's market is available from Sharelink (telephone 021-200 4610). More information can also be obtained from:

Lloyd's of London
Lime Street
London EC3M 7HA
Telephone 071-623 7100.

13

Where to Go for Professional Advice

One question often asked by investors is where to go to get reliable financial advice. In practice, there is no shortage of people or organisations willing to offer advice, from stockbrokers to solicitors and accountants, banks and various kinds of intermediary. The services offered also cover a wide range, from advice on specific types of investment, such as life assurance plans or stocks and shares, to overall financial management, including tax planning and long-term strategies as well as day-to-day affairs.

As well as scope, services differ in terms of independence, cost and the type of client they are aimed at. Traditionally, for example, stockbrokers, merchant banks and accountants focused on the top end of the market, so-called 'high net worth individuals', while smaller investors dealt mainly with insurance brokers and agents, or the local bank manager.

These two extremes have now come much closer together. The top end has spread downwards, as stockbrokers have made efforts to enlarge their appeal and appear more user-friendly. Some are even advertising on commercial radio in order to spread the message to a wider audience. At the same time, smaller firms of advisers have been expanding the range of services they offer, moving up the scale from simple life assurance into the realms of investment and, in some cases, tax planning.

There are perhaps three main reasons for these changes. In the first place, the substantial growth in home ownership before and after the Second World War has meant that far more people are

Boyton Financial Services

One of the first decisions that an investor must face is whether he is going to construct his own portfolio, or whether he is going to employ a professional and, if so, what type of professional.

Many independent financial advisers are paid by commission, some are paid by fees, and investors can be confused by the implications of both. However, John Golding, a member of the Institute of Financial Planning, has come up with an explanation of the two different methods of remuneration for independent financial advisers. He points out that:-

1. A commission is paid for the packaging, delivery and installation of a product. There may be little or no after-sales service. A COMMISSION REWARDS A TRANSACTION.
2. A fee is paid for an impartial, reliable, professional service. The service is usually ongoing and ADDED VALUE is the key.

The next fence that an investor must jump is to decide whether his portfolio is to be actively managed, either by himself, or by his advisers or, conversely, whether it is to be a passive portfolio, with the investor taking a more relaxed view to the ups and downs of the financial markets.

Asset managers Boyton Financial Services Ltd., which has operated solely on a fee basis since 1988, can provide investors with either type of management. Both the initial construction of the portfolio, as well as the ongoing advice, is totally fee-based.

It will be up to the passive investor to revert to his advisers as and when he thinks he needs further guidance.

Boyton Financial Services has created its Alert Service for those clients requiring ongoing management. This has proved particularly beneficial, either for those clients who have existing portfolios, constructed by themselves, or those who have retained the company to build the portfolio in the first place.

The Alert Service monitors the investor's funds on a daily basis, will make recommendations when Boyton Financial Services Ltd. feels the funds are fully valued, and make suggestions for re-investment.

The company calculates what it expects to spend on a time basis during the year, including a meeting if required, divides the resultant sum by twelve, and asks for payment on a monthly basis by standing order. On an annual basis, it compares the actual amount of time spent against the time that has been charged, and adjusts its fees accordingly.

Investors still refuse to pay sufficient attention to the fact that it is TOTAL RETURN – both income as well as capital gain – that is the important yardstick for portfolio performance. Significant numbers of investors do not utilise their Capital Gains Tax allowance and, if this allowance is not used, it cannot be rolled forward, and is therefore lost at the end of the tax year.

A married couple, for instance, can create £11,600 worth of capital gain totally free of tax under current legislation. It matters not whether they need income or capital. What they need in their pocket is money to spend that has been accumulated in a tax-efficient way.

Lastly, but most important of all, the investor should have his own ideas firmly set as to what it is that he wants his capital to achieve. Keep the portfolio simple, do not over-diversify as, although there may be protection from any serious falls, any gains will be minimised.

Invest in a 'phone call before you make your next investment

Boyton Financial Services Limited is one of the few Independent Financial Advisers that operates on a time-spent, fee charging only basis, passing on the total benefit of discounts and commissions directly to the client.

We also operate an *Execution Only Service* for those investors who merely wish us to carry out their own investment decisions.

If you are about to invest in any new fund launch, including investment trusts, with profit bonds or any other form of commission paying instrument – call us first to find out about about our *Execution Only Service.*

A few pence on your 'phone bill could well mean your chosen investment goes straight into profit, rather than standing still for a time whilst the dealing commission is recouped.

Our other services include:

❖ Advice on capital investment, both onshore and offshore.

❖ Analysis of in excess of 11,000 Institutional Funds worldwide.

❖ Specialised income or growth schemes with a high degree of security.

❖ A comprehensive financial planning service on a fee and retainer basis.

❖ A managed currency service, in conjunction with Robert Fleming's Managed Offshore Reserve Account, actively managed between the world's major currencies by BFS, with the client retaining a cheque book, and the facility of instant withdrawal of funds.

❖ Pension, personal corporate and self-administered.

❖ Annuities – information is held on all current annuity rates, which allows the annuitant enormous flexibility and personal control over the underlying investment funds.

❖ An association with Boyton, Stuart & Co Limited, a firm of Chartered Accountants set up to offer tax services to clients. A simple tax return and agreement starts from £125 (inc. VAT).

For further information and an explanatory brochure, 'phone: Richard Boyton on 0787 462462

BOYTON
FINANCIAL SERVICES LTD

**Boyton Financial Services Ltd., PO Box 14, Halstead, Essex CO9 4DY
Telephone: 0787 462462 · Facsimile: 0787 462114**

Member of the Financial Intermediaries, Managers and Brokers Regulatory Association. Registered Office: 12 Chequer Lane, Ely, Cambs CB7 4LN · Credit Licence No. 157049. Registered in England and Wales No. 1759368. Also at Piccadilly, London W1 and China Buildings, 29 Queens Road, Central, Hong Kong.

now inheriting property. In many cases, they already own their own homes, so the inheritance translates into a sizeable capital sum – even despite the recent fall in property prices. This creates a need not only for investment advice, but also tax planning; the nil rate band for inheritance tax of £150,000 can easily be surpassed where the estate includes a house.

Redundancy, sadly, is another source of increased demand for advice. Again, there are two sides to this. First, the redundancy payment may be a sizeable sum that needs careful investment, particularly if the redundancy happens fairly late in life and the person is not expecting to find another job, or not at the previous level. Second, the tighter job market has encouraged younger people to set up their own businesses, with a consequent need for advice on matters such as tax and pension arrangements.

Third, the spate of privatisation issues over the last few years has enticed many first-timers into the stock market, some of whom have then caught the bug and gone on to other share dealing. A good number, of course, have not stayed in the market, particularly as some issues gave exaggerated opportunities to take a quick profit. But this in itself encouraged the growth of cheap share-dealing services; while the issues could be bought very easily through application forms in newspapers, selling was more of a problem and 'no-frills' services sprang up as a convenient solution.

The Financial Services Act

In addition to these social changes, a major influence on the development of financial services, and the cause of much upheaval, has been the Financial Services Act, which became law in 1988. This is founded on the principle – which has been much questioned ever since – of self-regulation by the industry rather than statutory control by the government.

Nevertheless, it has still spawned a substantial amount of bureaucracy and one suspects that vast acreages of forest must have been expended on producing rule-books, which are continuously needing to be updated for amendments, and which are so complicated that further reams of paper are devoted to clarification of what it all might mean. If there has been one growth area during the recent recession, it has been the compliance departments of financial services companies, which are responsible for ensuring that all these rules are followed.

At the top of the regulatory tree is the Securities and Investments Board (SIB), which is responsible for supervising the whole show. At the next level down are the Self Regulatory Organisations (SROs), which take their authority from the SIB and carry out the day-to-day tasks of regulation. Hitherto, there have been four of these bodies: the Financial Intermediaries, Managers and Brokers Regulatory Association (Fimbra); the Life Assurance and Unit Trust Regulatory Organisation (Lautro); the Investment Management Regulatory Organisation (Imro); and the Securities and Futures Authority (SFA).

In future it is intended that there should be just three: Imro, the SFA and a new body, the Personal Investment Authority (PIA), which will be responsible for retail investment services. The plan is that current members of Fimbra and Lautro, plus those Imro members who deal primarily with private clients, will transfer to the PIA, which is due to become operational in July 1994, and Fimbra and Lautro will subsequently cease to be regulators. The SIB also hopes to stop having any regulatory role, concentrating wholly on supervision, although at the time of writing there are still some companies which are directly authorised by the SIB.

The PIA was originally conceived as an answer to funding problems experienced by Fimbra, particularly in relation to the Investors' Compensation Scheme. It was felt that a single regulator would be more cost-effective and financially sound; it would also offer a measure of control to life assurance companies, which had been repeatedly asked to subsidise Fimbra while having no say in how it was run.

But more recently the SIB decided that the creation of the PIA should also be the occasion for raising regulatory standards, with pre-vetting of members, a minimum capital adequacy requirement for all applicants of £10,000 and more public interest members on the PIA board. These proposals have not been universally welcomed by prospective members and there is still some doubt about whether the PIA will gain the full support of the industry.

In addition to the SROs, there are also Recognised Professional Bodies (RPBs). These cover professionals who offer investment advice and management services as part of their business, such as solicitors, accountants and insurance brokers. The Law Society, the Insurance Brokers Registration Council and various accountancy bodies act as RPBs.

Anyone who gives financial advice must be authorised through one of these various organisations. Assuming the PIA goes ahead as planned, it is likely to cover independent financial advisers, life assurance companies and their agents, and unit trust groups, while investment managers dealing mainly with institutional clients will continue to come under Imro and stockbrokers are governed by the SFA.

Anyone who offers financial advice without being authorised is breaking the law, unless it is on a casual, one-off basis and unpaid. This was once explained to me by a regulator as follows: if you are in the pub one evening and a friend asks you for some advice, you may obviously offer your opinion. But if you hold court at the bar every night, offering advice to all and sundry and perhaps accepting a few drinks in return, that would, strictly speaking, be against the law.

Polarisation

Authorised firms must display on all their literature, stationery, business cards and so on which of the regulatory bodies they belong to. In addition, they must make it clear whether they are offering advice in a wholly independent capacity, or as the representative of one particular company.

This distinction, which is known as polarisation, was one of the main planks of the Financial Services Act when it was first drawn up. Before then, it was quite common for some advisers to recommend products supplied by more than one company, but without professing to cover the entire market. For example, they might limit their suggestions to just a handful of companies because they lacked the resources to research all of them. Alternatively, they might act in the main for a single company, but occasionally recommend others if the required product was not offered by that one company.

The powers that be decided that this could prove much too confusing for the customer, who would not be sure whether the advice he was getting was genuinely free range or in fact limited to a small sector of the market. So they came up with the principle of polarisation, under which an adviser must be either completely independent and able to offer the products of any company in the market, or tied exclusively to one company and barred from offering the products of any other. Since then, there have been occasional proposals to modify the principle; for example, to allow 'multi-ties', under which an adviser could represent several specified companies, but so far it has not been changed.

To be independent, the cardinal rules laid down were 'know your customer' and 'give best advice'. The former still holds: advisers must complete a fact-find on their clients, covering circumstances such as age and tax position, the range of their financial needs and other relevant factors such as attitude to risk.

The 'best advice' principle has since been toned down to 'good advice'. The adviser is not expected to have a crystal ball to show which product will produce the best results at the end of the day – which could be 20 years hence – but he must select the most appropriate for his client from all those available, in terms of both the type of product and the track record of the company on charges, past performance and so on.

In practice, this means that the adviser may focus on particular companies if they are seen to be the market leaders. For example, if he identifies one company as being good for endowment policies, there is nothing to stop him recommending it to several different clients, but he must be prepared to justify his choice to inspectors from his regulatory body, who will make periodic visits to check that the rules are being satisfied.

While this is basically a sound concept – and what any good adviser should be following anyway – there are certain drawbacks in practice. First, advisers may be tempted to stick to big name companies, the choice of which would not be queried, rather than face having to justify a recommendation which might be based on gut feeling as much as hard facts.

Second, the considerable costs and pressures of being independent have meant that a large number of advisers have simply given up and become tied, so the availability of independent advice has shrunk considerably. It is arguable that the quasi-independent advice that existed before, for all its faults, at least gave investors a degree of choice.

Those tied to one company may work as part of a direct salesforce or be self-employed but acting as an appointed representative. Either way, they can offer only the products from that one company's range but, within that, they are still expected to recommend the most appropriate product. The obvious

INVEST IN YOUNG PEOPLE

Each year approximately 10,000 young people, aged between 16 and 18 years, leave the sheltered environment of residential or foster homes to make their own way in the community.

National research studies over the past five years show that:

- 75% of those in care leave school with no qualifications.
- 30% of homeless 16-17 year olds come from a care background.
- 50% of care leavers are unemployed.

At present the Society operates eleven projects in London and the South East assisting young people with education, training, employment, accommodation, and providing dependable adult relationships and advice.

This year the Royal Philanthropic Society, a charity which has been caring for young people since 1788, has pledged to spend a million pounds to help teenagers leaving state care.

If you would like to invest your money in these vulnerable young people by donating a lump sum, giving by covenant or gift aid, send your donations to:

Mrs Carol Williams
Appeals Administrator
The Royal Philanthropic Society
Rectory Lodge, High Street
Brasted, Kent TN16 1JE
Tel: 0959 561611

Charity Registration No: 229132

drawback is that the company may simply not provide the type of product that would best suit the client, in which case he may be persuaded into a poorer substitute.

In practice, the competition between companies to attract and retain good quality representatives does influence the product range, although it is still true that any single company is unlikely to be a market leader across the board. Naturally, both independent advisers and representatives will argue fiercely for their own merits: the former point out that they are free to select the best product on the market for any given need, while the latter claim that the closer relationship they have with the company can work to the client's advantage. The truth is that there are good and bad in both sectors; what really counts is honesty and competence.

For banks and building societies, polarisation presented a difficult problem. On the one hand, they did not want to give up offering independent advice, as that might mean losing their more discriminating (and more valuable) customers, but on the other, the branch network represented an excellent outlet for business from an associated operation.

Midland, Barclays and Lloyds already had associated life assurance and unit trust companies; a number of others have set up subsidiaries since, such as NatWest Life, Abbey National Life and Woolwich Life. In fact, 'bancassurance', as it is known, is becoming a growing force in the market and represents considerable potential competition to traditional operators because of the huge opportunities afforded by high street outlets.

Of the major banks, National Westminster was the only one to retain independent status at the outset, which it has now given up, while among the top ten building societies, only Bradford & Bingley offers independent advice. To some extent, though, banks and building societies have cut across polarisation by offering tied advice through their branches and independent advice through a separate arm. But where they have associated operations of their own, these would not normally be recommended through the independent side; the rule for that situation is that the recommendation would have to be 'better than best advice', which in practice would be almost impossible to prove.

With so many developments in the market, it is difficult to be categorical about what sort of advice is available from where.

What follows is therefore just a basic guide to current sources and the services they offer.

Merchant banks

Merchant banks still tend to operate very much at the top end of the scale, offering investment services mainly or wholly for six and seven figure portfolios. These would be based on UK equities and gilts and also on overseas investments, either directly into equities or, particularly for smaller markets, through the medium of unit trusts and other pooled funds.

Commonly they provide services on a discretionary basis, which means that they will take the decisions without previously referring to the client. You do, of course, have the chance to specify your aims and requirements; for example, whether you are primarily seeking income or capital growth and the degree of risk you are prepared to take.

The firm will take care of all the paperwork, but you will be kept informed of all the transactions and in addition will receive regular reports and valuation statements. The management fee will generally be based on a percentage of the portfolio value on an annual basis.

Stockbrokers

At one time, stockbrokers were generally regarded as inhabiting a rarefied world of high finance which had little to do with the man in the street. In recent years, though, the mystique has been all but dispelled. For one thing, Big Bang brought greater potential for competition between firms, stimulating the wider publicity of their services. For another, potential clients are no longer just the upper classes whose families have placed business with the same broker for generations. With privatisations, all kinds of newcomers have been drawn into share-buying and most stockbrokers are keen to attract this new business.

As a result, where choosing a broker was once largely a matter of personal recommendation, a number now advertise their services and provide information on what they offer. For example, the Association of Private Client Investment Managers and Stockbrokers produces a directory in which members set out brief but alluring guides to the facilities they provide. All this is very welcome, as it makes the choices much clearer.

Most brokers offer a range of services, from the very basic to the fully comprehensive, as follows.

1. *Dealing or execution-only service.* This is for people who simply want the broker to buy and sell shares, generally without any advice being given. Because there are no added frills, this is generally much cheaper than management facilities.

2. *Discretionary or portfolio management service.* This is suitable for those who have an overall idea of what they want, in terms of income or growth and degree of risk, but do not want to take part in the decision process. The broker will take full responsibility for managing the investments, but the client will be kept informed of the transactions carried out and will receive regular valuations and reports. While some brokers only offer this type of service to wealthier clients, many are happy to take on quite small portfolios and there may be no fees above the dealing commission.

3. *Advisory service.* This may cover dealings in individual shares or the whole of your investment portfolio. Unlike the discretionary service, the client takes responsibility for decisions; the broker will offer advice, based on the client's needs and objectives, but no transactions will be carried out without reference and express permission. Although some brokers specify a minimum portfolio size, which might be anywhere between £20,000 and £75,000, others are happy to consider any amount.

4. *Comprehensive financial planning.* In addition to investment management, this would include advice on any other financial needs; for example, retirement planning, school fees, tax planning, mortgages, life assurance and general cash management. In fact, it could go right down to advice on bank and building society deposit accounts and some brokers also offer banking facilities themselves.

Now that standardised commission scales no longer exist, costs can vary from one firm to another. As a rule, those based in the provinces are likely to be cheaper than those in London, simply because they have lower overheads, and with modern communications technology, location should not have any impact on the quality of service. If you are using an advisory service, it may be more convenient to choose a local firm; for a discretionary service, this is not particularly necessary, although you may need to make the occasional visit to update your objectives.

Accountants and solicitors

Traditionally, accountants have focused on tax affairs, while solicitors have touched on financial matters only indirectly, through business such as conveyancing and wills. Nowadays, however, the distinctions are becoming blurred and accountants in particular may offer overall financial planning services, generally on a fee basis.

Solicitors are becoming more involved in investment business and there is now a trade association for those who specialise in giving financial advice – the Association of Solicitor Investment Managers. A directory of members can be obtained free by telephoning 0892 870065. Work is undertaken on a fee basis, as solicitors are required by the Law Society to disclose and repay any commission earned.

Independent financial advisers

Independent financial advisers will generally come under the auspices of the PIA, but that, and the fact of independent status, are more or less the only things that any one may have in common with any other. In other respects, this group has enormous diversity, ranging from one-man bands to large firms and offering a wide variety of services.

In the first place, there are different categories of authorisation, depending on the type of business carried out. At the lower end, the adviser will not actually handle your money; you simply make out your cheque direct to the company supplying the product. Firms that do handle clients' money have to undergo more rigorous checks designed to ensure that they are not likely to make off with it.

The PIA will initially continue the training and competence arrangements set out by Fimbra. Under new rules introduced in January 1994, this means that all applicants are subject to a vetting process and must have passed the first paper of the Financial Planning Certificate, an examination which tests knowledge of regulations and products. This entitles the applicant to become an associate registered individual, but to become fully registered he must pass the remaining two papers within two years, as well as having at least two years' relevant experience. Those who were already registered before 1994 will count as fully registered but must pass all three examination papers by December 1995.

All registered individuals must also undertake at least 50 hours' training a year. There are also additional examinations that are required for certain specialist activities, such as discretionary portfolio management, broker fund management and dealing in options and warrants.

The Financial Services Act has led to greater costs for independent advisers and a considerable burden in time and money to comply with the morass of rules. One response has been the establishment of networks, linking together anywhere between a dozen and 800 advisers. Through either centralised or decentralised administration, a network can take over much of the burden of compliance with the rules, leaving advisers to concentrate on their main business, and may also offer technical support and training. Generally, network members will deal with their clients in the normal way, but they may also cross-refer for specialist products, which may be an advantage for the investor.

The range of services offered by independent advisers can include any or all of mortgage arrangements and related products, life assurance, pension planning, school fees planning, unit trusts and investment trusts. In the last two categories, some firms provide portfolio management facilities on a discretionary as well as an advisory basis. However, they do not normally offer advice about individual stocks and shares, or get involved in sophisticated tax planning techniques.

The majority operate wholly or mainly on a commission basis, but some are fee-based or may offer the client a choice. The organisation IFA Promotion runs a telephone service which can supply investors with the names of three independent advisers in their local area.

Insurance brokers

Insurance brokers are members of the Insurance Brokers Registration Council (IBRC). In addition to general insurance, such as
motor and household, they may also deal with life assurance,
pensions and a certain amount of investment business. In the case
of those who are authorised only by the IBRC, this last is
currently limited to a maximum of 49 per cent of total business,
but a number of insurance brokers have also been members of
Fimbra and may join the PIA, hence will not be subject to this
restriction.

Choosing an adviser

In addition to the above categories, financial advice is also offered
by banks and building societies, although, as mentioned above,
the majority of these act on behalf of one particular provider and
can only offer its products. Similarly, the appointed representatives and direct salesforces of life assurance companies can offer
advice within the range of the company they represent. Unit trust
groups may also offer portfolio management services within the
scope of their own trusts.

All advisers must clearly notify the investor of their status,
whether they represent one company or act as an independent.
The Securities and Investments Board maintains a central
register of authorised firms, so if you are in any doubt, you can
check whether a firm is authorised and the types of service it is
allowed to provide. The information can be obtained by telephone or through Prestel.

In principle, independent advisers offer the widest choice,
because they can select any product on the market. But if you are
happy to deal with one particular product supplier, a tied agent
can offer equally valid advice and, by virtue of his relationship
with the company, may be better placed to sort out any problems
that arise.

Types of service

Discretionary
With a discretionary service, you are effectively handing over all

control to the adviser. At the outset, you will, of course, set out your basic requirements, your investment aims and the degree of risk you are prepared to accept in trying to achieve them. But thereafter you must trust the adviser to carry out your wishes faithfully and effectively.

On the other hand, there is the advantage of speed of action. Since the adviser is not having to refer decisions to you for approval, he can act immediately on opportunities which might otherwise be missed.

Advisory

Advisory services give you complete control, while you still have access to professional advice. Of course, if you are simply going to agree to everything the adviser suggests, you may as well give him discretion and have done with it. But an advisory service can also provide a useful learning process, so that you gradually come to take a more active role.

Since every transaction will require your prior authorisation, it is important that you should be accessible to your adviser. Equally, he should be readily accessible to you whenever you need advice or to deal.

Execution-only

Execution-only services are aimed at those who are confident that they know what they want and do not want to pay extra for added frills. Since no advice is being given, the choice may be largely cost-based, but if you plan to deal actively, then you need to be sure that you can place an order easily and that it will be carried out quickly. Also, some execution-only share-dealing services do offer a few additional facilities, such as company reports or recommendations, and may also deal with the paperwork; for example, looking after share certificates and providing composite tax vouchers at the end of the financial year.

Commission versus fees

The commission versus fees issue has always been a sensitive one and has become more so lately. From the start of 1995, all independent advisers and insurance company salespeople will have to disclose what they stand to earn from a product sale before the client signs the application form. This will include not only commission but, for company salespeople, any relevant additional benefits provided by the company.

As there is no longer a maximum commissions agreement, companies are free to pay whatever levels they choose, which means there is the potential for advisers to be biased in their recommendations. In practice, rates are still based on the old scales and the differences between providers tends to be small. A more important issue is possible product bias, as products with similar functions may carry quite different rates of commission. In particular, if an adviser has spent considerable time checking a client's circumstances and requirements, he may be reluctant to recommend something like National Savings Certificates which carry no reward.

Commission disclosure, however, will not prove whether a product is good value for money. That depends on a number of factors, including the overall level of charges, the service provided and the total returns one might expect. To judge impartiality, an investor would need to know not only the levels of commission on all the possible alternative products, but also their relative merits in different circumstances; without that knowledge it would be difficult to prove a case of commission bias.

The obvious solution would be to move to a fee basis for all advice. But while this would increase independence, it is no guarantee of good advice. There is also the key question of whether people would be prepared to pay realistic fees. For those who are, there are a growing number of advisers who work on a fee basis or offer clients the choice. But this route is likely to prove more expensive for small investors, for whom percentage commissions can offer very good value.

Making complaints

If you feel that you have been badly treated by a company, or given inappropriate advice, the first step should be to take it up with the company itself, explaining why you are not happy and what action you expect. Always keep copies of any correspondence and also make a note of any telephone calls – when they were made, who you spoke to and what was said.

If you are not satisfied with the response, the next stage is to take your complaint to the appropriate SRO. Advisers and companies must indicate which SRO they are authorised by.

If you believe you are entitled to compensation, and this is not forthcoming from the adviser, you can take your case to an ombudsman. There are now ombudsmen covering each sector of the financial services market: banks, building societies, insurance, investment and pensions.

In some cases, you may be able to make a claim from the Investors Compensation Scheme. Claims should be made within six months of a default being declared and the maximum for any individual claim is £48,000. The main criteria for eligibility are:

- that you are a private investor;
- that the firm involved is fully authorised;
- that the firm cannot pay out claims;
- that the firm owes money or was holding investments on your behalf;
- that your claim relates to business regulated by the Financial Services Act.

But the Scheme cannot help in the following cases:

- the firm is not fully authorised;
- the firm has gone into liquidation but has not been declared in default;
- the firm is still in business;
- the business was conducted before 18 December 1986.

Bear in mind, too, that you cannot claim compensation simply on the grounds of bad performance if you have been fairly advised and warned of investment risk.

The various ombudsmen publish guides to their services, which are provided free of charge to investors. Product providers – whether life assurance companies, unit trust groups, banks or building societies – can also supply information on their complaints procedures, but if you have any doubts, further guidance is available from the Public Information Office at the SIB.

Useful contacts

Financial Intermediaries, Managers and Brokers Regulatory Association: 071-538 8860

Life Assurance and Unit Trust Regulatory Organisation: 071-379 0444

Investment Management Regulatory Organisation: 071-628 6022

Personal Investment Authority: 071-929 0072

The Securities and Futures Authority: 071-378 9000

The Securities and Investments Board, Central Register: 071-929 3652; Public Information Office: 071-638 1240

The Banking Ombudsman: 071-583 1395

The Building Societies Ombudsman: 071-931 0044

The Insurance Ombudsman: 071-928 4488

The Investment Ombudsman: 071-796 3065

The Pensions Ombudsman: 071-928 4488

The Investors Compensation Scheme: 071-283 2474

IFA Promotion: 0483-461461.

Further Reading from Kogan Page

Good Retirement Guide 1994, Rosemary Brown

How to Write a Will and Gain Probate, 4th edition, Marlene Garsia, 1993

How to Understand the Financial Press, 2nd edition, John Andrew, 1993

Letting Residential Property, Frances M Way, 1993

Living Abroad: The Daily Telegraph Guide, 7th edition, Michael Furnell, 1994

Retirement Made Easy, Rosemary Brown, 1994

Index of Advertisers

Index of Advertisers

Index